A Critical Study

DOS PASSOS'

U.S.A.

by DONALD PIZER

University Press of Virginia

Charlottesville

THE UNIVERSITY PRESS OF VIRGINIA
Copyright © 1988 by the Rector and Visitors
of the University of Virginia

First published 1988

Library of Congress Cataloging-in-Publication Data
Pizer, Donald.
    Dos Passos' U.S.A. : a critical study / by Donald Pizer.
      p.   cm.
    Bibliography: p.
    Includes index.
    ISBN 0-8139-1171-0
    1. Dos Passos, John, 1896-1970. U.S.A.   2. United States in
literature.   3. Modernism (Literature)—United States.   I. Title.
PS3507.0743U547 1988
813'.52—dc19   87-27905
                                                                     CIP

Printed in the United States of America

FOR CAROL

CONTENTS

PREFACE

J ohn Dos Passos' *significant place in twentieth-century literature has long been recognized. In an oft-cited comment, Jean-Paul Sartre in 1938 named Dos Passos "the greatest writer of our time."*[1] *Some thirty years later, when Dos Passos' reputation was at its lowest, George Steiner was still willing to state that Dos Passos had been "the principal American literary influence of the twentieth century."*[2] *A variety of approaches has been used in efforts to describe Dos Passos' centrality. He has been studied as a writer whose varying interests during the 1920s and 1930s clearly exemplify the broad changes occurring in American intellectual and literary life during those decades. He has also been examined as one of our principal literary modernists, as a writer who absorbed almost every vital avant-garde current of his day and evolved out of them a major experimental fictional technique. And he has been scrutinized for the paradigmatic character of his shift in political and social belief from the radical left to the extreme right during the course of his career.*

Slighted in these broad-sweeping studies is full and close attention to the work that is universally acknowledged to be Dos Passos' greatest, his trilogy of novels, U.S.A. To stress the preeminence of U.S.A., it should be clear, is not to polarize Dos Passos' work into a masterpiece and a body of minor writing deserving little attention. Much of Dos Passos' work up to U.S.A. will always be of interest, both intrinsically and on the various grounds I have noted. But U.S.A.—because of its length, complexity, and richness—requires a corresponding fullness of critical effort, and criticism of the book has not been afforded this opportunity within the relatively brief compass of a periodical essay or a chapter in a book devoted to Dos Passos' career as a whole. As both the greatest of Dos Passos' works and a classic of twentieth-century modernism, however, U.S.A. deserves a book of its own. This study is devoted to an effort to demonstrate its nature and its quality.

Despite my desire to write a full-scale study of U.S.A., I be-

lieve it necessary to view the work, at least initially, in relation to
Dos Passos' emerging themes and techniques of the most fertile period of his career, the 1920s. (It should be recalled that although
the completed trilogy was not published in a single volume until
1938, the work was begun in 1927.) I therefore devote the first
chapter to this purpose by selecting from the large body of Dos Passos' writing before U.S.A. three works to serve as an introduction
to the trilogy. The remainder of the study is devoted to U.S.A.,
from Dos Passos' planning and composition of the trilogy and his
concept of it as a whole to the function of its four modes and the
nature of the modal interrelatedness that constitutes the completed work of fiction.

Since it has become almost mandatory in a critical study to
announce one's theoretical position, lest the critic be thought ingenuous in his assumptions about his endeavor, let me say that I
sail under the good old flag of the beliefs that the literary object, as
a work of art, can be meaningfully studied in relation to the inter-
dependence of its themes and form and that, as a specific instance
within the institution of literature, it can be meaningfully studied
in relation to its author and his times. It seems to me that these
methods come closest to meeting the needs of most readers (both
academic and nonacademic) who are interested in literature but
who are less interested in linguistic or philosophical issues about
the nature of literature. It is to these readers that this study is
addressed.

I wish to thank Mrs. Elizabeth Dos Passos and the University
of Virginia Library for permission to quote from material in the
John Dos Passos Papers of the University of Virginia Library and
to reproduce in facsimile some pages from that collection. I have
benefited in the preparation of this study from grants provided by
the American Council of Learned Societies and the American Philosophical Society. I would also like to thank the editors of Modern
Fiction Studies and the Papers of the Bibliographical Society of
America for permission to reprint material that initially appeared—in different form—in their journals.

1

INTRODUCTION

Dos Passos before *U.S.A.*

Like most young writers, John Dos Passos at twenty (when he was graduated from Harvard in 1916) was self-preoccupied. In particular he was concerned with his lack of experience of the world and with the conditions of his family and class background that prevented him from either widening his experience or expressing his beliefs openly. At Harvard, many of the sketches and stories that he published in the *Harvard Monthly* deal with a young man's search for experience. He also made a corollary of this theme—the thwarting of the quest for a life of insight and feeling by repressive social forms and conventions—the subject of his first novel, *Streets of Night,* which he wrote largely at Harvard.

As early as his junior year, Dos Passos began to mythologize this personal theme of rebellion against authority and convention through his association of all that was repressive and destructive in society with a force he called "industrialism." In a notebook entry for February 23, 1915, he commented on his reading of Lowes Dickinson's *Appearances,* a book of travel essays. Dickinson's essays on America, Dos Passos wrote, "Unfortunately . . . don't attack the worst of the evils of our damned industrialism, of our beastly worship of Mammon, of our lack of intellect and plethora of intelligence. He doesn't realize the narrowness, the provinciality, the sickly sentimentality of our outlook. It seems as though our good healthy physical full blooded virtues were being stamped out, under a combination of corporations and YMCA's."[1] In embryonic and slightly hysterical form, this comment contains the core of a good deal of Dos Passos' early work and thought. On one side is the native vitality (the full-blooded virtues) of America; on the other, the increasing encroachment of a modern industrial system upon this innate strength both through economic power (the corporation) and through control of popular belief (the YMCA).

By the time Dos Passos left Harvard, he had expanded and sophisticated this position, but it was still basically intact. Two major essays of this period articulate the notion of a restrictive force on the one hand and a potentially liberating energy on the other. "A Humble Protest," published in the *Harvard Monthly* of June 1916, is devoted principally to an attack on an industrial, mechanical civilization for its "demoralizing" of man, "body and soul." "Has not the world today," he asked, "somehow got itself enslaved by this immense machine, the Industrial system?"[2] In "Against American Literature," which appeared in the *New Republic* on October 14, 1916, Dos Passos found American literary expression thin and effete. "The tone of the higher sort of writing in this country," he stated, "is undoubtedly that of a well brought up and intelligent woman, tolerant, versed in the things of this world, quietly humorous, but bound tightly in the 'fetters' of niceness, of the middle-class outlook." Russian literature, with its "primitive savagery" and its "freshness, rank and lush as the vegetation of early May," is offered as a literature of a better and different kind. And, again, "an all-enveloping industrialism" is named as a principal cause of the limited range and depth of modern American writing.[3]

Of course, for an American writer of 1916 to attack industrialism and to call for a literature of honesty and vitality was not much in the way of innovative thinking. Both positions have deep roots in nineteenth-century radical belief, with Emerson, perhaps, the most obvious example of the attitude. But 1916 was not like any other moment in American intellectual history. The European war was at its height, and America was inexorably (despite Wilson's election promises) being drawn into the war. "Industrialism" was therefore not merely a symbol for that in society which shapes and controls vision and action; it was a symbol of the war itself, of that which openly oppresses freedom in the name of freedom and which kills the innocent in the name of a moral crusade. Running through Dos Passos' life and work from his graduation from Harvard to the early 1920s is a schematic conception of modern culture, a conception that in its intensity and oversimplification reflects both Dos Passos' youth and the troubled times. Society through its various institutions increasingly stifles the individual capacity to think, feel, and act freely. The function of the writer is to seek out through personal experience evidence of this reality and to make it known to the world at large. At the center of this belief is the notion of the negative quest of the artist. One pursues experience less to affirm a faith than to reveal its corruption, though an affirmation of a kind is nevertheless implicit in the often bitter and satiric representation of the failure of society to live by its proclaimed values.

Dos Passos' own undertaking of this quest began during 1916–17 with his departure from Harvard, with the deaths of his parents, and with the personal adventure of a half year in Spain on his own. It reached full expression with the extraordinary widening of his range of experience that occurred through his service first as a volunteer ambulance-corps driver during 1917–18 and then as an enlisted man in the army during 1918–19. The initial major literary expression of this quest, and the seminal work for much of Dos Passos' writing until the mid-1920s, is his lengthy unpublished novel "Seven Times Round the Walls of Jericho." Dos Passos began this work in collaboration with his Harvard friend Robert Hillyer while the two were serving as ambulance drivers on the Verdun front in the summer of 1917. Hillyer, however, contributed only a few chapters. By the time Dos Passos left the Italian front for home (and army service) in the summer of 1918 he had completed three lengthy sections of the novel.

"Seven Times" tells the story of Fibbie Howe from a middle-class childhood through prep school and Harvard.[4] The general theme of the novel, much of which rehearses Dos Passos' own childhood and youth, is that family, school, and finally society as a whole attempt to force us into accepted conventions of belief and behavior. We therefore live in a sea of lies about life. Fibbie told yarns as a child; hence his nickname. But as Dos Passos wrote in a letter of January 4, 1918, in which he summarized the novel, "There's a general undercurrent of the feeling that instead of Fibbie being the liar—it is Society." The two central figures of the novel, Fibbie and Suzanne, therefore struggle "against the incomparable asininity of things in general—conventions, social ordinances, the lies of a civilization, living in the shell of a totally different way of life—now dead a hundred years or more."[5]

"Seven Times" is a typical first novel in its autobiographical literalism and in its concentration on adolescent malaise, and it is not surprising that Dos Passos was unable to find a publisher for it. He nevertheless drew upon various aspects of the work throughout his early career. Fibbie's uncle, a rebellious truth-sayer and a model for Fibbie's own later rebelliousness, is a playwright. His play, which is described at great length, becomes Dos Passos' own expressionistic attack on the lies of society, *The Garbage Man* (completed in 1923). A minor figure during Fibbie's Harvard years is John Andrews, a musician, who evolves into the central character of *Three Soldiers*. And on his way back from Italy in the summer of 1918, Dos Passos wrote a fourth section of "Seven Times" dealing with the experience of Fibbie (now Martin) as an ambulance driver. This section was published in 1920 as a separate work under the title *One Man's Initiation—1917*. Indeed, Dos Passos at one time also contemplated incorporating his almost completed *Streets of Night* into the portion of "Seven Times" set during Fibbie's Harvard years.[6]

This large body of work is linked not only by its common origin in or association with Dos Passos' unpublished novel but by a common underlying theme. On October 5, 1918, while serving as an enlisted man in a work detail at Camp Crane, New Jersey, Dos Passos wrote to a friend: "Organization is death. Organization is death. . . . I repeat the words over and over."[7] Dos Passos' melodramatic vehemence stems from the massive demonstration offered by army enlisted life of the capacity of an institutionalized structure to control and destroy the individual's freedom to think and act, whether by force or by manipulation of truth. Dos Passos' early ideas were thus fully confirmed by his army service and were soon afterwards fully expressed in his army novel, *Three Soldiers,* a work that interprets his military experience in the light of the myth of the industrial state and the free spirit. The army in *Three Soldiers,* as a machine that controls by strength and lies, symbolizes the merely more subtle manipulative devices of the social machine at large. Of the three soldiers in the work, Andrews and Crisfield are crushed by brute strength and Fuselli by false promises, but all are destroyed.

Dos Passos' work of this period has the force and integrity of his intense commitment to the ideal of freedom. Each of his three works of this phase of his career thus has considerable interest. *Streets of Night* (finally published, after much delay, in 1923) is perhaps the outstanding example in American literary history of a single-minded dramatization of T. S. Eliot's equation of social convention with emotional and spiritual impotency. And *One Man's Initiation* and *Three Soldiers* (1921) seek—in ways that instructed an entire generation—to distinguish between the reality of war and the social and rhetorical constructs required to bring men to accept that reality.

But the three novels are also predictable and conventional.

Whether or not the Sensitive Young Man is specifically present (and he is indeed prominent in *One Man's Initiation* and *Three Soldiers*), the novels are nevertheless pervaded with the same aura of personal hurt and frustration at the world's crassness and its failure to understand that is the principal tonal quality of "Seven Times Round the Walls of Jericho." For the most part, they also echo the conventional bildungsroman form of "Seven Times," in which the novel as autobiography structures almost all essential characteristics of the narrative. They are, in short, young men's books in which personal revolt is raised to the level of an all-encompassing Truth. Family, society, politics, literature—all are viewed as oppressive, with the war serving as the cumulative and climactic symbol of destructive repression. Dos Passos' maturation as a novelist during the 1920s (*Three Soldiers* was completed in 1920) was not gained by the denial of this deeply held belief. Rather, it was achieved by his discovery of new and compelling forms for its expression that both enlarged and deepened its implications.

The three works that best reveal Dos Passos' increasing artistic maturity during the 1920s are *Rosinante to the Road Again* (1922), *Manhattan Transfer* (1925), and "300 N.Y. Agitators Reach Passaic" (1926). Although these—and especially *Manhattan Transfer*—are major efforts in their own right, I will discuss each principally in relation to Dos Passos' movement toward the themes and techniques of *U.S.A.*

Rosinante to the Road Again has its origin in Dos Passos' visit to Spain in late 1916, between his graduation from Harvard and his father's death in early 1917, an event that brought him back to America and that also led to his two-year involvement in the war. As is clear from Dos Passos' "A Humble Protest" and "Against American Literature," both of which were written before he left for Spain, he went abroad predisposed to discover alternatives to the "industrialism" that he believed was vitiating American life. He was not disappointed. Within a month of arriving, he wrote in his notebook: "Compare the civilized savagery of Spain with the savage civilization of America."[8] And compare he did. In the music and theater of Spain, in many of its writers, and most of all in its village life he found evidence of a freedom and vitality lacking in America. His essay "Young Spain," which appeared in *Seven Arts* in August 1917, articulated this theme fully.

Whether Dos Passos contemplated in mid-1917 a further exploration of his Spanish matter we do not know. In any case, the war intervened, and with it "Seven Times Round the Walls of Jericho" and the works stemming from it. When Dos Passos was discharged from the army in mid-1919, he again visited Spain and spent almost nine months there. He gave most of his energy to completing *Three Soldiers,* but his extended reinvolvement in Spain also renewed his interest in the country as a literary subject. Indeed, the war itself served this purpose, for the basis of his fascination with Spain—its difference from other Western societies—was confirmed by his firsthand experience of the destructive chaos that was the principal "benefit" of modern industrialism. Between late 1919 and early 1921 Dos Passos wrote sixteen essays about contemporary Spain. These were published from October 1920 to April 1922, largely in the *Freeman.* With some revision (and with the inclusion as well of a revised version of his "Young Spain" article) the essays appeared as *Rosinante to the Road Again* in March 1922.[9]

The significance of *Rosinante,* and the basis of its relationship to Dos Passos' emerging literary sophistication during the early 1920s, lies in his ability to make a complex form express an increasingly complex version of his basic cast of mind. *Rosinante* consists of three different kinds of prose—a mythic search narrative, polemic personal essays, and discursive analytical essays. The book as a whole—as will be true of *U.S.A.*—combines these diverse forms into a work with a single powerful theme.[10]

The narrative portion of *Rosinante* comprises eight chapters, including the first, "A Gesture and a Quest," and the last, "Toledo"; the remaining six are dispersed throughout the book. The narrative element thus frames the work as a whole and also supplies it with pace and continuity. The two central figures in the narrative are Telemachus and his companion Lyaeus. In Madrid, at the opening of the book, they witness a performance by the flamenco dancer Pastora and sense that in the intensity of her dancing, an intensity that seems to dramatize the self at its most expressive and impassioned, there may lie the meaning of Spain. This meaning—which Tel calls the "gesture" of Spain—they determine to explore further by a journey to Toledo, the ancient soul of Spain. After various minor adventures on the road, they reach Toledo, where Tel decides that they have indeed discovered the import of the gesture.

This portion of *Rosinante* is built on an elaborate series of dualisms, each of which makes a contribution to the "gesture" theme. Tel, an intellectual with a conscience (symbolized by his mother, Penelope), and Lyaeus, a sensualist and carouser, are closely identified with a traditional soul/body dualism. They meet on the road a confirmation of this permanent division in human nature in the form of several figures resembling either Don Quixote or Sancho Panza. And in Toledo the theme is further reinforced by their arrival in the ancient religious city during the raucous carnival season. The meaning implied by Pastora's flamenco dancing—that a heightened and free expression of man's deepest nature, of both his body and soul, is still possible in Spain—is thus clarified and confirmed by the quest and its conclusion.

The narrative chapters of *Rosinante* reveal Dos Passos' closeness to several major literary currents of the early 1920s. The Tel and Lyaeus figures, as well as the *Don Quixote* reference underlying both the work as a whole and several individual segments, represent Dos Passos' use, in a manner recently popularized by Joyce and Eliot, of a mythic substructure and allusiveness to express the theme of the limitations placed on the feeling self by modern society.[11] But as is also true of Joyce and Eliot, Dos Passos uses myth to express a personal theme as well. The impulsive journey from Madrid to Toledo with a friend was based on Dos Passos' own adventure in December 1916, when he and a Harvard acquaintance decided to walk to Toledo while imagining themselves in Cervantes' Spain.[12] More significantly, Telemachus himself is a semi-ironic self-portrait. His inner compulsions, which Dos Passos represented as a conventional and censorious mother and an absent father, the finding of whom somehow constitutes meaning,[13] are both a universal configuration and Dos Passos' own specific state of mind during the early 1920s. In particular, Tel's fear of and attraction for the Lyaeus side of his nature was a characteristic of Dos Passos' temperament that both he (in his Camera Eye passages in *U.S.A.*) and Edmund Wilson (in his fictionalized portrait of Dos Passos in *I Thought of Daisy*) later fully confirmed.

Chapters 2 and 3 of *Rosinante*, "The Donkey Boy" and "The Baker of Almorox," comprise a second major prose form in the work, the polemic personal essay. Despite the few examples of the form in the work as a whole (only these two out of seventeen chapters), the portion given over to it constitutes the most important segment of the book, as is suggested by the strategic placing of the essays immediately after the announcement of the quest and by their being of far greater length than most other chapters. In these two chapters, a first-person narrator (the Tel quest chapters are in third person) recounts some lively, piquant experiences in out-of-the-way places—a mountain road in Andalusia and a small village near Madrid.[14] In both chapters, the experience serves as an excuse for the expression of a strongly held view—that the rough-hewn life of rural Spain, where one lives poorly in body but free in spirit, is far preferable to the "rich" but spiritually impoverished life of industrial America. But paradoxically—and this will be a paradox that will grow in Dos Passos' thought until it becomes (in his later career) an obsession—freedom lies, not in the pursuit of change, but in the preservation of the past, in maintaining one's sense of self in relation to an unchanging source of values in one's heritage.

> It was all so mellow, so strangely aloof from the modern world of feverish change, this life of the peasants of Almorox. Everywhere roots striking into the infinite past. . . . [There] always remained the love for the place, the strong anarchistic reliance on the individual man, the walking, consciously or not, of the way beaten by generations of men who had tilled and loved and lain in the cherishing sun with no feeling of a reality outside of themselves, outside of the bare encompassing hills of their commune, except the God which was the synthesis of their souls and of their lives.[15]

Here, too, as in the quest chapters, there is a deeply conservative note resembling that of Joyce and especially Eliot in the early 1920s. The free pursuit of the life of the spirit in the present requires an acceptance of the truths embodied in the great myths and undying culture of the past. Dos Passos, of course, was eventually to domesticate this conservative center of his thought, to find these truths and this culture in the civil religion of America's past. But the cast of mind disposed to discover remedies for present ills in past values is already powerfully present in *Rosinante*.

The third kind of prose in *Rosinante* is more conventional than the quest and personal-polemic forms. In a number of critical essays Dos Passos describes and analyzes several areas of contemporary Spanish literary, intellectual, and artistic life. There are six such essays (some of which also contain a personal element), and their subjects range from the novelists Pío Baroja and Blasco Ibáñez and the poets Antonio Machado and Juan Maragall to the intellectuals Franciso Giner de los Ríos and Miguel de Unamuno and to the Madrid theater. The underlying theme of these essays, which are interspersed among the "Talk by the Road" quest chapters, is the vitality of those aspects of Spanish life that seek to identify and perpetuate the strong roots of Spanish individuality, and the falseness of those aspects that purvey clichéd images of Spain for popular international consumption. The essay on Baroja is of particular significance for the direction of Dos Passos' own work. Baroja, Dos Passos writes, is a social satirist whose picaresque narratives set in contemporary Spain reveal "a profound sense of the evil of existing institutions."[16]

Rosinante to the Road Again achieves a unified effect through a variety of seemingly unconnected and disparate means. The quest by Tel for the gesture of Spain, for the meaning that is a celebration of life in the midst of death and of the soul in the embrace of the body, is the meaning that the first-person narrator finds in the ancient ways of the villages and mountains of Spain and that the analytical essayist discovers in the work of many contemporary Spanish artists and writers. And it is a meaning, as Dos Passos expressed overtly on several occasions and implied throughout, that is not found in contemporary America. The relationship of this theme and form to *U.S.A.* is striking. Here, for the first time, Dos Passos has broken through to a fully juxtapositional form, one in which the parts of various different formal structures contribute to a central theme both individually and in their underlying reinforcement of each other as the work progresses. (*Three Soldiers,* which might be considered Dos Passos' first effort along these lines, is in truth principally a variation on the Victorian novel of multiple plots.) Here, too, the search for one's own self, as Tel seeks to reconcile his divided nature during his quest for the gesture of Spain, leads to a recognition that the two searches constitute a single quest for meaning—the meaning that both Spain and Tel are inseparably body and soul and that freedom is the supreme human condition. *U.S.A.* is of course a novel rather than a collection of various kinds of nonfictional prose. But in that work, too, a personal search (that of the Camera Eye) will also lead to the discovery of the meaning of an entire culture; and in *U.S.A.* a rhetoric of strikingly diverse modes will also contribute to the central in-

sight that to live freely in the present we must recover the truths of
the past.

Although *Rosinante to the Road Again* is Dos Passos' first major
venture into literary modernism, it is not a fully successful work.
One source of weakness lies in its miscellaneous origin. The book,
as I have noted, had its genesis in a personal essay of 1917 ("Young
Spain"), which Dos Passos several years later supplemented with a
series of discursive critical articles about modern Spanish intellectual and artistic life. He then conceived and wrote, as a final stage
in the preparation of the volume, the only fully cohesive portion of
the book, a series of narrative chapters with a pseudomythological
structure.[17] The nature and shape of *Rosinante,* in brief, appears
to have evolved during its preparation rather than to have existed,
before composition, as a formal construct in Dos Passos' mind. As a
result the work has a number of anomalies. Most obviously, Chapter 7, "Cordova No Longer of the Caliphs," which Dos Passos included because it is among his Spanish journalism of 1919–21, is
principally political reportage about an Andalusian farmers' strike
and has little substantive or formal relationship to the other essays
of *Rosinante*. In short, in preparing *Rosinante* Dos Passos had yet
to discover the paradoxical modernistic truism that the more experimental a form, the more controlled intellectualization it requires in advance of its execution.

   Rosinante is also somewhat out of focus. Although the
underlying impulse behind the book is Dos Passos' dissatisfaction
with American life, the work communicates this theme in large
part indirectly through personal and national metaphor—that is,
through the adventures and character of Tel and the nature of
Spain. The book therefore has the effect of having been written by
an author who has something on his mind but who is expressing
his preoccupation so obliquely that the reader is in danger of missing this concern. The lessons offered to Dos Passos' burgeoning
modernistic imagination by *Rosinante* were thus twofold—that
conception of form should coincide with conception of subject
matter, and that subject matter should be closely allied to theme.
The triumph of *Manhattan Transfer* as a major expression of modernism lies in part in Dos Passos' successful absorption of these
lessons.

   Dos Passos was, in a sense, a New Yorker. His father lived
and worked there, and Dos Passos himself, during his peripatetic

youth, was in and out of the city, especially during his Harvard years, when he often stayed with his aunt and uncle on his mother's side, the Madisons. But his full experience of New York began in August 1920, when he arrived in the city as a young man of twenty-four after three years abroad. He plunged into the life of the metropolis and almost immediately began to view it in surreal terms, as if he were testing the city's potential for extended literary development. He wrote a French friend in September 1920 that "New York—after all—is magnificent." It is, he continued, "a city of cavedwellers, with a frightful, brutal ugliness about it, full of thunderous voices of metal grinding on metal and of an eternal sound of wheels which turn, turn, turn on heavy stones. People swarm meekly like ants along designated routes, crushed by the disdainful and pitiless things around them." The city reminds him of

> Nineveh and Babylon, of Ur of the Chaldees, of the immense cities which loom like basilisks behind the horizon in ancient Jewish tales, where the temples rose as high as mountains and people ran trembling through dirty little alleys to the constant noise of whips with hilts of gold. O for the sound of a brazen trumpet which, like the voice of the Baptist in the desert, will sing again about the immensity of man in this nothingness of iron, steel, marble, and rock. Night time especially is both marvellous and appalling, seen from the height of a Roof Garden, where women with raucous voices dance in an amber light, the blue-gray bulk of the city cut up by the enormous arabesques of electric billboards, when the streets where automobiles scurry about like cockroaches are lost in a golden dust, and when a pathetic little moon, pale and dazzled, looks at you across a leaden sky.[18]

Before Dos Passos could raise his "brazen trumpet" to translate these images into fiction, he had to bring to completion several other projects already under way. *Three Soldiers* and *Rosinante* had to be seen through the press, and *Streets of Night* and *The Garbage Man* required additional work. And Dos Passos had once again to satisfy his wanderlust, this time with an extended trip to Europe and the Near East from early 1921 to early 1922 and yet another visit to Europe in the spring and summer of 1923. But in the early fall of 1923, back in New York, he began *Manhattan Transfer.*

The New York that Dos Passos shaped into the narratives and images of the novel derived in part from his knowledge of the artistic and radical worlds of Greenwich Village, where he lived during the early 1920s. In particular, the theatrical setting of the Ellen Thatcher narrative, as well as of several minor narratives related to hers, owes much to Dos Passos' interest in the theater during this period. Ellen herself seems to be a composite of several "advanced" women—especially Elaine Orr Thayer Cummings and Esther Andrews—whom Dos Passos knew, while Dos Passos' middle-class relatives, the Madisons, served as models for the Merivales and supplied sources for various other business figures and narratives. And there was a rich vein of material in past and present newspaper accounts of events that appeared to Dos Passos to be characteristic of life in the metropolis, accounts that he drew heavily upon for several narratives.[19] In short, Dos Passos was beginning to acquire the ability to transmute all levels and kinds of experience, including researched "experience," into fictional representation, unlike his earlier reliance, in the "Seven Times" phase of his career, on a largely unmediated autobiographical method and subject matter.

One of the principal motifs in Dos Passos' account of the city in his letter of September 1920 is that New York is a place of rapid movement, of a frantic scurrying that is both animal and mechanical in character. To Dos Passos this motion was not only horizontal in the sense of movement to and from and within the city but also vertical in the conventional metaphorical sense of success and failure. One came to the city seeking success and one either found it and rose or was crushed and exiled.

The Garbage Man, a play that Dos Passos initially drafted in 1920 and that he completed in the spring of 1923, reveals his predilection, just before he began *Manhattan Transfer,* for the expression of ideas about success and failure in abstract form.[20] *The Garbage Man* is self-conscious expressionism. Its characters are archetypes; its scenes allegorical tableaux. Tom and Jane, the principal figures in the play, constitue Dos Passos' paradigm of the American myth of success. Tom, without a specific sense of direction, wants to live the good and full life while remaining free in spirit; Jane wants success. She becomes a popular actress; he is swept away by the Garbage Man. The play is painfully raucous and obvious. But it does point in a useful way to Dos Passos' parallel effort in *Manhattan Transfer* to use a stylized representation of the city as the setting for the playing out of the tragedy of the American dream. (*The Garbage Man* is also set largely in New York.) It anticipates as well his proclivity toward the division of the dream of success into the sexual roles of the male as reluctant and failed seeker and the woman as betrayer of the man in her eager pursuit of success.

Perhaps the most significant and far-reaching consequence of Dos Passos' New York experience of the early 1920s was his deep interest in the various artistic and literary movements of the period that encouraged the conception of fiction as a form of experimental pictorial art. Dos Passos himself later recalled the artistic ferment of the early 1920s, with its emphasis on the visual:

> Some of the poets who went along with the cubism of the painters of the School of Paris had talked about simultaneity. There was something about Rimbaud's poetry that tended to stand up off the page. Direct snapshots of life. Rapportage was a great slogan. The artist must record the fleeting world the way the motion picture film recorded it. By contrast, juxtaposition, montage, he could build drama into his narrative. Somewhere along the way I had been impressed by Eisenstein's motion pictures, by his version of old D. W. Griffith's technique. Montage was his key word.[21]

Dos Passos is referring principally to two major innovative art movements of the early twentieth century—cubism and other nonrepresentational forms (such as futurism) in painting, and the motion picture. He had been aware of avant-garde painting since his early Harvard days, when one of his classmates, Edward Nagel, was an enthusiast of the new movement. (Dos Passos' first two years at Harvard, 1912–14, coincided with the high point of cubism in France.) And like many others, he found the Armory Show (which he saw in Boston in the spring of 1913) "a real jolt."[22] Yet despite this interest, cubism and futurism (he had also read some of the futurist poets in Italy in 1918) had little impact on his writing until he began work on *Manhattan Transfer* in 1923.

A number of factors combined in early 1923 to impel Dos Passos toward an experimental fictional form based on visual analogies. First, he himself had begun—on his arrival in New York in 1920—to sketch and paint with a strong undercurrent of cubistic technique. This interest culminated in January 1923 when he and

Adelaide Lawson held a joint exhibition at the Whitney Studio Club.[23] (The best published example of this phase of Dos Passos' artwork is his watercolor sketch "Baghdad: The Bazaars That Burned" in his 1927 travel book, *Orient Express*.) Also, he began at this time to realize (along with many others in the avant-garde) the relevance of D. W. Griffith's work in film—principally *Birth of a Nation* (1915) and *Intolerance* (1916)—for those interested in the relationship of the visual arts to literature. For the film montage techniques of Griffith and Eisenstein, in which discrete images follow one another in time, had far more direct implication for the writer of narrative than had the single flat surface of a painting.[24] And, finally, if a relationship between these new art forms and New York as a subject was required, Dos Passos was provided one in the work of such New York cubists of the early 1920s as Joseph Stella and John Marin.[25]

The key terms in Dos Passos' recollection of the art scene of the early 1920s—simultaneity, juxtaposition, and montage—can serve as guides to an understanding of the impact of visual forms on his work of this period. The experimental stance that these terms seek to convey is that the artist, whether painter or writer, is not bound by a common sense representationalism in which the artwork must achieve a close approximation to what is generally accepted as reality. By the very act of isolating an object or event within the frame of a painting or within a narrative, the artist introduces his stylizing and conceptualizing consciousness into the art process. Art therefore is the product of an intellect brought to bear on an object in an effort to render it more truly. And for this particular moment in the history of art, truth appeared to be encompassed by simultaneity, juxtaposition, and montage.

Simultaneity and juxtaposition were derived principally from cubism and futurism.[26] As one historian has put it, at its most basic, cubism is an effort to construct a "pure geometry" of forms.[27] An object is not so much seen as perceived; that is, the components of its inherent but not superficially visible form are realized and then represented. The object is recreated with its underlying variety and complexity of form visible from the viewer's single perspective even though it required a multiplicity of angles of perception at different moments in time by the artist to gain this understanding of the object. Thus is achieved "the simultaneous juxtaposition in the same picture of aspects which can only be perceived successively in time."[28] As Dos Passos implied in his recollection of the impact of cubism on the literary scene of the early

1920s, the movement had more immediate resonance for poetry (hence the Rimbaud allusion) than for fiction. One could readily conceive of a sequence of symbolist images as an exercise in "simultaneous juxtaposition," as an effort to isolate out and then present as a seemingly single moment of apprehension a series of superficially unconnected but inherently joined visceral responses to an object or event. But the potential application of a cubist concept of art to narrative was perhaps not fully realized by the writers of the day until it was understood that montage, because it was basically a technique of juxtaposition, was both a cubist art technique and a device clearly adaptable to fiction.

Montage, like simultaneity and juxtaposition, assumes that the viewer—now the person viewing what the camera lens has viewed—need not see what can be seen only from a single perspective. The camera can move both in angle and distance within a single scene or it can photograph two entirely different scenes. The various angles, distances, and scenes can then be joined by editing (that is, by montage) into a single sequence. Of course, montage produces a somewhat different effect than a cubist painting, in that the consciously dissected object (the event) exists in a sequence of images rather than in one "frozen" image. But the illusion of simultaneity is nevertheless gained because we are encountering the event in swiftly juxtaposed images, as though the event were indeed frozen in time in order for it to be seen from various angles and distances.

Dos Passos now had several suggestive models for his own attempt to write a "rapportage" of New York. Like the cubist painters around him, he wished to peel the city down to its constitutent forms, to its underlying "geometry" of meaning, and in the technique of montage he had a device that was congruent to the narrative form of fiction. He would conceive of New York, not as constituting a single story (comparable to the traditional representationalist device of a single perspective on an object), but as comprising many stories (the cubist's multiple angles of vision). And he would combine these stories, which constituted the inherent form and meaning of the city, through montage, through the constant juxtaposition of a portion of one story and a portion of another.[29] He would thus recreate through juxtapositional simultaneity, through the constant relevance of one narrative thread to the others, the nature and meaning of the object that was a modern American city.

It might also be useful to clarify at this point the relationship

between the visual arts matrix of *Manhattan Transfer* and what is
today called the spatial novel.[30] Spatiality is a modern critical term
for fiction that seeks to involve us less in a forward-moving chronology (that is, action and plot) than in the interrelatedness
throughout the novel of image patterns, symbols, and leitmotifs.
This pervasive atemporal interconnectedness, it is argued, produces an illusion that we are encountering a static image rather
than participating in a forward-moving sequence of events. That
is, it produces the spatial novel. Of course, most major fiction is in
part spatial, but the term is usually reserved for works since the
late nineteenth century—*Ulysses* is often a prime example—that
are consciously experimental in nature. *Manhattan Transfer* and
U.S.A. are both spatial novels in the sense that each seeks through
its various parts to create an image of a single object, New York or
America. But the distinctive kind of spatiality that they exhibit can
probably best be studied and understood in relation to Dos Passos'
responsiveness to the implications for fiction of simultaneity, juxtaposition, and montage.

Manhattan Transfer is similar to two other major novels published
in 1925, *The Great Gatsby* and *An American Tragedy,* in its emphasis on the centrality of the myth of success in American life.
For Dos Passos, the American obsessive need to gain success had
always been linked to the nature of America as a modern industrial
society and had thus been a recurrent theme in his work from the
beginning of his career. For *Manhattan Transfer,* however, Dos
Passos found in the large metropolitan city a far more effective evo-
cation of the idea of "industrialism" than the abstractions that appear in *Rosinante.* Arrival in the city is to begin seeking success;
departure from it is to fail. The lives of the major figures in the
novel are jaundiced readings, in the context of this axiom of city
life, of legendary roles within the American myth of success. The
unscrupulous lawyer, the corrupt politician, the sharp-witted immigrant, and the conscienceless banker push ahead, while the
dull-minded country boy, the failed stock-exchange gambler, the
simple working girl, and the returned veteran go under.

The success myth is also the controlling force in the lives of
Jimmy and Ellen, the figures who receive the fullest attention and
the only characters whose lives we follow from childhood to climactic determining acts as adults. Jimmy is restless, unhappy, and
directionless because he cannot accept the drive to achieve suc-

cess that life in New York demands of him. Ellen, on the other hand, adapts to the constraining roles that an upward climb demands. The failure of their love and marriage, with Jimmy leaving the city a penniless wanderer and Ellen remaining, having gained comfort and prominence, is Dos Passos' schematic moral commentary on the myth of success. To fail is to be cast out but to preserve the possibility of continuing to live inwardly as a seeker after meaning; to win is to die spiritually. Indeed, so programmatic is Dos Passos' dramatization of the success theme that he seems himself to parody its obvious moralism in several of the minor narrative threads. So, for example, Cassie, a friend of Ellen's, is an arty dancer who is forced to popularize her "art" if she is to find work. "I feel," she says, "I've got it in me, something without a name fluttering inside, a bird of beautiful plumage in a howid iron cage." But McAvoy, her lover, takes little interest in her caged spirit. "I want money," he says. "Once you got money you can do what you like."[31]

Which is to say that we don't read *Manhattan Transfer* for an insight into human nature. Most of its minor figures are either types or caricatures, while Jimmy and Ellen belong to Dos Passos' extensive gallery of artist-manqué figures (he the writer, she the actress) whose spirits are challenged or destroyed by the materialism of American life. This is not to say, however, that Dos Passos' two major characters are entirely without interest. The youthful Jimmy in the First Section is one of Dos Passos' more engaging autobiographical portraits. And Ellen—as Linda Wagner has demonstrated[32]—can be sympathetically interpreted as a besieged feminine figure in a hostile masculine world. Nevertheless, one reads *Manhattan Transfer* not for depth of characterization but for the brilliance of Dos Passos' overall design, for his effort to achieve a formal expression of American life. One reads it, in other words, as one looks at a nonrepresentational painting, not for its "subject" but for its "shape."

Broadly speaking, the "shape" of *Manhattan Transfer,* its character as conscious artistic design, consists of two major elements—its multiple plots, which are themselves broken into multiple narrative segments, and its surreal image patterns. Of these, Dos Passos' manipulation of plot is the most significant—both for *Manhattan Transfer* and for his further development of the device in *U.S.A.* A brief account of the plotting in the First Section of *Manhattan Transfer* (approximately the first third of the novel) will indicate what is distinctive in the narrative technique of the

work. The section consists of thirty-six narrative segments, of
which all but seven are divided among five unrelated plot lines:
Ellen, Jimmy, Bud Korpenning (a farm boy in the city), George
Baldwin and the McNiels (a young lawyer and his working-class
clients), and Congo and Emile (two French immigrants). Their
narratives are broken into segments that are interspersed throughout the section. Each of the other seven segments of the section is
devoted to a brief vignette involving characters who do not reappear in the novel. Dos Passos' technique of multiple narratives is
comparable to the cubist technique of isolating out the underlying
components of the form of the object (here isolating out the "stories" that make up the city as a center for the American drive
toward success) and then arranging them into a geometric composition. The breaking up of the "planes of vision" that are the separate plots into brief interspersed fragments is Dos Passos'
adaptation of the techinque of montage in order to heighten the
illusion of simultaneity, the illusion that a narrative moment in one
plot line is occurring at the same moment as the narrative moments in immediately juxtaposed plot lines.[33] The unconnected vignettes have a literary analogue in the symbolist technique of the
abruptly interjected image that has little discursive relationship to
its adjoining images. But in more suggestive visual terms, the vignettes can be associated with collage in cubism, in which an object from "real life"—a piece of newspaper, a menu card, an
advertisement—is "pasted in" the painting as a form of concrete
referential imagery. The painter by this technique appears to validate and "explain" the abstraction of "real life" that is occurring
elsewhere in the painting, just as Dos Passos frequently offers in a
vignette a clear symbolic reading of a theme functioning more
obliquely in the extended and dispersed "geometric" narratives of
the novel.

    That Dos Passos sought to intellectualize the form of *Man-
hattan Transfer* from the onset of his composition of the novel is
evident from the surviving manuscripts of the work.[34] His notebooks and drafts reveal that each of the principal narratives was
initially written as a single consecutive narrative, usually in a small
separate notebook devoted to that narrative. Then, for his first holograph draft of the novel, Dos Passos engaged in two acts of abstracting: individual narratives were broken into segments and
spliced with other such broken narratives into an approximation of
the finished form of the novel; and individual vignette segments

were added. Then, after considerable juggling of segments,[35] a final order was achieved and the prose-poem epigraphs introducing each of the chapters were added.

How does Dos Passos' juxtapositional technique in fact work in *Manhattan Transfer?* Since my interest at this point is in the technique and not in a full reading of *Manhattan Transfer,* I will limit my discussion of the method to the single example of the opening of the novel, a portion that Dos Passos obviously crafted with some care in order to key the reader to the narrative form of the work. "Ferryslip," the first chapter of the First Section of *Manhattan Transfer,* comprises a brief prose-poem epigraph describing the docking of a ferry and four narrative segments. Of the four, three are devoted to narrative threads that will continue—two for Ellen and one for Bud Korpenning—and one to a vignette involving a Jewish immigrant. The common subject of the chapter is arrival—Bud and the immigrant coming to the city and the birth of Ellen—and the common theme is the necessity for evasion, disguise, and compromise if one is to succeed in the city. The narratives of Bud and Ellen will reinforce this theme in their later segments; the vignette states it with immediate dramatic force by its central event of a Jew shaving his beard in order to gain an American identity.

The opening chapter of *Manhattan Transfer* also reveals one of the principal paradoxical effects both of this novel and of *U.S.A.* The novel begins with a series of arrivals, and throughout the work characters move through the city at a feverish pace (a kind of inchoate "Brownian Motion," in Iain Colley's suggestive phrase[36]). The reader's sense of rapid motion is also enhanced by the discontinuous narrative lines that through imitative form suggest swift change. Moreover, *Manhattan Transfer* is a historical novel that takes the reader through an extended period of time. It contains many specific references to historical events from its opening in the late 1890s to its conclusion in the early 1920s. All in the novel, in brief, appears to be in motion in time and space. Yet the seemingly contradictory effect of simultaneity, of the representation of a single and static object, is also present. One way this effect is gained, as I have already noted, is by the underlying geometric design of Dos Passos' constant cross-stitching of theme in an apparently disparate group of narrative threads. Another is by the sense of stasis we have within characters. As the characters of *Manhattan Transfer* move forward in time and shift in space (that is, as

they reappear in new incidents), nothing changes in their essential
characters or in the direction of their fates. So George Baldwin and
Joe Harland (two major figures) remain what they are when we
initially meet them: the one on his way up, and the other down;
the one craftily planning each stage of his career, including the
purchase of love when he can afford it, and the other a Hurstwood
broken in spirit and accepting what the moment provides. Yet—
and here is where the paradox functions as a successful fictional
aesthetic—this potentially shallow repetitiousness affects us neither as shallow nor as repetitious, because figures such as Baldwin
and Harland are, within the work as a whole, compelling and significant as predictable planes of ascent and descent within the
geometric design of the work.

It was no doubt to strengthen the effect of carefully planned
intersecting planes within a conscious design that Dos Passos
adopted a narrative device that he would also use in *U.S.A.*, that of
bringing most of the major figures into some contact with each
other while maintaining the separate plotting of their individual
narratives. So, for example, George Baldwin plays a role in Ellen's
later career; Joe Harland is related to the Merivales and thus to
Jimmy; Congo frequently turns up in Jimmy's later narrative segments; and in one major scene, set in a roadhouse, most of the
major figures of the novel cross paths. Indeed, with some major
exceptions, by the close of the novel each of the principal characters has had some contact with at least one other principal character. Thus, inherent in Dos Passos' combining of the dynamicism of
the film and the stasis of the painting is the paradox that movement, including movement that contains the intersecting of otherwise distinct planes, exists to reveal a complex but static single
design.

Dos Passos also helps achieve the effect of simultaneity in
Manhattan Transfer through the more conventional device of repetitive threads of imagery and symbolism that contribute to the
spatial form of the novel. This device ranges from a generalized
image of the violent provided by the many accidents that occur
throughout the work to more specific recurrent images of the destructive in the fire and fire-engine symbolism. It also includes
particularized clusters of imagery attached to particular characters, such as the mechanical-doll images that recur in Ellen's
stream-of-consciousness reveries or the circular images central to

Jimmy's sense of himself. In these and other such leitmotifs, Dos Passos dramatizes—often through a surreal overemphasis—the compulsions both in the city as a whole and in its residents that are the static, permanent realities of life in the metropolis.

For all its suggestive approximation of a visual form, *Manhattan Transfer* contains a number of flaws. One weakness lies in the conventionality of the Jimmy-Ellen relationship, a conventionality not entirely disguised by the experimental form in which it appears. Theirs is a Jazz Age soap opera. Jimmy as the artist who almost fatally compromises himself for love, Ellen as the attractive woman who exploits her looks and sheds love as a hindrance to success, and Stan Emery (Ellen's one true love) as a drunken playboy who dies tragically touch too many bases of conventional 1920s sentiment. Much of the weakness in this aspect of the novel stems from Dos Passos' continuing difficulty with autobiographical characters. The problem is not that Dos Passos draws upon autobiographical detail for Jimmy but that once having done so he is unable to maintain sufficient distance from him to prevent the portrait from becoming that of yet another of his thwarted sensitive young men.

But the major limitation of *Manhattan Transfer*—a limitation principally from the perspective of the greater success of *U.S.A.*—lies in the unfulfilled potential of the work. Dos Passos had pushed on from *Rosinante* to a fully conscious and planned intellectualization of form, but he had not realized that the abstracting of objects into fictional form could go beyond the use of the narrative mode. One of the unintended effects of the almost total commitment of *Manhattan Transfer* to narrative (even most of the prose poems have a strong narrative element) is that despite Dos Passos' approximation of simultaneity, the novel—especially in its later portions—often functions like a Victorian novel of multiple plots in which there is merely the inconvenience of breaks and interruptions before a specific plot continues. The breakthrough to a more compelling and innovative cubistic form in *U.S.A.* occurs because of Dos Passos' recognition that there lay "buried" within the narrative form of *Manhattan Transfer* a number of other distinctive modes that he could separate out of narrative in order to intellectualize and abstract even more fully the object he was seeking to perceive and depict. His next major step, in other words, was to recognize that narrative itself is a conventional mode, something akin to representationalism, but that narrative contained elements of other forms of discourse that, when radically isolated and expressed, could contribute powerfully to his interpretive design.

Perhaps the most easily identifiable of these "buried" modes in *Manhattan Transfer* is that of the stream-of-consciousness passages devoted to Jimmy and Ellen. These are usually brief but intense moments in which surreal images of escape (for Jimmy) or oppression (for Ellen) prevail. In *U.S.A.* Dos Passos limited the fiction of introspection to one of the four modal divisions in the work—the Camera Eye—where it is not only the sole form of expression within the division but is used openly and exclusively for the depiction of Dos Passos' response to his own experience. Through this narrowing and intensification Dos Passos was able to solve two problems in the rhetoric of fiction that had plagued him since the beginning of his career. He was at last able to achieve a "draining off [of] the subjective" (as he later put it)[37] into a form appropriate to it rather than to have it appear in diffused and awkward form in semiautobiographical fictional figures. And he was able, because of the greater freedom and depth of introspection encouraged by the open and fully conscious exploration of self, to render his life and feelings with a force and pertinence he had never before gained.

As well as being a "private" novel in its stream-of-consciousness passages, *Manhattan Transfer* is full of the public trivia of modern life, of the verbal detritus of misleading newspaper stories, inflated speeches, and sentimental popular songs. Indeed, Dos Passos' satire of this aspect of American life, especially of newspapers and advertising, is a major current in the novel. (Some of this stems from Jimmy's job as a newspaperman, but much also arises out of Dos Passos' parody of 1920s journalistic style in the reporting of such events as Dutch and Francie's career as the Flapper Bandits.) Moreover, as a historical novel *Manhattan Transfer* contains frequent references to public events, especially to those involving the war. For *U.S.A.,* Dos Passos abstracted and isolated the historical and social context of the narratives in *Manhattan Transfer* into the distinctive nonfictional experimental modes of the Newsreels and biographies. Dos Passos thus seemingly defictionalized these two aspects of public life (just as in the Camera Eye he seemingly defictionalized the autobiographical) in order to express in more emphatic form their essential nature. I say seemingly because the separating out of the personal and the public from the narrative in *U.S.A.* in fact played a significant role in the creation of a new and striking overarching fictional design.

One final "buried" aspect of *Manhattan Transfer* that demands attention is the relatively minor theme in the novel of the modern corruption of language, of the falsification of life through the way we communicate our understanding of life.[38] This major concern of *U.S.A.*, which was to control much of its theme and form, appears in *Manhattan Transfer*, for example, in Phineas P. Blackhead, a figure who anticipates J. Ward Moorehouse of *U.S.A.* Blackhead, a shady corporation lawyer, remarks to two other lawyers of a similar kind: "The attitude of the railroad and docking interests that I represent is one of frankness and honesty, you know that. . . . I have confidence, I can say I have the completest confidence, that we can settle this matter amicably and agreeably. . . . Of course, you must meet me halfway. . . . We have I know the same interests at heart, the interests of this great city, of this great seaport. . . ."[39] Almost every formal address in the novel (a judge sentencing Dutch and Francie, Merivale making an imaginary speech, and so on) and every newspaper report reveal a similar misuse of the traditional language of probity and justice for various class and personal ends. No wonder that Jimmy, who is aware of much of this verbal corruption, says toward the end of the novel, "If only I still had faith in words."[40] But this theme is diffused in *Manhattan Transfer* within the "representational" nature of the various narratives in which it appears. Like the private and public modes I have been discussing, it, too, in *U.S.A.* will be made far more central and evident through a greater conceptualization of its expression.

Dos Passos' *New Masses* article of June 1926, "300 N. Y. Agitators Reach Passaic," is significant for the presence of two new important dimensions of his career and work that would be fully reflected in *U.S.A.*—his personal involvement in the activities and concerns of the radical left and his expression of this involvement through an all-enveloping ironic style.

Dos Passos first became deeply committed to the left in the early spring of 1926, on his return to New York after a lengthy stay abroad. Of course, he had been critical of American life from his earliest writings while still a Harvard undergraduate. But now, like many other American writers during the mid-1920s, he was

caught up by the possibility of translating criticism into political
and literary activism. Almost immediately upon his return he
joined the New Playwrights Theatre, a group committed to the
production of left-wing plays. Almost as promptly he agreed to become a member of the board of editors of the left-wing *New
Masses,* which published its first issue in May 1926. And in June
1926 Dos Passos journeyed to Boston to interview Sacco and Vanzetti in prison, an event that began his intense engagement during
1926–27 in the effort to save their lives. The failure of this effort, in
1927, was to play a major role in impelling him toward the writing
of *U.S.A.*

The Passaic textile strike (which also appears in the Mary
French narrative in *U.S.A.*) was one of the first large-scale attempts by the Communist party to control an industrial dispute.
The strike had already dragged through several difficult months
when early in April 1926 a group of picketing strikers had the Riot
Act read to them. From this time on, all public meetings and
speeches were forbidden. After several radical notables had tested
this prohibition and were arrested, Dos Passos journeyed to Passaic
with a group of left-wing intellectuals who were also seeking to
test and break the ban. His *New Masses* account of the incident,
since it is both brief and not widely known, is here reprinted in
full:

The people who had come from New York roamed in
a desultory group along the broad pavement. We were talking of outrages and the Bill of Rights. The people who had
come from New York wore warm overcoats in the sweeping
wind, bits of mufflers, and fluffiness of women's blouses
fluttered silky in the cold April wind. The people who had
come from New York filled up a row of taxicabs, shiny sedans of various makes, nicely upholstered; the shiny sedans started off in a procession toward the place where the
meeting was going to be forbidden. Inside we talked in a
desultory way of outrages and the Bill of Rights, we, de-
scendants of the Pilgrim Fathers, the Bunker Hill Monu-
ment, Gettysburg, the Boston Teaparty. . . . Know all men
by these present. . . . On the corners groups of yellowish
gray people standing still, square people standing still as
chunks of stone, looking nowhere, saying nothing.

At the place where the meeting was going to be forbidden the people from New York got out of their shiny se-

dans of various makes. The sheriff was a fat man with a
badge like a star off a Christmas tree, the little eyes of a
suspicious landlady in a sallow face. The cops were waving
their clubs about, limbering up their arms. The cops were
redfaced, full of food, the cops felt fine. The special deputies had restless eyes, they were stocky young men
crammed with pop and ideals, overgrown boy-scouts; they
were on the right side and they knew it. Still the shiny new
doublebarreled riot guns made them nervous. They didn't
know which shoulder to keep their guns on. The people
who had come from New York stood first on one foot then
on the other.
　　Don't shoot till you see the whites of their eyes. . . .
　　All right move 'em along, said the sheriff.
　　The cops advanced, the special deputies politely held
open the doors of the shiny sedans. The people who had
come from New York climbed into the shiny sedans of various makes and drove away except for one man who got
picked up. The procession of taxis started back the way it
had come. The procession of taxis, shiny sedans of various
makes, went back the way it had come, down empty streets
protected by deputies with shiny riot guns, past endless fa-
cades of deserted mills, past brick tenements with ill-
painted stoops, past groups of squat square women with
yellow grey faces, groups of men and boys standing still,
saying nothing, looking nowhere, square hands hanging at
their sides, people square and still, chunks of yellowgrey
stone at the edge of a quarry, idle, waiting, on strike.[41]

Thematically, the report looks forward to the climactic Camera Eye (51) of *U.S.A.* where—in the setting of the Harlan miners'
strike of 1931—Dos Passos was again to depict himself as a member of a group of radical intellectuals attempting to test the validity
of the "old words" from America's revolutionary past in a context of
suppression of these ideals by the economic and political power
symbolized by a sheriff. The report thus anticipates one of the major themes of the entire trilogy. But the piece is especially significant because of its control, through a stylized irony, of Dos Passos'
anger and frustration. Individuals (including Dos Passos, who is
one of "the people who had come from New York") are subsumed
under their group identity, with this identity subject to a critical
irony arising from the reporter's awareness of the futility of this ex-

ercise in free speech. In the end, as in most irony, the essay reverses expectation and assumption. The "agitators" and the police, well fed and comfortable in their roles, appear to be vocal and in motion. But in a deeper sense both are speechless and immobile in the face of the seemingly insoluble social conflict that divides them and all American life. The strikers, both before and after the empty confrontation, stand "still as chunks of stone, looking nowhere, saying nothing." But they are in fact expressing mutely but powerfully a demand for a resolution to their need.

Dos Passos uses in this report an ironic detachment and stylization lacking both in *Rosinante* and *Manhattan Transfer* but fully present in *U.S.A.* The report reveals that he has not only found a way to distance himself from his experience but has also discovered the uses of irony as a means toward the expression of his deepest feelings. That is, he has on the one hand dismissed through irony the excessive presence of a Tel or Jimmy, and he has on the other expressed the beliefs and values of a Tel or Jimmy through the stylized ironic shape of the report as a whole. *U.S.A.* is thus a novel in which the "personal" appears to be limited to the Camera Eye. But it is, in fact, a work in which the other modes— the biographies, Newsreels, and narratives—although impersonal and ironic in cast, aid in the creation of a total construct that expresses above all Dos Passos' most deeply felt beliefs.

2

U.S.A.

Genesis and Basic Character

Although the themes and techniques of *U.S.A.* are present in embryo form in Dos Passos' work of the early 1920s, the trilogy also owes much to Dos Passos' specific thought and activities of the period of its composition and publication, from mid-1926 to early 1938.

Chief among the events impinging on the origin and character of the trilogy was Dos Passos' spirit-wrenching participation in the efforts to save Sacco and Vanzetti during 1926 and 1927, the years in which *U.S.A.* was taking shape in his mind. After six years in prison, Sacco and Vanzetti had, by early 1926, exhausted most of their legal appeals. The attempts by the left, as well as by many other shades of American opinion, to gain a new trial for the convicted men, and, barring that, at least a commutation of their death sentences, thus intensified greatly, and Dos Passos joined fully in these activities. In June 1926, he journeyed to Dedham and Plymouth prisons to visit the two men. (His report of these visits appeared initially in the *New Masses* for August 1926, and later both in a Sacco-Vanzetti Defense Committee publication and in Dos Passos' own 1927 pamphlet *Facing the Chair.*)[1] Like many others, Dos Passos was especially struck by Vanzetti's intelligence and articulateness. But he was also moved in a more personal way by the circumstance of an Italian immigrant imprisoned for his beliefs. As he later recalled in connection with his attitude toward Vanzetti, "In college and out I had . . . felt the frustrations that came from being considered a wop or a guinea or a greaser."[2] Sacco and Vanzetti were thus like Dos Passos—at once stigmatized outsiders and believers in the American dream of a better life for all men. The two prisoners were "all the wops, hunkies, bohunks, factory fodder that hunger drives into the American mills through the painful sieve of Ellis Island. They are the dreams of a saner social order of those who can't stand the law of dawg eat dawg."[3] As he talked with Vanzetti in Plymouth prison, however, Dos Passos also realized the possibility, given the site of the prison, of extending the significance of the two men beyond the personal and contemporaneous to the mythic center of the American dream of freedom. On that same coast, he wrote, "about three hundred years before, men from the west of England had first sailed into the grey shimmering bay that smelt of wood and wild grape, looking for something; liberty . . . freedom to worship God in their own manner . . . space to breathe."[4]

The execution of Sacco and Vanzetti in August 1927, evoked a deep and initially destructive anger in Dos Passos, an anger caught by the "all right we are two nations" exclamation by the Camera Eye persona in *The Big Money* (*BM*, 462). "I had seceded privately the night Sacco and Vanzetti were executed," he later wrote."[5] But soon after their deaths he determined to turn his anger to more productive use. "It is up to the writers now," he wrote in the *New Masses* of November 1927, "to see to it that America does not forget Sacco and Vanzetti."[6] It is possible, within a limited but nevertheless suggestive prospective, to view *U.S.A.* as a memorial to the two martyred anarchists. As I will discuss fully later, much of the Camera Eye portion of the trilogy is directed toward the climax of the Camera Eye persona's recognition of the meaning of the deaths of Sacco and Vanzetti for his own personal and artistic life. The translation of this insight by the persona into a radical vocation, into an acceptance of the need to portray the entire American experience of the twentieth century as a betrayal of the ideals of opportunity and freedom that brought all the "immigrants" to America (from the Pilgrims to Dos Passos' grandfather to Sacco and Vanzetti)—the fulfillment of this vocation is *U.S.A.* as a whole.

But of course this is to simplify both the origin and the nature of the trilogy. Given Dos Passos' emerging radical commitments during 1926 and 1927, he was both responding to the plight of Sacco and Vanzetti and using them to force into conscious centrality already established beliefs. He found especially evocative the capacity of the two figures to lend themselves to the deeply resonant, almost sacred language of the American dream ("liberty," "freedom," "space to breathe"), a language that Dos Passos was to designate the "old words." And once Dos Passos began to envision Sacco and Vanzetti in this way—as he did in 1927 while undertaking the early chapters of *The 42nd Parallel*—the two figures transcended their personal significance and became imaginative symbolic constructs to which could adhere a large body of fictional reality only remotely connected on the surface to their specific fates. It is thus difficult to overestimate the importance of the Sacco-Vanzetti case as a crystallizing event in Dos Passos' imaginative life. All the hopes and fears about the American experience and about his own role as an artist in relation to American life that he had been holding in cloudy solution now came into sharp focus. And out of this clarity of vision came much of the strength of purpose and of belief necessary to carry the vast project of the trilogy to completion.

During 1926 and 1927, the crucial years in the genesis of *U.S.A.*, Dos Passos' principal interest—aside from his radical activism—was the theater. He had returned to America in early 1926 specifically to become a member of the New Playwrights Theatre, and he devoted much time during 1926–27, before he became fully engaged in the writing of *U.S.A.*, to the affairs of the company and to the writing of a new play, *Airways, Inc*. In fact, however, these theatrical activities cannot be considered as more "literary" than "radical," since the New Playwrights board included Mike Gold and John Howard Lawson (both staunch Communists) and since many of the plays produced by the company, including *Airways, Inc.*, were socially or politically on the left. But the ideals and practices of the New Playwrights did contain an additional feature of some importance in the emergence of *U.S.A.*

Dos Passos had in the late 1920s already begun to characterize himself as a "historian" of American life, and he was to use this designation for the remainder of his career.[7] (Indeed, he was later to call his novels "chronicles.") Once a writer begins consciously to conceive of himself as a recorder of national life, he is forced into the need to discriminate among the kinds of social life he will include in his fiction and the means he will employ to render this material. To Dos Passos, prepared as he was by the earlier methods of *Manhattan Transfer* (the novel includes songs, advertisements, and newspaper stories), and stimulated afresh by the mixed-media experimental practices of the New Playwrights Theatre, the problem was in fact a nonproblem. The New Playwrights, as Dos Passos noted in a 1929 defense of the group, were seeking "to break down the pictureframe stage" by treating a play like a "musical composition" in which multiple stages and the devices of opera, burlesque, and ballet would "move the audience with a slice of the history of a race instead of with episodes in the lives of individual puppets."[8] Of course, each play produced by the group had its own character, but many of the plays relied on heavily accentuated theatrical devices—expressionistic sets, jazz music, and dance movements—to communicate a social theme directly and repetitiously. As the principal historians of the group have noted, the New Playwrights were pioneers in "rhythmic intergration. Action would be taking place on various levels simultaneously, to the accompaniment of music and supported by techniques of dialogue, such as the repetition of phrases and sentences in interwoven but continuous rhythmic patterns."[9] The New Playwrights thus offered a compelling model for a self-consciously avant-garde artist seeking to be a historian of his own time. It was necessary to include all ranges of twentieth-century American life, and it was necessary to do so in forms appropriate to twentieth-century American life.

Dos Passos was, of course, to conceive and write *U.S.A.* as fiction, not drama. Thus the visual and aural simultaneity and repetition of the stage received in *U.S.A.* their own distinctive fictional expression, as did the general thrust toward "breaking down barriers" between an art form and its audience. As Dos Passos later recalled, in what is perhaps his fullest account of the origin of *U.S.A.* (in fact, he wrote remarkably little about the genesis of the trilogy), he wanted to write "objectively" about America—that is, to shape a historical rather than a personal representation of twentieth-century American life. He would thus draw inspiration from the tradition of the chronicle novel—the fiction of Stendhal, Thackeray, and Tolstoy—and from the satirical picaresque novels of Baroja. And he would also seek to use in fictional form the ideals of simultaneity and montage that he had absorbed from cubism and the film. He continued:

> I dreamed of using whatever I'd learned from all these methods to produce a satirical chronicle of the world I knew. I felt that everything should go in: popular songs, political aspirations and prejudices, ideals, hopes, delusions, crackpot notions, clippings out of daily newspapers.
>
> The basic raw material is everything you've seen and heard and felt, it's your childhood and your education and serving in the army, and travelling in odd places, and finding yourself in odd situations. . . . A novelist has to use all the stories people tell him about themselves, all the little dramas in other people's lives he gets glimpses of.[10]

The reader of *U.S.A.*, in other words, would be exposed to the concrete actuality of American life, as in a "chronicle" of such life, drawn both from the writer's knowledge of that actuality through his own experience and from his seeking out further evidence of it in the experience of others. The rendering of this actuality would be in the forms best suited to recreate it directly and "purely"— songs as songs, for example, "real" lives as semidocumentary biographies, and "stories" about people's lives in narratives in which an authorial hand appears to be completely absent. And the whole would constitute an immense exercise in juxtapositional relatedness, in which the varied ways of depicting the varied aspects of American life would nevertheless communicate a single and coherent satirical vision of the American experience—satirical because of the need to portray critically the vast failure of the American ideal of freedom in the twentieth century. Like the New Playwrights, Dos Passos would seek to engage his audience directly and immediately in what was ostensibly an objective—that is, unmediated—encounter with American life. What he in fact produced was a representation of American experience that was fashioned with a high degree of sophisticated artistry in order to render a powerful indictment of American life. Like Whitman before him (and others to follow), Dos Passos was engaged in that distinctively American effort of writing a "natural" and "impersonal" epic of American life that was in fact a highly wrought and deeply personal work of art.

The idea for a long panoramic novel about twentieth-century American life occurred to Dos Passos during the winter of 1926–27 when he spent several months in Mexico.[11] There he met Gladwin Bland, a former IWW radical long settled in Mexico, who told him his life story and thus supplied much of the detail for the opening Mac narrative in *The 42nd Parallel*. But Dos Passos seems to have done very little other than preliminary planning and the writing of some of the Mac segments during 1927 and early 1928, as he was engaged in the concluding phases of the Sacco-Vanzetti case and in the completion of his play *Airways, Inc.* In the late spring of 1928, Dos Passos left for a trip of almost eight months to Europe and Russia. In Russia, he met the publicist Ivy Lee, who supplied him with the model for J. Ward Moorehouse. By the time Dos Passos returned to America in the winter of 1928, he was fully committed to his project and undertook to work steadily on it. The

summer of 1929 finds him in Chicago consulting the Chicago
Tribune for Newsreel material. He completed *The 42nd Parallel* in
December 1929.

Initially, Dos Passos had no thought of writing a trilogy;[12] nor
had he conceived of the title *U.S.A.* But once he began to work
steadily on the project, on his return from Russia in early 1929, he
realized that he could not fulfill his intent within the compass of
the traditional novel. By the summer of 1929 the notion of a trilogy,
as Edmund Wilson noted at the time, was established in his
mind.[13] The title *U.S.A.* came very late in the history of the project.
In Dos Passos' notes, his working description (and perhaps title)
for the trilogy as a whole appears to be "The New Century."[14] It
was not until July 1937, when he was preparing the three novels
for publication in a single volume, that he wrote to his agent that
he had "finally decided to publish the collected volume under the
name of U.S.A."[15]

The 42nd Parallel was published by Harper and Brothers in
February 1930. Dos Passos had begun *Nineteen-Nineteen*[16] even
before this event, and he completed it in the summer of 1931. He
and Harpers then became involved in a controversy over the biography of J. P. Morgan in *Nineteen-Nineteen*. Morgan had come to
the aid of Harpers some years earlier, and the firm was reluctant to
publish Dos Passos' extremely sardonic portrait of "The House of
Morgan." Dos Passos sought another publisher, and it was Harcourt, Brace that published *Nineteen-Nineteen* in March 1932.

There now occurred a major interruption in the completion of
the trilogy, caused principally by a series of lengthy and debilitating illnesses suffered by Dos Passos during the early 1930s. Indeed, he did not give his full attention to *The Big Money* until
1935, after three years of little work on the novel. This hiatus had
two notable effects on the nature of the trilogy as a whole. *The Big
Money,* most critics agree, is the most finished and thematically
rich of the three novels. It is as if the three-year lapse before Dos
Passos returned to the trilogy permitted a greater unconscious
preparation for the work and hence a greater sophistication of
theme and method. But also, and perhaps even more apparent,
Dos Passos' political beliefs had undergone a major reorientation
between the completion of *Nineteen-Nineteen* in mid-1931 and the
composition of *The Big Money* in 1935 and early 1936. He had begun the trilogy, in the late 1920s, in a spirit of cautious hope about
the role of the radical left (and more specifically the Communist
party) in the solution of America's social and political dilemmas.

(This attitude is best revealed in his reportage from the Soviet Union during his visit of 1928.) But as the Stalinist hold on the Russian revolution and the American Communist party intensified over the next several years, Dos Passos became increasingly disillusioned with the methods and goals of the far left. The key events that stimulated Dos Passos' shift in attitude were his recognition of the party's self-serving use of the Harlan miners' strike in November 1931 and his dismay over the party's disruption of a socialist meeting at Madison Square Garden in February 1934.[17] By January 1935, Dos Passos could note in a letter to Edmund Wilson that he had lost all faith in the party.[18] *The Big Money,* as I will discuss later, reflects this change in a number of significant ways, especially in the dramatization of the ideals and methods of the far left in the stories of Ben Compton and Mary French.

With the publication of *The Big Money* by Harcourt, Brace in August 1936, Dos Passos could undertake the preparation of the three novels as a single-volume trilogy. He felt that the work as a whole had an integral character and force, and he wished to make these apparent both to those who had read the novels as they appeared and to a new generation of readers by making the entire work available in a single volume. The first task in the preparation of such a volume was to reconcile the different formats of the three novels. As I have noted, *The 42nd Parallel* was published by Harpers, while *Nineteen-Nineteen* and *The Big Money* were published by Harcourt, Brace. Whether through editorial influence, house styling, or Dos Passos' own insistence, the last two novels differed sufficiently from the first in typography and format to constitute a major anomaly if the three books were to appear together unchanged in a single volume. Most obviously, in *The 42nd Parallel* each new modal segment (except the biographies) begins on a new page, while in the last two novels the format is that of continuous run-on from segment to segment. In addition, the type size for the various modes in *The 42nd Parallel* is completely different from the same modes in the last two novels. *The 42nd Parallel,* in short, had to be completely reset to bring it into conformity with *Nineteen-Nineteen* and *The Big Money.*

This resetting in fact occurred before the appearance of the single-volume trilogy when—apparently in anticipation of that event—*The 42nd Parallel* was published in the Modern Library series by Harcourt, Brace in November 1937. The significance of this new edition of *The 42nd Parallel* is that Dos Passos took advantage of the need to reset to make a number of changes in the novel, including an extensive cutting of the Newsreels. The Newsreels were far more prominent in the first edition of *The 42nd Parallel* than in the other two novels, both because they are longer and because of the large type font used in their printing. In Dos Passos' revision, no one Newsreel was omitted entirely, but almost all were cut, some by as much as a third.[19] In addition, their typography was brought into conformity with that of the Newsreels in the last two novels. Late in his life, when questioned by a graduate student who had discovered the editing of the Newsreels, Dos Passos expressed surprise and denied any participation in or authorization of the cuts.[20] But this was a lapse of memory. In a letter to his agent Brandt and Brandt in late July 1937, he enclosed a blurb for a Harcourt, Brace house newsletter in which it was noted that "*The 42nd Parallel* by John Dos Passos will be reprinted this fall in the Modern Library. Mr. Dos Passos . . . has made many corrections in this forthcoming edition of his novel."[21]

Three other revisions of *The 42nd Parallel* for the Modern Library resetting are worth noting. Since the other two novels in the trilogy have no interior divisions, the division of the novel into five parts was dropped.[22] Dos Passos also discarded the epigraph, in which he cited a passage from a book on the American climate as a partial explanation of the title of the novel. (Storms in North America move from West to East along several paths; the 42nd parallel latitude is the most central of these paths.) This omission has caused considerable perplexity to later readers of the trilogy, who have been left without a clue as to the relevance of the title of its first novel. (It is also of some interest that the dust jacket of the 1930 Harper edition of *The 42nd Parallel* depicted a map of the United States marked with longitude and latitude lines and indicating that the 42nd parallel crossed the east coast at approximately Plymouth, Massachusetts. This would have had a private symbolic meaning for Dos Passos.) The third significant revision of *The 42nd Parallel* consisted of a juggling of the order of the segments of the novel from Newsreel XVI through the Proteus biography (pp. 274–328 of the revised edition). Nothing is omitted in this revision, but the order in which we encounter the ten segments is much altered. The importance of this revision is less its effect on this portion of the novel than its reflection of Dos Passos' basic cast of mind in the shaping of the trilogy. The task of finding a satisfactory juxtapositional balance did not end even with publication if an opportunity was provided for yet a further refinement of the effort.[23]

The Harcourt, Brace edition of *U.S.A.*, published in January 1938, used the plates of the 1937 Modern Library edition of *The 42nd Parallel* and the plates of the 1932 and 1936 editions of *Nineteen-Nineteen* and *The Big Money*, which means that Dos Passos made no further changes in the text of the trilogy for its single-volume edition.[24] Nevertheless, for this initial publication of the entire trilogy, Dos Passos had two additional tasks. One was to devise a title for the work as a whole, which, as I have noted, he did in the summer of 1937. The other was to write an introduction to the trilogy. This, after many drafts, he completed in late 1937 and also titled "U.S.A." Since The final segment of *The Big Money*, "Vag," was itself a late addition to Dos Passos' plan for the novel,[25] and since "U.S.A." and "Vag" have a number of striking similarities in structure and theme, the two appear to be Dos Passos's conscious effort to frame the work as a whole within a prologue and an epilogue.

Dos Passos made no changes in the text or format of *U.S.A.* after its 1938 Harcourt, Brace publication. The later publication history of the work, however, contains two notable events. The first was the reprinting of the Harcourt, Brace edition in the Modern Library in 1939; several generations of readers encountered the trilogy in this form. The second was the resetting of the trilogy in a deluxe edition by Houghton Mifflin in 1946, with illustrations by Reginald Marsh that sought to render the element of caricature in Dos Passos' narrative style.

U.S.A. is an extraordinarily rich and complex work of fiction. Any effort to reduce the work to a single overarching theme will thus inevitably produce a distorted oversimplication. Yet, if the depth and quality of the trilogy are to be adequately appreciated, some of its larger dimensions require recognition at the outset of any critical discussion. What follows is an attempt to use a key passage from *U.S.A.* as a means of bringing to the fore some important aspects of the work as a whole. The ideas thus introduced will serve as the basis for the more detailed analysis of the full trilogy that is to come.

The passage, one remarked upon by a number of recent critics of *U.S.A.*,[26] occurs at the close of Camera Eye (51) in *The Big Money*. Camera Eye (51), which is the final Camera Eye in the trilogy, stems from Dos Passos' participation in the visit of a committee of left-wing writers, led by Theodore Dreiser, to Harlan

County, Kentucky, to investigate conditions arising out of a miners'
strike. The miners epitomize working-class life in early 1930s
America in that they are poor, exploited, and oppressed. They are
kept in this condition not only by the mine operators but by the
manipulators of language—the law and the press—who are in the
pay of the operators. The committee visits a group of jailed strikers
and encounters the red-faced, armed sheriff sitting at his desk, the
sheriff who, in the final words of this final Camera Eye, feels behind him

> the prosecutingattorney the judge an owner
> himself the political boss the minesuperintendent
> the board of directors   the president of the
> utility the manipulator of the holdingcompany
>   he·lifts his hands toward the telephone
>   the deputies crowd in the door
>   we have only words against   (*BM*, 524–25)

The unendstopped "we have only words against" is followed on the
same page (after three-quarters of an inch of white space) by the
words POWER SUPERPOWER, the title of the biography of Samuel Insull. This juxtaposition of the final words of the Camera Eye
persona and the title of the biography of a utility holding company
magnate is a crystallization of theme and form in the work as a
whole. The startling thrust of meaning across the modal barrier
between the final Camera Eye and the final biography raises and
extends the level of abstraction of the entire moment. Words are all
we have against power, and power extends through the economic
and political system from a county sheriff to an Insull. But the anger communicated by the Harlan County segment and the satiric
irony of the Insull biography illustrate that POWER SUPER-
POWER is vulnerable to attack through literary art. We have only
words against power in every aspect of American life, and in that
uneven conflict lies our despair and our hope.

One way of approaching *U.S.A.* is to recognize that the trilogy
is in large part about the relation of language in America to the
American experience.[27] The one continuous "story" in the trilogy
as a whole is that of the Camera Eye persona. The artist in this
story, after many misdirections and uncertainties, comes at last to a
realization that the ideals on which the country had been founded,
the "old words" of freedom and justice and equality, have been perverted during his own lifetime, and that his duty as a writer is to

seek their radical revitalization through a portrayal of their distortion. This warping of the "old words" is dramatized in two major ways in *U.S.A.* The three strategically placed "impersonal" biographies that structure the trilogy—the opening "U.S.A.," "The Body of an American" (which occurs at the close of *Nineteen-Nineteen*), and the final "Vag"—are a concise symbolic dramatization of a failure within American life to find meaning in language. And the other modes of the trilogy—the narratives, biographies, and Newsreels—constitute a massive representation of the corruption of American values as revealed by a corruption of language.

Dos Passos' belief that language was the principal means both for understanding national character and for bringing about social change is revealed in a number of his comments during the years he was preparing *U.S.A.* In the Introduction to a new edition of *Three Soldiers* in 1932 he wrote: "The mind of a generation is its speech. A writer makes aspects of that speech enduring by putting them in print. He whittles at the words and phrases of today and makes them forms to set the mind of tomorrow's generation. That's history. A writer who writes straight is the architect of history."[28] This notion of the writer as a bridge between generations is made even more explicit in one of the most revealing statements ever made by Dos Passos about his intent in *U.S.A.* In "The Writer as Technician," a speech he prepared for delivery at the 1935 American Writers' Congress, Dos Passos wrote that "The professional writer discovers some aspect of his world and invents out of the speech of his time some particularly apt and original way of putting it down on paper." If he is good enough, he "molds and influences ways of thinking to the point of changing and rebuilding the language, which is the mind of the group. . . . There is no escaping the fact," Dos Passos continued, "that if you are a writer you are dealing with the humanities, with the language of all the men of your speech of your generation, with their traditions of a past and their feelings and perceptions." And if you probe deeply enough, you find yourself on the side of "liberty, fraternity, and humanity. The words are old and dusty and hung with the dirty bunting of a thousand crooked orations, but underneath they are still sound. What man once meant by these words needs defenders to-day."[29]

A kind of historical/linguistic/artistic vocation underlies these statements and *U.S.A.* itself. The "old words" are an Edenic past; at one time they were believed in and practiced with full honesty and commitment. But now they have been corrupted and are used falsely, just as the nation itself has been diverted from a practice of

their intent and meaning. The function of the artist is to depict this
postlapsarian decay of both life and language and thereby to aid in
the possible restoration of Eden.

The most schematic dramatization of this conception of a national language and character occurs in the "U.S.A.," "The Body of
an American," and "Vag" journey narratives of archetypal Americans. As has often been noted, the "young man" of "U.S.A." is a
Whitmanesque seeker.[30] He is attempting to find communion and
meaning as he restlessly wanders the cities and regions of America
and as he undertakes various occupations. But his search is unsuccessful, and he remains isolated until he realizes that "Only the
ears busy to catch the speech are not alone." The idea is pursued:

> It was not in the long walks through jostling
> crowds at night that he was less alone, . . .
> but in his mother's words telling about longago,
> in his father's telling about when I was a boy, . . .
> it was the speech that clung to the ears, the link
> that tingled in the blood; U. S. A.

U. S. A., the vignette concludes, is many things, "But mostly
U. S. A. is the speech of the people." The implications of this "prologue" to *U.S.A.* for the work as a whole are clear. Language as
used by the people is the means toward recognizing and represent-
ing the essential nature of a society, and the writer must seek out
this source of meaning in every corner and every activity of the
country. The trilogy will itself replicate this quest both in its representation of the great variety of life in America and in its depiction
of the artist's search for his own role in relation to the meaning of
America. His own self-reflexive presence, in other words, as a
wanderer in search of meaning will authenticate what he eventually discovers in the world at large, and which is depicted in the
remainder of the novel. In brief compass and in archetypal form,
"the young man" of "U.S.A." is thus the Camera Eye persona of the
trilogy as a whole.

This identification of Dos Passos with the Whitmanesque
seeker of an American national identity is even more apparent in a
portion cut from a draft version of the "U.S.A." vignette. In this
passage, "the young man" is for a moment specifically a writer attempting to understand what he has found during his wandering:

> (From the lighted window the writer looks down into the
> empty street, sees the figures tiny among the dark oblongs

of buildings that rise against the city's golden haze, reads
carefully sentence[s] men wrote with quill pens a century
and a half ago, feels in his nose the dusty smell of old
newspapers in the Public Library   eyes smart with
blurred newsprint, head aches to remember the hopes the
wants the walks, the halfcaught turn of a phrase the line of
talk, the speech) Before I can do I must know the country
the speech.[31]

Although this passage was probably best excised, it nevertheless
usefully illustrates the extent to which Dos Passos identified himself with a historical/linguistic vocation. Realizing what the men
with quill pens have written, he will seek out what remains of the
belief underlying their language in the speech of today—in the
newspapers in the library and in the turn of phrase of the street—
and out of this twofold awareness he will seek to "do": to depict in
U.S.A. what he knows.

"The Body of an American" is a summation of what the
seeker has discovered about American life and language in the
first two decades of the century, a period that climaxes with America's participation in the war and in the peace conference. John
Doe, the unknown soldier, is the Whitmanesque wanderer transformed with biting irony into the archetypal American victim of
the falsification of belief and language of the period. He is an average commonplace American, his life devoid of any noble purpose
or ideals, his mind full of the verbal debris of his time. ("Now is the
time for all good men knocks but once at a young man's door, It's a
great life if Ish gebibbel"—NN, 471). He becomes separated from
his unit during combat and wants only to return to it, but a stray
shell kills him. His death symbolizes the immense chasm that has
developed between reality and language. Dos Passos' account of
the vacuity of his motives and the emptiness of his "sacrifice" ("the
brains oozed out of the cracked skull and were licked up by the
trenchrats, the belly swelled and raised a generation of bluebottle
flies"—NN, 472) is ironically interwoven with the "dirty bunting"
of resolutions, oratory, and newspaper reports that stress the honor
and glory of his death and that parade him as an example of the
"justice of his country's cause" (NN, 470). "The Body of an American" epitomizes a central theme in the first two novels of the trilogy in that its emphasis on the corruption of the language of belief
that the war occasioned expresses in symbolic form a principal

cause of the failure of the "old words" in twentieth-century American life.

"Vag" begins with the same phrase that opens "U.S.A."—"The young man." But whereas in "U.S.A." the verb following is "walks," in "Vag" it is "waits." The seeker has now experienced the America of the 1920s and early 1930s; he has been in transient camps and in jails and has been beaten up by cops and driven out of towns. Exhausted and hungry, he waits by the side of the road for a lift while overhead a transcontinental plane flashes by with its well-to-do passengers, signifying the "two nations" (*BM*, 462) that America has become under the impact of the quest for the big money. For the young man, however, the quest is over; what remains are the false promises of American life: "went to school, books said opportunity, ads promised speed, own your home, shine bigger than your neighbor, the radiocrooner whispered girls, ghosts of platinum girls coaxed from the screen, millions in winnings were chalked up on the boards in the offices, paychecks were for hands willing to work, the cleared desk of an executive with three telephones on it" (*BM*, 561). The buoyancy of the seeker in "U.S.A." as he set out to discover the link between a national language and national ideals has met with two powerful shocks. The war revealed the discrepancy between a language of honor and the reality of war itself, and the postwar period revealed the distinction between a language of opportunity and freedom and the reality of a business society. The journey comes to an end as the archetypal American, his mind still filled with the language of possibility and accomplishment, waits "with swimming head, needs knot the belly, idle hands numb, beside the speeding traffic" (*BM*, 561).

The Camera Eye persona, as I have noted, also undergoes a Whitmanesque range of experience, and he too is engaged in a search. But unlike the archetypal twentieth-century Americans depicted in "The Body of an American" and "Vag," he matures in insight until he has achieved a firm sense both of his own identity and of his function as a Whitmanesque reviver ("I too Walt Whitman") of the "old words" of "our storybook democracy" (*BM*, 150).

Contrary to an initial impression (as I will discuss in the next chapter), the Camera Eye is less Joycean in technique than in the motifs of the search by the artist for a home and a father. Since *U.S.A.* is a work of the 1930s, the Camera Eye persona depicts the successful completion of the search as an acceptance by the artist of his committed role within the class struggle. But since *U.S.A.* is also a work of the 1920s, the persona, now more covertly and often principally through image and symbol, identifies specific social values, attitudes, and activities with specific sexual values, attitudes, and activities. While Dos Passos was not seeking to render his life in explicit sexual terms, he nevertheless often does so in the sense that his recollection of his life by means of image and symbol is closely related to psychoanalytic self-revelation, in which there is a constant intertwining of the sexual and almost every other phase of one's experience. Thus, in the Camera Eye Dos Passos depicts his maturation into literary radicalism both as a development into a proper masculinity and as a discovery of a literary creed that is symbolically a father and a home.[32]

The general texture of Dos Passos' early life as depicted by the Camera Eye in *The 42nd Parallel* is of constant physical movement within the social world of the upper middle class.[33] Within this world, Dos Passos' mother and father (the "He" and "She" of the Camera Eye persona's consciousness) play conventional parental roles. The mother is a figure who initially expresses accepted class attitudes ("Workingmen and people like that laborers travailleurs greasers") (*FP*, 25) and a feminine aversion to violence and conflict (as in the first Camera Eye when she and Dos Passos take refuge under a shop counter during a riot) and who later fades into a debilitating illness ("He was very gay and She was feeling well for once") (*FP*, 173). The father, the "strong, athletic man . . . immensely energetic," described by Townsend Ludington,[34] is powerfully masculine in thought and action. Willing to state and act on unpopular opinions ("What would you do Lucy if I were to invite one of them [a Negro] to my table?" and "Why Lucy if it were necessary for the cause of humanity I would walk out and be shot any day") (*FP*, 13), he is also a man who carries his flask wherever he goes, recites *Othello* in cabs, and enjoys swimming and yachting.

Early in the Camera Eye, Dos Passos beings to associate his upper-class experience with his mother's feminine conventionality and lack of strength and the lower-class world, which he occasionally encounters, with his father's masculinity, both because of the greater vigor of this world and because of its more openly expressed sexuality. This pattern of association is probably indebted to Dos Passos' knowledge of his father's Portuguese immigrant background and his mother's roots in a socially prominent Maryland family. But it is also, more clearly, a product of the sexual conventions of Dos Passos' youth, in which a Victorian gentility still

masked the expression of sex in upper-middle-class life, while
working-class experience was assumed to be more openly and ag-
gressively sexual. Initially, this association is communicated
largely by images and brief incidents in which the boyish Dos Passos is fearful during moments when a masculine sexuality is
linked to his father or to the working class. Traveling by train at
night with his mother through an industrial landscape, he peeks
"out of the window into the black rumbling dark suddenly ranked
with squat chimneys and you're scared of the black smoke and the
puffs of flame that flare and fade out of the squat chimneys" (FP,
25). And when challenged at school about his political opinions
(opinions that are also his father's), he can only reply "all trembly"
(FP, 58).

Camera Eye (7), which describes Dos Passos on an ice-
skating pond during the period when he was attending Choate,
brings to the surface his permanent association of class and sexual
roles.

> skating on the pond next the silver company's
> mills where there was a funny fuzzy smell from the dump
> whaleoil soap somebody said it was that they used in clean-
> ing the silver knives and spoons and forks putting shine on
> them for sale   there was shine on the ice early black
> ice that rang like a sawblade just scratched white by the
> first skaters   I couldn't learn to skate and kept falling
> down   look out for the muckers everybody said bo-
> hunk and polack kids put stones in their snowballs write
> dirty words up on walls do dirty things up alleys their folks
> work in the mills
> we clean young American Rover Boys handy
> with tools Deerslayers played hockey Boy Scouts and cut
> figure eights on the ice Achilles Ajax Agamemnon I
> couldn't learn to skate and kept falling down   (FP, 81)

The immigrant background "muckers" play roughly and unfairly
and revel in an unclean sexuality; the Rover Boys lead clean American lives of ritualized activities, codes, and roles. Dos Passos at
this point identifies with and aspires to the Rover Boys ("*we* clean
young American Rover Boys"), a group that includes hockey and
figure skating among its activities. But "I couldn't learn to skate
and kept falling down." His ineptness signifies that he is between
two worlds. As his father's son his true identity is with the outsider

"muckers," but as his mother's son he condemns their overt sexuality and endorses the conventional and derivative upper-class roles of the Rover Boys. Dos Passos' illegitimacy probably strengthened his sense of not belonging to the world he aspired to and hence his ineptness in its skills. (Metaphorically speaking, his father and mother had also done "dirty things up alleys.") He therefore carries with him throughout his upper-middle-class boyhood and early youth a sense of displacement. He responds deeply to the story of a man without a country (*FP*, 147–48) and considers himself without either a home ("I wished I was home but I hadn't any home," *FP*, 224) or a religion (*FP*, 206–7). But as a "displaced person," Dos Passos' life also increasingly takes on the shape of a search for a home and a father—that is, for a creed and a course of action that will embody in compelling symbolic form the values he attributed to his father.

In other Camera Eye passages in *The 42nd Parallel*, Dos Passos' overt condemnation yet underlying desire for the greater sexual vitality and experience of lower-class life emerges clearly. Near his parents' Virginia farm he meets at a freight crossing a youth who "couldn't have been much older 'n me . . .   he had curly hair and whisps of hay in it and through his open shirt you could see his body was burned brown to the waist I guess he wasn't much account" (*FP*, 92–93). Dos Passos' early encounters with girls also bring into the open his association of a desirable sexual freedom with lower-class life and of a cold formality with upper-class experience. He sits in a well-to-do suburban Pennsylvania church listening to girls singing "chilly shrill soprano" in the choir and watching them in their "best hats and pretty pink green blue yellow dresses" (*FP*, 108). Then, in the Camera Eye that follows, he has his first sexual experience, as Jeanne, the young family maid from the Jura, takes him into her bed one night, "and afterwards you knew what girls were made like" (*FP*, 130).

As Dos Passos moves into adolescence, he discovers further confirmations of his linking of sexual attitudes and values with class. At a summer resort he meets a Methodist minister's wife, who "loved beautiful things and had had stories she had written published in a magazine . . . and she wore thin white dresses and used perfume and talked in a bell-like voice about how things were lovely as a lily" (*FP*, 238). With this woman, with her thin aestheticism and suppressed sexuality, Dos Passos "felt you ought to put your arm round her and kiss her only you didn't want to" (*FP*, 238). Rather, you "wished you had the nerve to hug and kiss Martha the

colored girl they said was half Indian" (*FP*, 239). And though he
does not have the nerve, "but Oh God not lilies" (*FP*, 239).

Parallel to this scene is Dos Passos' visit to "historic Quebec"
with a group of students in the care of several older men. One of
these guides, a singer, takes a homosexual interest in Dos Passos
and talks incessantly about

> the Acropolis and the bel canto and the Parthenon and
> voice culture and the beautiful statues of Greek boys and
> the Winged Victory and the beautiful statues
> > but I finally shook him . . .
> > and the gray rainy streets full of girls   (*FP*, 284–85)

Dos Passos' identification of effeminacy and homosexuality
with the upper class and of masculinity with the lower continues
in the Harvard portions of the Camera Eye in *The 42nd Parallel*. As
in his Quebec visit, experience now presents Dos Passos with clear
choices. There is the world of Jeanne, the colored servant, and the
Quebec girls, and there is the world of shrill sopranos, the minister's wife, and the baritone. But the Harvard Camera Eye passages
add an important new element to this distinction. Now the upper
class becomes associated in Dos Passos' mind not only with sexual
inadequacy but with a destructive social blindness. In a sharply
ironic Camera Eye section dealing with the Lawrence strikes of
1912, the Rover Boys of Choate reappear as young Harvard men
who become scabs on a streetcar line:

> what the hell they were a lot of wops anyway bohunks hun-
> kies that didn't wash their necks ate garlic with squalling
> brats and fat oily wives the damn dagoes they put up a no-
> tice for volunteers good clean young
> > to man the streetcars and show the foreign agita-
> tors this was still a white man's   (*FP*, 245)

Yet despite Dos Passos' restlessness ("can't sleep") because of
his realization of the social blindness of his world, he doesn't have

> the nerve to break out of the bellglass
> > four years under the ethercone breathe deeply
> gently now that's the way be a good boy one two three four
> five six get A's in some courses but don't be a grind be in-

terested in literature but remain a gentleman don't be seen
with Jews or socialists   (*FP*, 301–2)

The Harvard bellglass is that of a sexless or effeminate aestheticism—"grow cold with culture like a cup of tea forgotten between
an incenseburner and a volume of Oscar Wilde cold and not strong
like a claret lemonade drunk at a Pop Concert in Symphony Hall"
(*FP*, 302). Opposed to it is an "outside" of raucous activity and
striving in the "real" world of industrial America—"the streetcar
wheels screech grinding in a rattle of loose trucks round Harvard
Square and the trains crying across the saltmarshes and the rumbling siren of a steamboat leaving dock and the blue peter flying
and millworkers marching with a red brass band through the
streets of Lawrence Massachusetts" (*FP*, 302). But Dos Passos concludes, "I hadn't the nerve" (*FP*, 303).

Dos Passos' occasional efforts to break out of the bellglass
end, not in action or commitment, but in a seemingly inevitable
return to his class. He and a friend attend some radical meetings
in New York, and afterwards "we had several drinks and welsh rab-
bits and paid our bill and went home, and opened the door with a
latchkey and put on pajamas and went to bed and it was comfortable in bed" (*FP*, 350). The concluding Camera Eye of *The 42nd
Parallel* finds Dos Passos on his way to Europe during wartime.
Perhaps, it is implied, he will discover in the upheaval of war an
answer to his dilemma of how to identify and commit himself to
the home and father that he senses are somewhere in the world of
radical struggle.

The initial Camera Eye in *Nineteen-Nineteen* sets the tone
for all the Camera Eye segments in this portion of the trilogy. It
begins with a coalescing of the news of the deaths of Dos Passos'
parents—his mother in May 1915, his father in January 1917.
With their deaths, the "bellglass" is "shattered" (*NN*, 11). Gone is
the protective shield they provided (a shield that included Choate
and Harvard) and gone too, therefore, is the barrier between himself and experience that their protectiveness included. Both they
and Dos Passos' earlier life are now dead:

we
          who had heard Copey's beautiful reading voice
and read the handsomely bound books and breathed deep
. . . of the waxwork lilies and the artificial parmaviolet scent

under the ethercone and sat breakfasting in the library
where the bust was of Octavius
          were now dead at the cableoffice   (*NN,* 11)

The Camera Eye continues by juxtaposing this rejected effete
world ("*I'm so tired of violets / Take them all away*") (*NN,* 10) and
the experiences of men at war, experiences ranging from ordinary
tasks—

          washing those windows
          K.P.
          cleaning the sparkplugs with a pocket knife
                                                  (*NN,* 11–12)

—to whores, bombardments, and death. Now that the barriers are
down, the war can provide Dos Passos with the kind of experience
that might lead to a full discovery of his true identity and role. The
initial Camera Eye in *Nineteen-Nineteen* thus ends: "tomorrow I
hoped would be the first day of the first month of the first year"
(*NN,* 12).

In the Camera Eye sections that follow, the experiences that
represent to Dos Passos a powerfully attractive combination of
masculinity and of integrity of feeling and expression have a distinctive Hemingway cast. It is while threatened by death or when
engaged with his comrades in drinking, eating, and adventure that
Dos Passos begins to have a sense of a new life. His response to
coming under bombardment at the Marne, with the shells "pound-
ing the thought of death into our ears" (*NN,* 71), is both sexual and
intoxicating: "the winey thought of death stings in the spring blood
that throbs in the sunburned neck   up and down the belly
under the tight belt   hurries like cognac into the tips of my
toes and the lobes of my ears" (*NN,* 71–72). And the Camera Eye
that describes Dos Passos' trip to Italy with his ambulance section
combines the lush richness of the French landscape with the camaraderie of men eating and drinking while on the loose.

War as a "real" masculine experience supplies the matrix for
the emergence of the motif that is to dominate the Camera Eye
from this point on, the motif of the distinction between life as Dos
Passos now understands it and the language conventionally used
to disguise the true nature of experience. Thus, in a Camera Eye
passage that is filled with the horrors of war—"remembering the
grey crooked fingers the thick drip of blood off the canvas the bub-
bling when the lungcases try to breath the muddy scraps of flesh

you put in the ambulance alive and haul out dead" (*NN*, 101)—the physical images of man's destructiveness are combined with the heroic language of patriotism and, in particular, with Patrick Henry's "Give me liberty or give me death" (*NN*, 102–3). Such language is now corrupt, it is implied, both because it drives men into the horror of war and because it then disguises that horror. During their trip to Italy, the ambulance section is accompanied by a living example of a failure in truth-telling about this horror, a "Successful Story Writer   . . . it turned out he was not writing what he felt he wanted to be writing What can you tell them at home about the war?" (*NN*, 150).

Dos Passos has at this point reached a felt though still not clearly articulated understanding of the basic relationship between art and life. Life is experience in its masculine cast of the complete range of human feelings and activities, and art is the effort to render this kind of experience with virile honesty and full attention to its frequent ugliness and injustice. Apparently believing, however, that he is still deficient in experience, Dos Passos enters the army as an enlisted man and is exposed to the drudgery, squalor, mindlessness, and destructiveness of life on its lowest level. But the army, though it contributes to Dos Passos' "education," is itself a prison of the spirit. Dos Passos' temporary release from service in the early spring of 1919 to study in Paris is thus like a second rebirth as he once again escapes a repressive world for one of a new freedom. In Paris, he feels the richness of life with a masculine sexual energy and excitement and with an imagery of rebirth that echoes almost precisely the imagery of his earlier escape from the bellglass:

> Paris comes into the room in the servantgirl's eyes the warm bulge of her breasts under the grey smock
> . . .
> Today is the sunny morning of the first day of spring We gulp our coffee splash water on us jump into our clothes run downstairs step out wideawake into the first morning of the first day of the first year   (*NN*, 343, 344)

But France offers Dos Passos no means for the expression of his emerging sense of his identity as an artist. In the 1919 May Day riots, he is the outsider who takes refuge in the back room of a cafe where he drinks "grog americain" (*NN*, 401). And the French radical movement itself lacks energy and direction, as is suggested

by its degeneration into an anarchist picnic where Dos Passos
meets a girl who "wanted liberty fraternity equality and a young
man to take her out" (*NN* 420). Like the girl in a New York taxicab
in an important *Big Money* Camera Eye passage, the French girl
does not provide Dos Passos a means for the expression of a radical
masculinity, despite the sexuality of their encounter. Beneath her
revolutionary activities she is really a girl in search of a good
time—"she wanted l'Amérique la vie le theatre le feev o'clock le
smoking le foxtrot" (*NN*, 420)—and thus threatens to deflect the
radical artist from his goals.

The final Camera Eye in *Nineteen-Nineteen* sums up Dos
Passos' development by the close of the second novel of the trilogy.
He has returned to service near Paris and is an army casual load-
ing scrap iron onto railcars in the morning and unloading it in the
afternoon while his discharge is delayed because his service record—that is, his identity—has been lost. Thus, the two "rebirths"
of *Nineteen-Nineteen* are, in truth, false dawns. Although Dos Passos had escaped from the prisons of both Harvard and the army,
neither his full identity nor his role as an artist has been discovered, and he is still engaged in the meaningless tasks that life presents him.

In *The Big Money* the Camera Eye passages are dominated
by the related motifs of traveling and of trying on literary roles—of
search as both physical and artistic restlessness. The theme of
search begins with the initial Camera Eye of *The Big Money* with
Dos Passos' reaction to postwar America on his return from
France. The harbor scenes evoke memories of place and season,
but once he is fully in touch with America the images shift to those
of a 1920s world of crushing normalcy on the one hand and social
oppression on the other: "the crunch of whitecorn muffins and coffee with cream gulped in a hurry before traintime and apartment-
house mornings stifling with newspapers and the smooth powdery
feel of new greenbacks and the whack of a cop's billy cracking a
citizen's skull and the faces blurred with newsprint of men in jail"
(*BM*, 27). Escape into art appears to be the only response to these
conditions, but escape into the two available roles of "artist as
world traveler" or "artist as successful novelist" brings no relief. In
each instance, Dos Passos must adopt a false identity appropriate
to the role, as is suggested by the borrowed dress suits he is forced
to wear both in Beirut and New York. The 1920s Greenwich Village cocktail party also does not provide a context for self-discovery.
In the Camera Eye segment devoted to such a party, the imagery of

effeminate artiness and of role-playing clearly relates the falsity of
this world to that of Eliot's Prufrock setting. At the party, "the narrow yellow room teems with talk" (*BM*, 125), and the hostess finds

> every man his pigeonhole
> the personality must be kept carefully adjusted
> over the face
> to facilitate recognition she pins on each of us a
> badge   (*BM*, 125)

To escape being pinned, Dos Passos must

> walk the streets and walk the streets inquiring of
> Coca Cola signs Lucky Strike ads pricetags in storewindows
> scraps of overheard conversations stray tatters of newsprint
> yesterday's headlines sticking out of ashcans
> for a set of figures a formula of action an address
> you don't quite know   (*BM*, 149)

In this search, "a formula of action" now has a special appeal—"to
do to make there are more lives than walking desperate the streets
hurry underdog do   make" (*BM*, 149)—and he briefly adopts
the role of social agitator, of "a speech urging action in the crowded
hall" (*BM*, 149). But he finds himself merely sloganizing and dis-
appointedly returns home "after a drink and a hot meal [to] read
(with some difficulty in the Loeb Library trot) the epigrams of Mar-
tial and [to] ponder the course of history and what leverage might
pry the owners loose from power and bring back (I too Walt Whitman) our storybook democracy" (*BM*, 150).

New York in the early 1920s thus provides Dos Passos with
the opportunity to choose between two opposing literary roles, neither of which is satisfactory. He can be the class-conscious radical
who is ineffectually seeking a way to contribute to the restoration
of our "storybook democracy." Or he can be the successful artist
who finds excitement in the intimate connection between sex and
money:

> money in New York (lipstick kissed off the lips of
> a girl fashionablydressed fragrant at five o'clock in a taxicab
> careening down Park Avenue . . .
> dollars are silky in her hair soft in her dress
> sprout in the elaborately contrived rosepetals that you kiss

become pungent and crunchy in the speakeasy dinner sting
shrill in the drinks   (*BM*, 150–51)

But this kind of sexual excitement is not an adequate conclusion to
his search. "[I]f not why not?" he asks; and from "somebody in
[his] head" comes the answer, "liar" (*BM*, 151). The sexuality of
the big money betrays rather than affirms and supports a masculinity of strength and purpose. So Dos Passos must still search
while "peeling the speculative onion of doubt" (*BM*, 151)—doubt
imaged in the Camera Eye that follows as a harbor fog that hinders
his efforts to begin his true journey.

Dos Passos' search for a fully expressive masculine literary
identity and role ends in the related settings of the Plymouth of the
Sacco-Vanzetti case and the Harlan County of the miners' strike.
In these examples of the organized oppression of freedom and democracy by the very institutions established to safeguard them,
Dos Passos discovers his theme and his function as a writer. He is
to tell the truth about America, and particularly about the corruption and subversion of the "old words" of freedom and justice by
those in power, and thus play an active role in the struggle to return us to our "storybook democracy." As he walks through Plymouth, "pencil scrawls in my notebook the scraps of recollection the
broken halfphrases the effort to intersect word with word to dove-
tail clause with clause to rebuild out of mangled memories un-
shakably (Oh Pontius Pilate) the truth" (*BM*, 436). Returning to
Boston, he asks,

how can I make them feel how our fathers our uncles
haters of oppression came to this coast   how say
Don't let them scare you   how make them feel who
are your oppressors America
              rebuild the ruined words worn slimy in the
mouths of lawyers districtattorneys collegepresidents
judges   without the old words the immigrants haters
of oppression brought to Plymouth how can you know who
are your betrayers America   (*BM*, 437)

With the deaths of Sacco and Vanzetti the struggle appears to be
lost—"there is nothing left to do   we are beaten   . . . our
work is over" (*BM*, 462). But in fact,

the old words of the immigrants are being renewed in
blood and agony tonight do they know that the old Ameri-

can speech of the haters of oppression is new tonight . . .
the language of the beaten nation is not forgotten in our
ears tonight
      the men in the deathhouse made the old words
new before they died   (*BM*, 463)

"We stand defeated America," this Camera Eye ends (*BM*,
464). "We stand defeated," however, only in the sense of the failure
to save Sacco and Vanzetti. The "old words" were brought to life
again in the courage of Sacco and Vanzetti and in the beauty and
power of Vanzetti's language of freedom and hope in his letters.
And in these examples the writer can find his true task. The two
"false" rebirths following the deaths of his parents and his escape
from the army have now been superceded by a "true" rebirth following the martyrdom of Sacco and Vanzetti. The "old words . . .
renewed in [their] blood and agony" are now the writer's living
faith. Dos Passos' journey forward in time in search of his identity
has led him paradoxically to the discovery that his identity lies in
the past, in the "old words" as a form of faith and in his father's
independence and strength of mind as a guide to the fulfillment of
this faith.

The full political and personal implications of this faith are
realized by Dos Passos at Harlan. In his account in *Harlan Miners
Speak* of the Kentucky miners who attend a "free speech speakin,"
he recalled that

These were the gaunt faces, the slow elaborations of talk
and courtesy, of the frontiersmen who voted for Jefferson
and Jackson, and whose turns of speech were formed in
the oratory of Patrick Henry. I never felt the actuality of the
American revolution so intensely as sitting in that church,
listening to these mountaineers with their old time phrases,
getting on their feet and explaining why the time to fight
for freedom had come again.[35]

But the miners are not the only strangers in their own land because of their wish to live the old ideal of freedom. The investigat-
ing committee, including Dos Passos, are—in an oft-repeated term
in the Harlan County Camera Eye—also "foreigners." As Dos Passos notes, in terminology loaded with resonance for himself as a
second-generation American striving to preserve old American values, the sheriff and his deputies "have made us foreigners in the

land where we were born" (*BM*, 524). No wonder, then, that the
crushing of the Harlan County miners by corporate and state
power represented to Dos Passos in microcosm the betrayal of
America, and that he ends the Camera Eye in *U.S.A.* with the de-
fiant and challenging charge to himself, "we have only words
against / POWER SUPERPOWER."

The corruption of the language of belief and value in America is an
implicit theme in the narratives, biographies, and newsreels of
U.S.A. But the theme is also frequently present in more direct
expression, as a kind of reminder of its centrality in a lengthy work
that is otherwise free of authorial editorializing. The relationship of
language to experience in America, in other words, is often a specific subject at various points in the trilogy. Occasionally the subject appears in a "positive" cast, recalling to us the potential
benefits of a truthful use of the "old words," as when the Camera
Eye persona states that "*If you hit the words Democracy will
understand*" (*NN*, 102–3), or when Jack Reed is praised as a west-
erner for whom "words meant what they said" (*NN*, 14). But more
often we are reminded openly of the perversion of language that
has occurred throughout the twentieth century in America, a perversion stimulated by the relationship between a predatory capitalism and the war. This quantum leap in untruthfulness from before
to after the war is neatly charted within the career of Doc Bingham. When we first encounter Bingham in Mac's narrative early in
The 42nd Parallel as proprietor of the "Truthseeker Literary Dis-
tributing Company" and as a man who signs his correspondence
"Yours in search for Truth" (*FP*, 29–30), he is a small-town shyster
and charlatan. When he reappears, in the Richard Savage narrative at the close of *The Big Money*, he is head of a national patent-
medicine company that is about to employ Moorehouse's public
relations firm. The firm's mandate, to convince the American public that self-medication fulfills the American ideal of "selfservice,
independence, individualism" and is thus an endorsement of
"Americanism" (*BM*, 494), illustrates the raising of the principle of
the inversion of truth for self-interest—Bingham's permanent operative mode—from that of petty huckstering to national ethic. To
Dos Passos' mind, an exponential legitimization of the falsification
of language under the guise of endorsing national goals occurred
at the time of the war. Some of his most explicit editorializing on

verbal corruption is thus found in such passages as that in Randolph Bourne's biography, when Wilson's verbal gymnastics are satirized: "for *New Freedom*, read *Conscription*, for *Democracy, Win the War*, for *Reform, Safeguard the Morgan Loans*" (*NN*, 105). A similar blatancy is found in a passage in Eleanor's narrative. America is about to enter the war, and Eleanor and Moorehouse, who have never had a profound or genuine or compassionate sentiment in their lives, find the prospect "too beautiful; she burst into tears and they talked about Sacrifice and Dedication" (*FP*, 353).

This last example illustrates an important additional characteristic of Dos Passos' dramatization of the interplay between language and experience. For in this instance, Eleanor and Moorehouse are not consciously manipulating language to gain a financial or political advantage, as are Bingham and Wilson in the earlier examples cited. They have instead absorbed and are using words to serve their unconscious need to validate a commendable and self-satisfying emotional and "spiritual" dimension in their otherwise sterile inner lives. It is this kind of "old words"—the language of personal belief and value, and often of love and sex—that Dos Passos also frequently openly depicts as having undergone a profound corruption in the twentieth century, one equal in significance, as well as complementary to, the failure in the language of political belief. An obvious example occurs early in Richard Savage's narrative. The adolescent Dick is told by an Episcopalian priest that "he must avoid temptations and always serve God with a clean body and a clean mind, and keep himself pure for the lovely sweet girl he would someday marry, and that anything else led only to madness and disease" (*NN*, 78). This passage is both a parody of conventional Christian sexual wisdom and—more suggestively for the trilogy as a whole—an indication of how the "old words" of sexual behavior can be warped. Such terms as *clean, pure,* and *sweet* draw upon the traditional language of love and romance to inculcate a specific kind of personal belief and behavior as falsely and powerfully as do the terms *Sacrifice* and *Dedication* in the area of political belief and behavior. Dos Passos' subject in *U.S.A.*, in brief, is not only the language of public attitudes but that of private conviction. His theme is that freedom is not merely a political concept; it involves our every value and act, and language is the best reflection of the degree of freedom that we exercise in every sphere of life.

As well as illustrating Dos Passos' preoccupation throughout

U.S.A. with the connection between language and life in America, the "only words against / POWER SUPERPOWER" passage also reveals how we must read the trilogy. We must read it as a vast canvas in which theme is potentially present both in the immediate connections between closely linked modal segments and in the implications of this connection for widely separated segments through the trilogy. The passage itself is a useful but somewhat misleading example of Dos Passos' technique, since theme is seldom revealed elsewhere so dramatically and directly. Rather, theme is far more obliquely, though densely and pervasively, rendered by the deep layers of interaction inherent in the montage form of the trilogy. For example, in the "only words against" passage, theme seems to be encapsulated in the visually immediate crossing of the modal barrier and in the direct reference to language. But this is only the beginning (though a profound beginning in this instance) of the juxtapositional implications of the passage. The Camera Eye persona is participating in a miners' strike, as have Mac and Mary French in their narratives earlier in the trilogy. Mac is a printer, Mary is a secretary, the Camera Eye persona a writer; all have used "words" to aid the miners' cause, but only the Camera Eye persona realizes fully that words are both their enemy and their weapon. On the other side of the modal division, the Insull biography is one of many inverted American success stories in the biographies and narratives. (Charley Anderson and Mary Dowling are other examples.) An immigrant youth, he works hard, pushes ahead, and then accepts the need for deception and dishonesty if he is to gain power and the big money. Almost immediately preceding the Insull biography, the final Richard Savage narrative depicts in detail Savage's adoption of this ethic in a modern public-relations firm and his parallel moral collapse. And in Savage, the Harvard poet turned public-relations executive, there is a swing back in ironic juxtapositional implication to the Camera Eye persona and his growth. The juxtapositional richness of the trilogy is, as these few examples suggest, almost infinite. A modal segment (a biography, for example) may obliquely refer to immediately adjacent different modal segments, to similar kinds of experience in biographies elsewhere in the trilogy, or to similar kinds of experience in other modes elsewhere in the trilogy. And other modal segments immediately adjacent to the biography (a narrative, for example) may be similarly engaged along independent thematic lines. *U.S.A.* as a whole is thus like a cubist painting at the height of the movement. It is a single object (America) rendered through multiple angles of vision (the varying modes and their varying subject matter) and it therefore requires of its audience a willingness to accept simultaneity (and thus a search for juxtapositional implication) as its operative aesthetic principle.

3

U.S.A.

The Modes

Viewed in their finished state, the four modes of U.S.A.—the Camera Eye, narratives, biographies, and Newsreels—appear to be almost inevitable and thus "natural" parts of the trilogy. It is difficult, in other words, to imagine U.S.A. without one of the modes or with one taking a different form, so balanced and functional is each in the total design of the work. But this, of course, is to mistake art for nature. The four modal devices of the total fiction that is U.S.A. are highly stylized and sophisticated versions of various kinds of early-twentieth-century imaginative discourse, and each was additionally refined to play a highly stylized and sophisticated role in the trilogy as a whole. There is, in short, nothing "natural" about them. They constitute, rather, an intellectualization of the raw material of American life into a made artwork of great complexity and intricacy.

Although Dos Passos never explained the specific meaning of the title "The Camera Eye," it would appear that he intended to imply the dual potential of this image of vision. The camera is a symbol of impersonal and "objective" depiction. But it is also possible to look through the "eye" or lens of the camera to see within the camera itself. Translated into the material of U.S.A., the Camera Eye mode is the consciousness of the author; the remainder of the work is the American world at large that the author has sought to depict as accurately as possible. This interpretation is confirmed by first impressions of the Camera Eye segments, since they indeed seem to be miscellaneous collections of stream-of-consciousness fragments from various moments of Dos Passos' life. Dos Passos himself later tended to support this notion of the Camera Eye as principally unfocused autobiography when he commented that his purpose in including this material was to increase the objectivity of the rest of the trilogy. "That's why I put the Camera Eye things in *U.S.A.*," he noted; "it was a way of draining off the subjective by directly getting in little bits of my own experience."[1] The architectonics of the Camera Eye segments in *U.S.A.* also seem to confirm a largely negative role for this material. The fifty-one brief Camera Eye segments are widely dispersed in an extremely long work (about 1,500 pages in the 1938 edition), which makes it difficult for readers to maintain a sense either of the relationship of one Camera Eye segment to another or of the distinctive form of the mode.

The Camera Eye, however, is a coherent autobiography (as I have already attempted to show) with a coherent form, and its account of Dos Passos' inner life is not merely a negative "draining off" of the subjective but also plays a major role in the juxtapositional form of the trilogy as a whole. To find the sources of the Camera Eye in Dos Passos' life[2]—a task made easier since the publication of his autobiography in 1966 and of two lengthy biographies in recent years—is thus not to diminish the character of the Camera Eye portion of *U.S.A.* as a created or made object. Dos Passos' choice of which events in his life to depict, and his careful molding of each of these into a contribution to the emerging theme of the search for identity and role by the Camera Eye persona, constitute an artistic recreation of life. Nor are the individual segments of the Camera Eye the product of a free-association stream-of-consciousness memory act. The available manuscript evidence reveals that Dos Passos often did begin the composition of a segment by jotting down several images. (The Camera Eye contains some of the obsessive images found elsewhere in his writing, such as night journeys by train as a child, or the cook's red-haired daughter of his adolescence, or his garden "retreat" at Verdun.) But after this beginning, the segment underwent careful expansion and revision, both in content and form, until it reached its finished state.[3] Both the origin and the nature of the Camera Eye thus suggest that it can be most profitably discussed as a form of autobiographical symbolic poetry. A segment of the Camera Eye does not render dramatically the workings of a consciousness at a specific moment of experience, as in conventional stream-of-consciousness expression. Rather, it renders a frame of mind or attitude from a phase of Dos Passos' psychic life by means of a series of carefully selected and ordered personal images that evocatively express the phase.

Of course, some Camera Eye segments fulfill this function

more fully and directly than others. *The 42nd Parallel*, which has a greater number of Camera Eye segments than the other novels in the trilogy, contains several that serve principally to capture the anecdotal debris of the memory of childhood. But as the trilogy advances and as the consciousness re-creating the past focuses more directly on the crises of his youth and adulthood, each of the Camera Eye segments takes on the character of a unified and complete poem—of a re-creation through image and symbol of a state of mind and feeling—that is also a stage in the larger poem of the coming into maturity and vision of the artist's imagination.

These symbolic poems, which constitute the episodes in the traditional romantic subject of the journey of the artist's spirit, reveal several major influences on their style and form. Joyce obviously contributed some of the conventional "signals" for the representation of the inner life in the superficial discontinuities and unconventional punctuation of the Camera Eye form.[4] But the principal influences on Dos Passos' style in the Camera Eye are undoubtedly Whitman and Eliot.[5] From the first comes an emphasis on grammatical and verbal parallelism as a basic structural device within an unmetrical form, and from the second the organization of each of the Camera Eye segments into a series of brief narrative or dramatic vignettes that themselves rely largely on private image and symbol. A Camera Eye segment is therefore a stylized recreation of feeling rather than an attempt to render immediate feeling, as in stream-of-consciousness writing. I state the difference again because in it lies an explanation not only of the sophisticated obliqueness of the Camera Eye style but also of the carefully wrought relationship of each segment to parallel (though differently expressed) moments in the lives of juxtaposed biographical and narrative figures. To stress that each Camera Eye segment is an individually conceived poem also helps explain the great variety of form and tone among them. Some are largely narrative or anecdotal; some detail only one incident, others combine several; some are comic and farcical, others angry and passionate. Each, to use the inevitable term, is an objective correlative to Dos Passos' state of mind, feeling, or spirit at a specific moment of his development, and each takes a form appropriate to that moment. Dos Passos' Camera Eye style is thus Joycean, not in the adoption of a Joycean form of the interior monologue, but rather in the bravura variations of style used for the expression of the interior self.

Camera Eye (28) is a good example of the form of the Camera Eye. The segment occurs early in *Nineteen-Nineteen* and is devoted to the impact on Dos Passos of his parents' deaths (in May 1915 and January 1917) and of his army service (during 1918–19).

THE CAMERA EYE (28)

when the telegram came that she was dying (the streetcarwheels screeched round the bellglass like all the pencils on all the slates in all the schools) walking around Fresh Pond the smell of puddlewater willowbuds in the raw wind shrieking streetcarwheels rattling on loose trucks through the Boston suburbs   grief isnt a uniform and go shock the Booch and drink wine for supper at the Lenox before catching the Federal

I'm so tired of violets
Take them all away

when the telegram came that she was dying the bellglass cracked in a screech of slate pencils   (have you ever never been able to sleep for a week in April?)
and He met me in the gray trainshed my eyes were stinging with vermillion bronze and chromegreen inks that oozed from the spinning April hills   His mustaches were white the tired droop of an old man's cheeks   She's gone Jack grief isn't a uniform and the   in the parlor   the waxen odors of lilies in the parlor   (He and I we must bury the uniform of grief)
then the riversmell the shimmering Potomac reaches the little choppysilver waves at Indian Head there were mockingbirds in the graveyard and the roadsides steamed with spring   April enough to shock the world

when the cable came that He was dead I walked through the streets full of fiveoclock Madrid seething with twilight in shivered cubes of aguardiente redwine gaslampgreen sunsetpink tileochre   eyes lips red cheeks brown pillar of the throat   climbed on the night train at the Notre station without knowing why

I'm so tired of violets
Take them all away

the shattered iridescent bellglass the carefully
copied busts the architectural details the grammar of styles
it was the end of that book and I left the Oxford
poets in the little noisy room that smelt of stale oliveoil in
the Pension Boston   Ahora   Now   Maintenant
Vita Nuova   but we
who had heard Copey's beautiful reading voice
and read the handsomely bound books and breathed deep
(breathe deep   one   two   three   four)   of the
waxwork lilies and the artificial parmaviolet scent under the
ethercone and sat breakfasting in the library where the bust
was of Octavius
were now dead at the cableoffice

on the rumblebumping wooden bench on the
train slamming through midnight climbing up from the
steerage to get a whiff of Atlantic on the lunging steamship
(the ovalfaced Swiss girl and her husband were my friends)
she had slightly popeyes and a little gruff way of saying *Zut
alors* and throwing us a little smile a fish to a sealion that
warmed our darkness   when the immigration officer
came for her passport he couldn't send her to Ellis Island la
grippe espagnole she was dead

washing those windows
K.P.
cleaning the sparkplugs with a pocketknife
A. W. O. L.
grinding the American Beauty roses to dust in
that whore's bed   (the foggy night flamed with proclamations of the League of the Rights of Man)   the almond
smell of high explosives sending singing éclats through the
sweetish puking grandiloquence of the rotting dead

tomorrow I hoped would be the first day of the
first month of the first year   (*NN,* 9–12)

The theme of Dos Passos' release through his parents' deaths and
his military service from a death in life to a potential rebirth is ex-

pressed in personal images that are knitted together by a parallel
rhetorical form. So the death of the mother—"when the telegram
came"—is in the context of restrictive Harvard images (the bellglass above all) and of an April funeral journey to the family's Virginia estate (itself echoing "When Lilacs Last in the Dooryard
Bloom'd"), which suggest a possible life out of death as the genteel
shackles of family and school begin to loosen. The father's death
("when the cable came") confirms a belief in an emergent freedom
as activities associated by Dos Passos with restriction (the architectural studies imposed on him by his father, the ethercone and lilies
of Harvard) "were now dead at the cableoffice." (The dense and
complex flower imagery of the segment, culminating in the crushing of the American Beauty roses in the whore's bed, is worthy of
Eliot at his richest.) The death of the young Swiss girl on the journey home to America appears to stress the need for the young to
pursue life before death overtakes them. And then abruptly life itself overtakes Dos Passos in the ironical "freedom" of his army service, in which he is thrust into the stark physicality of empty tasks,
raw sexuality, and violent death. Is this the freedom and life he
wished to break through to and hold? The poem does not answer
the question; rather, it dramatizes the emotional reality of this
phase of Dos Passos' life as he is released from the protective co-
coon of youth into an ambiguous freedom—"tomorrow I hoped
would be the first day of the first month of the first year."

Camera Eye (44), which occurs early in *The Big Money*, deals
with Dos Passos' travels in the Near East in the fall of 1921 and
with the notoriety he gained both from this adventure and from the
publication of *Three Soldiers* while he was abroad.

THE CAMERA EYE (44)

the unnamed arrival
(who had hung from the pommel of the unshod
white stallion's saddle
a full knapsack
and leaving the embers dying in the hollow of
the barren Syrian hills where the Agail had camped when
dawn sharpshining cracked night off the ridged desert had
ridden toward the dungy villages and the patches of ses-
ame and the apricotgardens)
shaved off his beard in Damascus
and sat drinking hot milk and coffee in front of

the hotel in Beirut staring at the white hulk of Lebanon
fumbling with letters piled on the table and clipped streamers of newsprint

addressed not to the unspeaker of arabic or the
clumsy scramblerup on camelback so sore in the rump
from riding

but to someone

who

(but this evening in the soft nightclimate of the
Levantine coast the kind officials are contemplating further
improvements

scarcelybathed he finds himself cast for a role
provided with a white tie carefully tied by the viceconsul
stuffed into a boiled shirt a tailcoat too small a pair of dresstrousers too large which the kind wife of the kind official
gigglingly fastens in the back with safetypins which immediately burst open when he bows to the High Commission-
er's lady   faulty costuming makes the role of eminent
explorer impossible to play   and the patent leather
pumps painfully squeezing the toes got lost under the table
during the champagne and speeches)

who arriving in Manhattan finds waiting again
the forsomebodyelsetailored dress suit

the position offered the opportunity presented
the collarbutton digging into the adamsapple while a
wooden image croaks down a table at two rows of freshly-
pressed gentlemen who wear fashionably their tailored
names

stuffed into shirts to caption miles lightyears of
clipped streamers of newsprint

Gentlemen I apologize it was the wrong bell it
was due to a misapprehension that I found myself on the
stage when the curtain rose the poem I recited in a foreign
language was not mine in fact it was somebody else who
was speaking it's not me in uniform in the snapshot it's a
lamentable error mistaken identity the servicerecord was
lost the gentleman occupying the swivelchair wearing the
red carnation is somebody else than

whoever it was who equipped with false whiskers was standing outside in the rainy street and has man-
aged undetected to make himself scarce down a manhole

                    the pastyfaced young man wearing somebody
        else's readymade business opportunity
                    is most assuredly not
                    the holder of any of the positions for which he
        made application at the employmentagency   (*BM*, 29–31)

The unkempt and inept desert traveler finds himself cast into new
and "improved" roles, first of eminent explorer, then in New York
of eminent author, both of which are symbolized by ill-fitting borrowed costumes. In his dismay, he recalls a slightly earlier incident
(at Tiflis) of mistaken identity that had forced him into an uncom-
fortable public role ("I found myself on stage"). The need to escape
these roles is paramount, and in the counterdisguise of "false whiskers" he "make[s] himself scarce down a manhole." Whatever he
wanted out of life, these were not "the positions for which he made
application at the employmentagency." As in the previous example,
Dos Passos in this Camera Eye was attempting to render a specific
phase of his personal life. But the inherently comic and farcical
aspects of the reluctant public figure—the roles pressed upon him,
the frantic efforts to escape—result in a different kind of Camera
Eye. The entire segment is built on the incrementally comic image
of the costumes Dos Passos is forced to wear, and the segment concludes with his burlesque adoption of yet another disguise to escape further persecution. In addition, the narrative pace is swifter
in this Camera Eye, as befits its lighter tone. The segment, in
brief, has its own poetic coherence—that of comic escape—that
lends the entire piece its own successful shape and character. It is
one of the obvious paradoxes of Dos Passos' literary career that
though he wrote and published much poetry throughout his early
career, almost all his poems are weakly derivative exercises in an
impersonal imagism.[6] It was only when he turned to the deeply
personal themes and images of his own life in the seemingly non-
poetic form of the Camera Eye that his poetic voice found its best
expression.

It was long common in general discussion of twentieth-century
American writing to regard the narratives of *U.S.A.* as evidence of
Dos Passos' allegiance to the naturalist tradition in American fiction. In flat, colorless prose, the argument goes, Dos Passos in endless detail tells of the external experience of flat, colorless

characters who exhibit little or no control over their destinies.
There is some truth to this view, in that the total effect of the narratives of U.S.A. is of human inadequacy and social coercion. But the
means used to achieve this effect are in fact very different from a
nonselective accumulation of the externals of life. Like the other
modes of U.S.A., though less obviously so, the narrative mode in
the trilogy is fully intellectualized and stylized. At its best—which
is most of the time—a narrative in U.S.A. is at once a dramatic representation of the relationship between a specific temperament
and its world and an interpretation of the large-scale designs operative in that world.

It might be expected that Dos Passos would use the opportunity afforded by the need to depict twentieth-century American life
through the experience of a sizeable number of fictional characters
to select figures who in their totality would constitute a cross section of American life. The narrative figures in U.S.A., however, fail
to achieve this kind of representativeness. The group lacks a
farmer, factory worker,[7] businessman, or professional (lawyer, doctor, etc.). Almost all the figures are from the Midwest or the East
Coast, and there is not a satisfactory (or even a more than miser-
able) marriage in the lot. This last failure in representativeness—
or, more cogently, Dos Passos' impulse toward thematic emphasis
through repetition—suggests a possible alternative principle of selection to that of sociological balance, despite the appearance of
random sampling and therefore of objectivity in the choice of narrative figures. That is, the division of the "plot" of U.S.A. into
twelve narrative figures who initially have widely differing backgrounds has something of the same purpose as the use of the documentary in the biographies and Newsreels. In all the modes other
than the Camera Eye, Dos Passos wished to create an impression
of objective truth, of historical accuracy in fictional form. Hence
the use of the documentary in some modes and of a seemingly balanced cross section of American lives in the other. The narrative
figures, however, have no special objectivity either in source or in
fictional expression. Rather, the narratives of U.S.A. are remarkably similar in characterization and plotting to those of conventional novels. The figures usually stem from prototypes in Dos
Passos' own experience, and Dos Passos recasts the lives of his
prototypes into narratives that approximate specific themes. The
narratives of U.S.A. are thus stylized, not in constituting a representative sociological spectrum of American life, but rather in sug-

gesting such a representativeness while, in fact, expressing above all Dos Passos' personal vision of American life.

The clearest evidence that Dos Passos sought to rely on some of the traditional thematic devices of fiction in the narratives occurs about halfway through *The 42nd Parallel,* when Eleanor Stoddard and J. Ward Moorehouse, two narrative figures who have already had narrative segments devoted to them, meet in New York.[8] This technique, which I will call interlacing, increases as the trilogy goes forward. It ranges from a casual reappearance of a figure (Moorehouse momentarily drifts into Mac's narrative in Mexico) to the love affairs of Daughter and Richard Savage and of Charley Anderson and Margo. The technique peaks on the several occasions (as in a Paris restaurant at the close of *Nineteen-Nineteen*) when as many as five or six narrative figures are thrown together at a social function. So pervasive is the interlacing of narrative figures in *U.S.A.* that by the close of the trilogy only Mary French has not appeared in the narrative of another figure.

The effect of this device is to bring the narratives of *U.S.A.* close to one aspect of the plotting of a conventional novel. As characters we know fully become involved with other characters we know fully, theme emerges more clearly and powerfully than it would otherwise. An obvious example is the group of narrative figures (Janey, Eleanor, and Savage) who eventually gather around Moorehouse, a clustering that confirms the emptiness of each figure. Another is the love affair between Ben and Mary, in which Mary's abortion and the breakup of their relationship because of their commitment to a radical ideology epitomizes the antihumanism of the far left. These and the many other instances of interlacing in the trilogy appear to work against the logic of the initial and continuing device of separate narratives, the logic that the frequent meeting of such widely dispersed characters would be unlikely. By taking the narratives strongly in the direction of this "unlikelihood," Dos Passos was introducing a self-conscious, and to the reader clearly evident, abstract element as a means of heightening theme. He was, in other words, writing narrative that frequently runs counter to expectation, and he often gained his greatest thematic emphasis at these "points of surprise."

The narratives contain several other conventions that also reflect a stylization of the narrative mode. One such convention is that Dos Passos, though a third-person narrator, does not provide a synopsis or summary of a character's previous experience at the opening of a narrative segment, even though several hundred pages may have elapsed since a narrative segment was last devoted to that character. Another is that the reappearance of a major character in the narrative of a different character does not elicit a sign of recognition from the narrative voice. It is as if the narrator is encountering the figure, whom we as readers are fully acquainted with, for the first time.

Both of these conventions originate in Dos Passos' fidelity to the technique of free indirect discourse as the means of telling the life stories of his narrative figures. Free indirect discourse, or *style indirect libre* as it is commonly called in European literary criticism, is a basic tool of the novelist and can take a variety of complex forms.[9] But to describe it in broad strokes, the author adopting the device writes of a character in the third person but seeks to describe his or her thoughts, feelings, and even actions in an idiom closely associated with that of the character. The extremes in the use of free indirect discourse are the occasional presence of the device for specific moments and figures (as in Dickens) and the complete adoption throughout a novel of the verbal style of the principal characters, in which style becomes part of milieu (as in Zola or in Mailer's *The Executioner's Song*). Dos Passos' use of the technique in the narratives of *U.S.A* approaches a full commitment to the device. Each narrative has its own verbal style, one seeking to suggest and approximate (rather than to reproduce exactly) the habitual modes of speech and therefore of thought of its narrative figure. In each narrative, Dos Passos is in effect communicating the total personality of the narrative figure by a narrative style that is an expression of that figure. Hence the convention of authorial nonpresence on occasions when a third-person narrator would ordinarily feel free to comment. The illusion that we are confined to the consciousness of the narrative figure through the narrative voice is thus preserved.

Although free indirect discourse has been common in fiction since the origin of the novel, it has had a special fascination for the modernist author since the late nineteenth century. The device permits the combination of two of the major impulses of modern fiction—the desire to depict the commonplace realities of life and the desire to dramatize consciousness. By portraying everyday action and thought in the everyday language habitual to a character, a language that thus powerfully reflects the consciousness of the character, the writer appeared to fulfill both aims simultaneously. Another appeal of the device for the modern novelist is its potential for irony. As most commentators on the technique have noted, it has the capacity to express either the author's sympathetic identification with or his ironic detachment from his central narrative figure. Irony is achieved, of course, by the difference between what a character's mode of expression suggests about his unconscious motives or unexamined values and what we as readers, either from evidence in the narrative or from external bases of judgment, sense are the inadequacies of these motives or values.

Dos Passos' free indirect discourse narrative style in *U.S.A.* exhibits only occasionally the most obvious verbal signs of the device.[10] His third-person narrative contains little vulgarity and few grammatical lapses, and he does not sharply differentiate among regional or ethnic voices. (Opportunities for this kind of distinction were present in the Jewish and Southern backgrounds of Ben Compton and Janey, for example.) He concentrates rather on an effort to render the stereotyped in thought and feeling through stereotypes of language—through the platitudes and clichés, the commonplace evasions and half-truths, the verbal disguises that constitute much discourse. So unobstrusive is the technique that many early (and some later) readers of the trilogy failed to recognize the extent and depth of its ironic intent. Even so ordinarily astute a critic as Edmund Wilson complained to Dos Passos in 1939 that the characters of *U.S.A.* seemed to talk only in clichés.[11] Other critics, however, such as Sartre in 1938 and Claude-Edmonde Magny in 1946, were quick to realize that Dos Passos was attempting to write the narratives in what Sartre called a "public" voice and that this voice constituted both the form and the theme of the narratives.[12]

The impulse behind this vast exercise in free indirect discourse was of course clearly announced by Dos Passos in the trilogy itself, when he concluded the "U.S.A." prologue with the words, "mostly U. S. A. is the speech of the people." As he had also noted in 1935, "language . . . is the mind of the group."[13] To render the language of America is to render the mind of the nation and thus the true nature of the national experience. And since Dos Passos undertook the trilogy with the belief that America had betrayed its "storybook democracy" of equality, freedom, justice, and opportunity and was attempting to disguise and even defend this betrayal by distorting the language of democratic idealism, he was at special pains to render ironically throughout the narratives the vast failure of belief and thus of language that was the twentieth-century American experience.

There is, of course, no single, uniform free-indirect-discourse technique in the narratives of *U.S.A.* Occasionally Dos Passos' own sensibility seems paramount in descriptive or narrative passages that seem to be beyond the verbal ability of the narrative figure. Occasionally, too, a verbal shrillness, suggestive of an authorial editorial voice, enters the narrative, as in the accounts of the suppression of civil rights during the war (*NN,* 173–74). At the other extreme, we are sometimes plunged into the chaotic and fragmented workings of a mind in a manner resembling stream of consciousness. This occurs especially during the closing portions of Charley Anderson's narrative, when he is drunk or seriously ill.[14] Perhaps the clearest and most pervasive indication of the dominance of free indirect discourse as narrative style occurs on the many occasions at the opening of a narrative when the childhood of the narrative figure is described.[15] Here, for example, is the first paragraph of Eveline Hutchins' narrative:

> Little Eveline and Arget and Lade and Gogo lived on the top floor of a yellowbrick house on the North Shore Drive. Arget and Lade were little Eveline's sisters. Gogo was her little brother littler than Eveline; he had such nice blue eyes but Miss Mathilda had horrid blue eyes. On the floor below was Dr. Hutchins' study where Yourfather mustn't be disturbed, and Dearmother's room where she stayed all morning painting dressed in a lavender smock. On the groundfloor was the drawingroom and the diningroom, where parishioners came and little children must be seen and not heard, and at dinnertime you could smell good things to eat and hear knives and forks and tinkling companyvoices and Yourfather's booming scary voice.   (*NN,* 107)

The irony in this passage is readily apparent but genial as the child's view of her world is gently mocked. More characteristic of the narratives as a whole, however, are the many instances when a narrative figure's thoughts, especially those involving politics or sex and marriage, are rendered in a blatantly clichéd verbal style that clearly reflects the painful inadequacy of his or her stereotyped belief. So, for example, Janey is working at the outbreak of the war as a secretary in a law firm in which one of the partners is of German background. "Mr. Dreyfus was very polite and generous with his employees but Janey kept thinking of the ruthless invasion of Belgium and the horrible atrocities and didn't like to be

working for a Hun, so she began looking around for another job"
(*FP*, 285). At the other extreme of political awareness, but revealing an equally suspect reliance on the inevitable and hackneyed
phrase, is Ben's motive for studying hard and reading Marx. "He
was working to be a wellsharpened instrument" (*NN*, 431). As for
love, there are J. Ward Moorehouse's aspirations as a young man:
"He was twenty and didn't drink or smoke and was keeping himself clean for the lovely girl he was going to marry, a girl in pink
organdy with golden curls and a sunshade" (*FP*, 177).

In general, however, the narrative prose of *U.S.A.* is far less
blatant in its free-indirect-discourse dramatization of the platitudes
and clichés that guide the lives of the characters. Rather, Dos Passos' more common method is to suggest by the jaded and worn
language of the narratives the underlying failure of individuality of
those who approach life without independent vision and who are
therefore strangled by the hold of the conventional upon their
lives. Here, for example, is a typical passage of narrative prose, one
in which without any bold ironic touches Dos Passos describes
Janey's new position in a Washington law office:

> Working at Dreyfus and Carroll's was quite different
> from working at Mrs. Robinson's. There were mostly men
> in the office. Mr. Dreyfus was a small thinfaced man with a
> small black moustache and small black twinkly eyes and a
> touch of accent that gave him a distinguished foreign diplo-
> mat manner. He carried yellow wash gloves and a yellow
> cane and had a great variety of very much tailored over-
> coats. He was the brains of the firm, Jerry Burnham said.
> Mr. Carroll was a stout redfaced man who smoked many
> cigars and cleared his throat a great deal and had a very
> oldtimey Southern Godblessmysoul way of talking. Jerry
> Burnham said he was the firm's bay window. Jerry Burnham
> was a wrinklefaced young man with dissipated eyes who
> was the firm's adviser in technical and engineering matters.
> He laughed a great deal, always got into the office late, and
> for some reason took a fancy to Janey and used to joke
> about things to her while he was dictating. She liked him,
> though the dissipated look under his eyes scared her off a
> little. She'd have liked to have talked to him like a sister,
> and gotten him to stop burning the candle at both ends.
>
> (*FP*, 152)

On the one hand, the passage merely records Janey's impressions of the various members of the firm and thus renders in a mildly ironic manner several of her received opinions: that fine clothes represent distinction, that speech mannerisms signify character, and that there are clear physical stigmata of moral decay—in short, that life is as superficially apparent as she finds it. But the passage also records, with a far deeper and more significant irony, Janey's unconscious absorption in Jerry Burnham and her fear of that absorption, a conflict that she seeks to resolve by adopting the role of "sister" toward him. Janey thus reveals in the seemingly bland prose of this passage her fear of her own emotions and desires, a fear that leads her to erect barriers of conventional and life-denying attitudes between herself and the world.

Each of the narratives of *U.S.A.* demonstrates that its major character is locked in an analogous prison of stereotyped thought and action that is reflected in his language. Of course, Dos Passos' degree of ironic distance varies in his portrayal of the twelve narrative figures, despite the limitations of all the figures. The range extends from Eleanor, whom Dos Passos characterized elsewhere as a "drawing room bitch,"[16] to Margo and Mary, toward whom he felt considerable sympathy. When Margo and Charley become lovers, for example, we are told in Margo's narrative that "Mr. A., as she called him, kept offering to set Margo up in an apartment on Park Avenue, but she always said nothing doing, what did he think she was, a kept woman? She did let him play the stockmarket a little for her, and buy her clothes and jewelry and take her to Atlantic City and Long Beach weekends" (*BM*, 327). The irony in this passage, though clear enough, is also deflected by Dos Passos' identification with Margo's buoyant nature, with her only token and halfhearted self-deception, and thus is more amusing than condemnatory.

This wide variation in the degree and kind of satiric irony in the narratives is significant for its suggestion that the characters differ in their inner natures, that they are not uniformly shallow echoing chambers of the shallowness of their society. Such figures as Eleanor and Moorehouse have indeed found linguistic formulas that at once express an emotional and spiritual aridity and serve as vehicles for social advancement, and Dos Passos' ironic rendering of their formulaic attitudes is usually biting. But for many of the other figures—far more than is usually acknowledged—the acceptance of formulas and roles causes an intense pain as a sensibility buried within the figure struggles in vain against the

life-denying modes of belief and speech that the formulas demand.
Such characters as Charley Anderson and Richard Savage approach tragic dimensions in this conflict. A number of other figures, such as Janey or Joe Williams or Ben, though lacking the
depth or centrality of Charley or Savage, also exhibit sufficient
traces of a repressed emotional nature to engage Dos Passos and
us in a complex mix of ironic critique and sympathetic understanding.

Two other pervasive devices in the narrative technique of
U.S.A. that are related to free indirect discourse are the verbal motif and the paradigmatic act. Both express with repetitive emphasis
the basic cast of a character's mind. The verbal motif is a word or
phrase habitual to a character's thought or speech that defines the
character's response to experience; the paradigmatic act occurs
early in a character's life and then reappears again and again in
varied guises. Both the motif and the act are unconscious refuges;
they create a safe and comforting enclosure of feeling and thought
from which a character can maneuver without undertaking dis-
turbing explorations of himself or experience. So, as obvious examples of motifs, Eleanor's constant use of "refined," Eveline's of
"tiresome," and Charley's of "only a mechanic" are forms of response to the world or to self that effectively block any fresh or true
vision of world or self. Clear instances of the paradigmatic act are
when the youthful Mac is sent to distribute strike handbills and
finds himself distracted by spring and the thought of girls, when
Janey as a child gives up her friendship with a black girl because
she is instructed that it is not proper to have black friends, and
when Moorehouse as a youth unconsciously exploits and then deserts the lonely spinster piano teacher who has befriended him.
The presence of these devices that dramatize the predominance of
the permanent and unchanging in character suggests that in
U.S.A. characters do not develop in reaction to their experience.
Rather, they remain static, and what changes in the course of time
and event is our own understanding of the pattern of failure in the
nation as a whole. Dos Passos has substituted developing thematic
links among the narrative figures for the more common device of
individual character devlopment.

Dos Passos' preoccupation with overall design is thus one of
the most significant aspects of the narrative portion of *U.S.A.* Not
that the narrative figures are crudely cast as symbols of specific
limitations of American life within a rigid plan. The detailed speci-
ficity of the narratives is that of a conventional realism, of our im-

mersion in the commonplaces of life—of place, dress, speech, and event—in order to suggest an actuality of character and action. We are not in the traditional allegorical world of a starkly bare microcosm. But there is nevertheless an aspect of realistic characterization that can push it toward the generalized, abstract, and allegorical in theme and form. As George Lukács has noted,

> The central category and criterion of realist literature is the type, a peculiar synthesis which organically binds together the general and the particular both in characters and situations. What makes a type a type is not its average quality, not its mere individual being, however profoundly conceived; what makes it a type is that in it all the humanly and socially essential determinants are present in their highest level of development, in the ultimate unfolding of the possibilities latent in them, in extreme presentation of their extremes, rendering concrete the peaks and limits of men and their epochs.[17]

An author's predilection for types that have a solid base in his contemporary society can take two directions. One is to caricature specific social types with satiric intent, as Sinclair Lewis does. The other is to manipulate the lives of the types portrayed in order to stress in their combined fates a large-scale moral vision of life, as Thackeray or Balzac do. *U.S.A.* contains both of these devices. The first is evident principally in the minor characters—as in Sally Emerson, one of Eveline's Chicago friends, who epitomizes an upper-class phoney artiness, or in the Whalleys, the parents of Charley Anderson's wife, who are a blatant caricature of Southern gentility. Far more central, however, is Dos Passos' casting of his major narrative figures into social types whose lives and whose patterns of interlocking fates indeed do constitute "the peaks and limits of men and their epochs."

There are occasional blatant signs in *U.S.A.* of a symbolic moralist's rendering of American life. One is the severe telescoping of time in the narratives of Charley and Moorehouse in order to dramatize through their physical degeneration in the 1920s (when in fact they are in early middle age) the moral consequences of having succumbed to the temptation of the big money.[18] Another instance of Dos Passos' heavy hand as a symbolic moralist occurs in Bill Cermak's death late in Charley Anderson's narrative. In the death of Bill, who is Charley's alter ego in that he is truly only a mechanic, Charley's own total moral collapse is signaled. More commonly, however, the entire pattern of the life depicted in a narrative constitutes the paradigm for that type and thus lends the narrative the cast of social allegory. To cite a clear example from the political side of social life, Mac's life exemplifies the history and fate of the IWW. Mac's unsuccessful effort to maintain his radical faith in the face of bourgeois temptations is less an account of an individual weakness than of a failing of early-twentieth-century native American radicalism in general. In a similar manner, Ben's narrative, in which a Marxist ideologue is expelled from the Communist party for failure to follow the party line, is above all a representation of the struggle within the far left during the 1920s and 1930s between Marxist purists and Stalinist pragmatists. This tendency to pattern the lives of types into full-scale social themes is found in all the narratives and even extends into the most personal of relationships, that of the love affairs of the narrative figures. So, Mary French's history of love affairs with left-wing lovers, in which she is constantly deserted or betrayed by the man she loves, is a kind of allegory of the ways in which the aroused social conscience can be left unfulfilled in America. The love affair between Savage and Daughter illustrates a different kind of moral symbolism. Here a headstrong, emotional girl from Texas who represents the underlying generosity and thus the vulnerability at the heart of the American character is made pregnant and is abandoned by a charming and self-serving manipulator of the needs of others. That Savage goes on to become Moorehouse's right-hand man in the public relations business deepens the suggestion that in his relationship with Daughter we are seeing an allegorization of the fate of the American public at the hands of the Moorehouses and Savages.

The stylization of the narratives of *U.S.A.*, a device most evident in the "artificial" interlacing of the lives of narrative figures, thus in fact pervades every aspect of the narratives. The technique of free indirect discourse, as used by Dos Passos, is a means toward dramatizing conventional belief and therefore social types, and the actions of these types are then patterned into what in Dos Passos' eyes was the fate of each type in twentieth-century America. Beneath the seemingly shapeless flow of the events that are the lives of the narrative figures there lies a carefully structured and often openly allegorical vision of the American experience.

In his recollections of the origin of *U.S.A.*, Dos Passos was characteristically vague yet suggestive when recalling the purpose of the

miniature biographies of major twentieth-century American public
figures that are one of the four modes of the trilogy. He told an
interviewer in 1964, for example, that "It's awfully hard to say how
I came to add the portraits. I was trying to get different facets of
my subject and trying to get something a little more accurate than
fiction, at the same time to work these pieces into the fictional picture. The aim was always to produce fiction."[19] Dos Passos' intent
to depict "different facets" of the single subject of modern American life is of course related to the underlying cubist aesthetic and
technique of the trilogy as a whole. His goal of "accuracy" pertains
to his self-assumed role as "second-class historian" of his age.[20]
And his insistence that he wished to integrate the biographies fully
into the fiction testifies to the conscious juxtapositional energy in
his compositional method.

An even more suggestive, though indirect, comment by Dos
Passos on the function of the biographies occurs in his 1927 review
of Paxton Hibben's biography of Henry Ward Beecher. Hibben,
whom Dos Passos knew and admired and whom he later included
as a biographical figure in *Nineteen-Nineteen,* had written a de-
bunking biography of the late-nineteenth-century American religious leader. Why bother to dig up "dead and forgotten worthies,"
Dos Passos asked, when fiction can express the same themes to a
wider audience. He replied: "It seems to me that history is always
more alive and more interesting than fiction. I suppose that is because a story is the day dream of a single man, while history is a
mass-invention, the day dream of a race." We need more biographies such as Hibben's of Beecher, who flourished during a period
when American values began to founder. We need, Dos Passos
concluded, "more accurate and imaginative studies of the American past to set our compasses by."[21]

Dos Passos was soon to respond to this challenge himself in
the biographical portraits of *U.S.A.* As far as accuracy of fact was
concerned, he did his home—or rather library—work. Aside from
a few figures (Edison, Hearst, and Ford, for example), all of the
twenty-six public personages he included in the biographies were
dead, which meant that an authorized standard biography was
usually available. He also frequently consulted, as is clear from his
inclusion of verbatim material from them, such other sources as
autobiographies, feature stories, and *Who's Who*–type biographical
summaries.[22] His research method, as his notes reveal, was, not to
attempt to record all the pertinent facts about a life, but rather to
note a detail here and a detail there from various phases of the

life.[23] Whether the method was prompted by the biographical form he had in mind, or whether it helped stimulate that form, is not clear. What is clear is that the method is closely related to Dos Passos' finished biographical technique of the shaping of highly selective concrete detail into an interpretive portrait. For as Dos Passos' equal stress on "imagination" and "accuracy" in his Hibben review suggests, he was not interested in writing the kind of biography that is accurate in the negative sense of the author's disinterested and judicious treatment of his subject. Dos Passos wished to mold decisively, or "imaginatively," selected biographical detail into a portrait with archetypal relevance. The lives of public figures are the "day dreams of the race" in that we should be able to find in them in heightened form what we have all hoped for in our own lives—accomplishment, success, and happiness. And if they are to be accurate in a far deeper sense than verifiability, they must also portray the hazards and costs of the effort to fulfill the American dream. If we set our compasses accurately, we can better confront the dangers of the voyage ahead.

The problem that Dos Passos faced in the selection of biographical figures for inclusion in U.S.A. resembled but was more difficult than that present in the selection of narrative figures. On the one hand, he again wished to suggest representativeness—in this instance, the representative avenues toward success in American public life. On the other, he was now limited by the need to choose public figures. In addition, he wished to select biographical figures whose lives were related to already chosen narrative figures. His notes contain several lists of possible portraits and include among the discarded possibilities figures ranging from General Pershing and Dick Norton for Nineteen-Nineteen to John D. Rockefeller, Huey Long, Charlie Chaplin, Al Capone, and Babe Ruth for The Big Money.[24] In the end, with some exceptions, he chose figures principally from politics, business, and science. The exceptions—those from entertainment, the arts, and the left wing—are present because of their specific relevance to narrative figures or to central themes in the trilogy as a whole.

Dos Passos had available to him in the 1920s an emerging convention for the kind of biography he wished to write. Lytton Strachey in England and Thomas Beer in America, among others, had popularized the ironic impressionistic biography in which a seemingly miscellaneous body of biographical detail produced a devastating reversal of received opinion about a major public figure. Gamaliel Bradford, a noted critic of the day, had even invented a term for the biographical study in which incisive interpretation rather than full-length description was the goal. "Psychography," he declared, "is the condensed, essential, artistic presentation of character."[25] Dos Passos' biographies in *U.S.A.* vary in length (from two to over ten pages, with a tendency toward greater length as the trilogy goes forward), but all are of course "condensed" in comparison to a conventional biography and all are "artistic" in form. Indeed, they are superficially similar to the Camera Eye in their reliance on the Whitmanesque unmetrical long line and on grammatical and verbal parallelism.[26] But within this broad similarity their style differs from that of the Camera Eye in two related and significant ways. The concrete evocative details or "images" of the biographies are drawn from what notable men said and did—often directly from such documentary sources as speeches, interviews, and memoirs—rather than from the interior, feeling self. And these public images are then invariably selected and arranged to produce an ironic effect that is itself reflected in the almost uniformly ironic titles of the biographies. Indeed, the title of a biography often blatantly overstates the theme within the biography that the figure portrayed is something less or more or otherwise than he is conventionally assumed to be. So Jack Reed, who struggled and died for socialist causes, is far more than a "Playboy"; Carnegie, who made his fortune as a ruthless entrepreneur before he became a philanthropist devoted to international peace, is something less than a "Prince of Peace"; and Steinmetz, who despite his inventive genius was only a piece of apparatus to General Electric, was no "Proteus." Within a biography, the details of the life are stylized into similar kinds of ironic reversal, with a heavy reliance on incremental verbal motifs to render the essential weaknesses or strengths of the figure portrayed.

Two biographies that illustrate these characteristic techniques are "The House of Morgan" (*NN*, 335–40) and "Fighting Bob" (*FP*, 365–69). The first begins with a passage from J. P. Morgan's will in which Morgan commits his soul *"into the hands of my savior,"* followed immediately by the announcement that "into the hands of the House of Morgan" he committed vast economic holdings. A largely neutral account of the early Morgans, Joseph and Junius, concludes with the principal ironic motif of this biography, a motif that derives from the first great financial coup of the Morgans during the panic of 1857—"(wars and panics on the stock exchange, bankruptcies, warloans, good growing weather for the House of Morgan)" (*NN*, 337). These two ironic themes—the piety

and art interests of the Morgans in contrast to their financial ra-
pacity, and their fattening on the misery of others—control the
choice of incident and detail in the remainder of the biography.
The physical appearance of J. P. Morgan—"a bullnecked irascible
man with small black magpie's eyes and a growth on his nose"
(*NN*, 338)—serves to reveal the raw and ugly acquisitiveness of
the Morgans beneath their overlay of culture and religiosity. The
biography concludes with details of the even greater accumulation
of wealth and power by the Morgan firm during the world war and
the reminder that

> (Wars and panics on the stock exchange,
> machinegunfire and arson,
> bankruptcies, warloans,
> starvation, lice, cholera and typhus:
> good growing weather for the House of Morgan.)   (*NN*, 340)

This, of course, is not biography in any conventional sense,
just as the Camera Eye is not conventional autobiography. Like the
Camera Eye segments, each of the biographies is essentially a
prose poem in which a specific theme is created out of the selec-
tively chosen details of a life and by the artful manipulation of repetitive motif. The principal differences in form between the two
modes arise out of the difference between the exploration of private
and public lives. The biographies have a looser, less intense style.
They are longer; their "lines" are often flat prose sentences; their
parallelism is less severe; and they substitute repetitive ironic motif for repetitive personal symbol as sources of internal structure.

Both "The House of Morgan" and "Fighting Bob" rely, as do
the great majority of the biographies, on an American-success-
story archetype as an implicit ironic parallel to the life being
recounted. J. P. Morgan rises, not because a grateful God has
rewarded him for his faith, but because of his magpie acquisitiveness. Similarly, Robert La Follette, an incorruptible, independent
thinker, is rewarded by his nation with contempt and ignominy
when he refuses to support the war hysteria of 1917. A young man
bred on ideals of honest public service, he bucks the dishonest politics of his state and national party machine and rises to be gover-
nor and senator. But in Washington he is finally defeated—not by
the corrupt, but the the "crazy steamroller" (*FP*, 368) of war madness orchestrated by Wilson. He becomes "an orator haranguing
from the capitol of a lost republic," and, in a final ironic reversal of

Wilson's attack on him, "a wilful man expressing no opinion but his own" (*FP*, 369).

As in "The House of Morgan" and many other biographies, Dos Passos' dependence in "Fighting Bob" on ironic structure and ironic verbal repetition pushes the biography toward a powerful conclusion in which the last appearance of a verbal motif nails down an ironic theme one final, climactic time. Unlike the Camera Eye segments, which depend to some degree on images that extend over several segments (the bellglass, for example), each biography is fully complete in itself both in theme and in form. It is this characteristic of the biographies that has led to individual biographies being more commonly anthologized than any other portion of *U.S.A.*

The biographies as a whole contribute to the major theme in *U.S.A.* that public discourse often falsifies truth in twentieth-century America. Much of the trilogy seeks in various ways to dramatize that the verbal coinage of American life, its language of democratic idealism, has been debased. In the biographies it is the images of public life that have been perverted, and we have thus been led to worship false heroes and have failed to understand and value our true heroes. True heroism, in this distinction, is not conventional achievement or fame but rather the ability and strength to live and speak the truth about national life. Dos Passos' biographies in *U.S.A.* of the "great" of twentieth-century American life therefore divide into clusters of analogous life stories. These clusters, broadly speaking, either confirm the possibility of the heroic life in America despite ostensible failure or deny the success of the seemingly great. They are thus basically exercises in the redefinition of the American myth of success.

There are three clusters of bitterly ironic portraits of the presumed great: the robber barons (Minor Keith, J. P. Morgan, and Samuel Insull); the misguided or hypocritical do-gooders (W. J. Bryan, Theodore Roosevelt, Carnegie, Wilson, and Hearst); and the industrialists (Taylor and Ford). Among these almost entirely negative portrayals, Dos Passos' deepest anger and longest biographies are reserved for those who have risen through a reliance on the rhetoric of American idealism but who have betrayed that rhetoric because of class or religious bias (Roosevelt and Wilson) or ambition (Hearst). Considerably less biting in tone are the biographies of a cluster of artists and inventors (Burbank, Edison, the Wright brothers, Steinmetz, Isadora Duncan, and Valentino) who, while themselves not directly culpable, have nevertheless permitted their genius to be controlled by the powerful and wealthy in America. Here the fault, as with Edison, is often that of detachment from the realities of American life, or, as with Valentino, that of naiveté. Nevertheless, though used by the system, all—whether consciously or not—have also used the system to gain success. All are therefore portrayed ironically, in that their fame as artists or inventors resonates with the falseness and hollowness of the society that has both rewarded and manipulated them.

On the other hand, several biography clusters are devoted to the possibility of the heroic life in America—to a life dedicated to the pursuit of truth in words and action by those willing to be ignored or vilified or martyred because they run against the grain of American life established by the powerful and corrupt. One such cluster is of failed leaders: Big Bill Hayward, La Follette, and Eugene Debs. These three prewar leaders sought to express through a radical ideal—the IWW, progressivism, socialism—a vision of a better life for all Americans. Each, in the more innocent days before the war, met with some success. But the career of each was destroyed as old enemies exploited the superpatriotism of the war to crush all forms of liberalism. Another cluster consists of the martyred radicals Jack Reed, Joe Hill, and Wesley Everest. All are Westerners who seek to translate the "old words" into action and who die or are killed in the attempt. And finally there is the cluster of the vilified truth-sayers, writers and thinkers and artists such as Bourne, Veblen, Hibben, and Frank Lloyd Wright. These are men who struggled to say something true about the war or economics or diplomacy or architecture. Each, like Veblen, found that so much falsehood was accepted as truth that he "couldn't get his mouth round the essential yes" (*BM*, 98), and thus each, like Wright, is "not without honor except in his own country" (*BM*, 433).

The biographies of *U.S.A.* are thus indeed beacons to set a compass by. They are so both in the sense of our own lives as Americans and in the sense that Dos Passos fully exploited in *U.S.A.* of the juxtapositional allusiveness between the lives of the biographical figure and the lives portrayed in the Camera Eye and in the narratives.

Dos Passos did not visit Chicago to take notes for the Newsreel portions of *The 42nd Parallel* until the summer of 1929, when he was well into the composition of the novel. There is little doubt, how-

ever, that his general plan for the trilogy included from the beginning the notion of a sardonic documentation of the vacuousness of
popular belief and expression in America.[27] As many commentators have noted, there is an attractive symmetry in an epic of
American life that ranges in angle of vision from a single consciousness to the mass mind, and the Newsreels were necessary to
complete that symmetry. In seeking to document popular expression through the verbatim use of newspaper headlines and stories
and of popular song lyrics, Dos Passos was, of course, scarcely
breaking new ground. He himself had used newspaper stories, advertising slogans, songs, and jazz in *Manhattan Transfer* and *The
Garbage Man,* and there was much comparable reliance on this
material of American culture during the 1920s, ranging from
Mencken's satiric exhibitions of specimens of American provincial
silliness and barbarism to the contrary tendency on the left to
sanctify the wisdom and strength of American folk expression.[28]

For *U.S.A.,* Dos Passos narrowed down his interest in the documentation of the popular mind to newspaper writing and the
song. The newspaper offered a rich source for the dual effects he
wished to achieve in the Newsreels of "the clamor, the sound of
daily life" and of "an inkling of the common mind of the epoch."[29]
Newspaper stories also provided a series of immediate chronological markers. A good many of the events reported in the headline
and story excerpts reprinted by Dos Passos are obscure now and
were indeed obscure to a 1930s reader. But many—from presidential elections to the sinking of the *Titanic* and Lindbergh's flight—
are part of common historical awareness and thus chronologically
site not only a specific Newsreel but also the portion of the novel in
which the Newsreel appears. The presence of many items dealing
with a particular occasion will also key the reader to the centrality
of that event both historically and fictionally, and the initial announcement of a major event in the Newsreels (the Armistice, for
example) will prepare him for its full-scale appearance in the other
modes. (These obvious functional uses of the Newsreels in relation
to major cultural and historical events stressed elsewhere in *U.S.A.*
perhaps explain why Dos Passos prepared the Newsreels comparatively late in the composition of each of the novels of the trilogy.)
The songs probably appealed to Dos Passos as a further and often
comic extension of a prominent feature of newspaper writing in
their mindless expression of the platitudinous heart of American
feeling and belief.

Dos Passos' method of preparing each Newsreel was to make

extensive notes from a single newspaper of items appearing over a period ranging from several days to several months, though occasionally a specific Newsreel will contain material that appeared more than a year apart.[30] He used the Chicago *Tribune* for *The 42nd Parallel* and the New York *World* for *Nineteen-Nineteen* and *The Big Money*. He tended to concentrate on first-page stories— sensational crimes and major international and national news— and he omitted almost entirely material about the arts, theater, books, and society. From his notes, he would compose a Newsreel by careful selection, cutting, rearrangement, repunctuation, and even verbal revision. One curious feature in Dos Passos' preparation of the Newsreels was his habit of leaving blank spaces for the late entry of a song lyric on the otherwise completed typescript of a Newsreel. This practice stemmed, it seems, less from uncertainty about which lyric to include than from doubts about the specific wording of an already chosen lyric. Song lyrics were not available in libraries, and rather than depend on his own memory, Dos Passos had learned to delay their inclusion until he acquired a correct wording.[31] He came to depend especially on his old college friend Ed Massey, who had a reliable and encyclopedic recollection of old popular songs.[32]

There are a number of ways to categorize the Newsreels. Some, as I noted, have a single subject to highlight a major historical event; others have a preponderance of material bearing on an event both because of its historical importance and because the event is prominent elsewhere in the trilogy, as with the Paris peace conference and the Sacco-Vanzetti case. Occasionally, a Newsreel will derive from only one portion of a newspaper in order to stress an aspect of an adjoining modal segment, as when a Newsreel consisting entirely of help-wanted ads is followed by a narrative segment in which seeking a job is prominent. But the great majority of the sixty-eight Newsreels in *U.S.A.* are true miscellanies. Each consists of from roughly ten to twenty items of largely unrelated headlines and news stories, among which brief passages from one or two song lyrics are interspersed. Each is an approximation in verbal form of what its title would imply to readers of the 1930s who were familiar with the movie newsreel—a miscellany of news items mixing the significant (war scenes, for example) and the trivial (a bathing beauty contest).[33]

This pasting up of the miscellaneous "verbal artifacts"[34] of the American popular mind into a kind of surreal collage permitted Dos Passos a number of obvious ironic effects within specific

Newsreels. So, for example, a particular news item or song lyric can stand in clear ironic relationship to the bulk of other items in a Newsreel. In Newsreel XVII various items on the European war are concluded with the stark headline, "BROTHERS FIGHT IN DARK." In Newsreel XIX, the patriotic lyrics of "Over There" are interspersed among a series of news items on increased profits and restrictive social legislation at home. And in Newsreel LXII, items about a devastating Florida hurricane are accompanied by the lyrics of "It Ain't Gonna Rain No More." Far more common, however, is the Newsreel that is a true pastiche in the sense that no dominant ironic device or thread is found. Rather, a number of chords are struck, some with resonance to other chords, others seemingly isolated. Here, for a brief but full example, is Newsreel XLVIII in the *The Big Money:*

> truly the Steel Corporation stands forth as a corporate collosus both physically and financially

> *Now the folks in Georgia they done gone wild*
> *Over that brand new dancin' style*
> *Called   Shake   That   Thing*

CARBARNS BLAZE

GYPSY ARRESTED FOR TELLING THE TRUTH

Horsewhipping Hastens Wedding

> that strength has long since become almost a truism as steel's expanding career progressed, yet the dimensions thereof need at times to be freshly measured to be caught in proper perspective

DAZED BY MAINE DEMOCRATS CRY FOR MONEY

> *shake that thing*

Woman of Mystery Tries Suicide in Park Lake

shake that thing

OLIVE THOMAS DEAD FROM POISON

LETTER SAID GET OUT OF WALL STREET

BOMB WAGON TRACED TO JERSEY

Shake   That   Thing

Writer of Warnings Arrives

BODY FOUND LASHED TO BICYCLE

FIND BOMB CLOCKWORK

(BM, 46)

Several items in the Newsreel are linked and thus comprise a possible ironic theme. The two items on the strength of the American steel industry, couched in public-relations prose, are perhaps in ironic juxtaposition to the last five items on a Wall Street bombing.[35] All is not as secure in American business life as American business life believes it to be. The other items are far more miscellaneous, though an underlying theme—one present in many of the Newsreels—is the indiscriminate violence of American life (fire, beatings, suicides). The lyrics of "Shake That Thing," a popular song of the early 1920s, seem to be totally unrelated to the news items except for a possible tenuous link to "Horsewhipping Hastens Wedding." Newsreel XLVIII (and many like it) thus has a few suggestive ironic threads but also much that appears to be a challenge to a reader's capacity for ingenious overreading. The effect is therefore much like that of a surreal collage in which discernible "meaning" is mixed with material that is present principally to startle or to amuse. One significant consequence of this effect is that the Newsreels as a whole appear to be a kind of hoax, though a hoax that is intimately related to the intent of the trilogy. The "history" of our times, as preserved by our major device for recording events, is a meaningless "noise" and "clamor" both in the lies purveyed by sources of public information and in the chaotic mix of the trivial and the momentous that is the "news." The Newsreels are carefully constructed to render this cacophony, to heighten and intensify it to a point at which we can recognize fully its essential emptiness. The Newsreels are therefore only seemingly documentary. More significantly, they communicate through imitative form, through their fragmented meaninglessness, the understanding of American life possessed by most Americans. It is the task of the other modes of the trilogy—the Camera Eye, biographies, and narratives—to make "sense" of the events recorded in the "nonsense" form of the Newsreels.

4

U.S.A.

The Shaping of the Whole

Each of the modes of *U.S.A.* is a distinctive literary form. Put over-simply, the Camera Eye is prose-poem bildungsroman; the biographies are ironic impressionistic pen portraits; the Newsreels, surreal collages; and the narratives, free-indirect-discourse renderings of archetypal lives. Each mode is also characteristic of a major tendency in the literary expression of the 1920s and is thus not strikingly original to Dos Passos. Although Dos Passos was extending the range and the level of execution of these experimental forms, he did not discover them. What is unique in *U.S.A.* is thus not the modal devices themselves but their combination in a single work that seeks to exploit the special quality of each to achieve an effect that is at once complex and unified.

Dos Passos himself always stressed in accounts of the genesis of *U.S.A.* that his principal creative act in the writing of the trilogy was the placing of the modal segments in relation to each other. His meeting with Sergei Eisenstein in Russia in 1928 confirmed, he later recalled, his belief in "the importance of montage" in expressing theme in all serial art.[1] "By that time I was really taken with the idea of montage," he remarked elsewhere.[2] As he explained to an interviewer, "I always had an interest in contrast, in the sort of montage Griffith and Eisenstein used in film. I was trying to put across a complex state of mind, an atmosphere, and I brought in these things [the Newsreels and biographies] partly for contrast and partly for getting a different dimension."[3]

Several commentators early in the critical history of *U.S.A.* remarked that the trilogy seemed to have been prepared in a manner similar to a film that relies heavily on montage. Delmore Schwartz noted in 1938, for example, that Dos Passos seems to have "put the book together as a motion-picture director composed his film, by a procedure of cutting, arranging, and interposing parts."[4] But in fact *U.S.A.* is far more complex in origin and nature than a film, in that the units that are being cut, arranged, and interposed are strikingly different from each other, while in a film the visual image is the single mode. In other words, by relying on montage in a work that already had a mix of four different literary modes, Dos Passos was raising the stakes, so to speak, beyond those present either in most films or in the fiction of other modernists (Faulkner, for example) who depended on montage. Now a reader would not only be asked to find connections and an ultimate spatial unity in juxtaposed scenes that derive from different plot lines, points of view, and chronologies. He would also be asked to perform the same task in response to modes of expression that were very different from each other both in substance and in manner. And since, as in most writing, the reader's task is also the author's, it is no wonder that Dos Passos recalled his intense preoccupation with this phase of his preparation of the trilogy.

It is possible, with the aid of Dos Passos' surviving notes and manuscripts, to trace with some confidence the way in which he wrote *U.S.A.* Although *The 42nd Parallel* and *Nineteen-Nineteen* are available only in incomplete notes and drafts, *The Big Money* is extant in an almost cradle-to-grave genealogy, from early notes to final printer's copy typescript (only proof is lacking). And since the three novels are essentially similar in form, it is reasonable to extrapolate from *The Big Money* (with confirming details from the manuscripts of the other two novels) to the trilogy as a whole.

Dos Passos began the preparation of each novel in the trilogy by drawing up lists of the characters he wished to include and of the focus of their activities. An early plan for *Nineteen-Nineteen*, entitled "Geography of *Nineteen Nineteen*" (see fig. 1 at the end of this chapter),[5] reveals his method.[6] We know that this is an early sketch, drawn to help Dos Passos scheme out the basic plan of the novel, because Richard Savage is here "Donald Savage" (a name not used in any of the surviving manuscript drafts) and because Alsace and Constantinople are not centers of action in the completed work. Another hint as to Dos Passos' method of construction is present in his early notes for *The Big Money*. Here, a group of notes that includes a list of "Characters for last volume" (some of whom do not appear in the novel) (fig. 3) also contains both a list of biographical figures for possible inclusion (fig. 4) and a page in which the two kinds of figures appear together (fig. 5).[7] That Dos Passos' method was to begin each novel by thinking principally of the narrative and biographical figures (and thus of their relationship) is fully confirmed by the initial three draft tables of contents for *The Big Money* (see figs. 6–8),[8] which are (except for the first Camera Eye and the first two newsreels) limited to these two modes. These plans also precede full composition of the novel, since several of the biographies cited (Norris of Nebraska, Oil King, Kingfish the First) do not appear in *The Big Money* and seem never to have been written.

We know from other manuscript evidence that Dos Passos wrote each of the modes independently of the others. That is, for each unit of modal expression—a biography or Newsreel or Camera Eye or complete narrative—there exists a separate and distinctive body of notes, drafts, and final typescript. Thus, the first full typescript of *The 42nd Parallel* (before a missing clean printer's copy was prepared) and the final printer's copy of *The Big Money* have crossed out pagination sequences that reveal that each modal unit had an independent pagination before its inclusion in the full typescript of the novel.[9] (An analogy with assembly-line production, in which independently manufactured components are at last brought together, inevitably comes to mind.) But the separate composition of each mode did not mean that Dos Passos suddenly plunged into the montage process at the completion of the writing of the modes. The evidence of his early lists, charts, and tables of contents is that he was thinking from the beginning both of the relationship of narrative figures to each other, including interlacings (as asides to himself in his notes reveal),[10] and of the relationship of narrative to biographical figures. That Dos Passos began the montage process in this fashion is not surprising. The two modes that allowed him the greatest latitude and thus required the greatest initial planning were the narratives and the biographies. For the Camera Eye and the Newsreel he had in a sense both substance and sequence in hand before composition. The events of his own life supplied a core subject matter and a chronology for the Camera Eye, and the major events of each period served a similar purpose for the Newsreels.

Relying both on manuscript evidence and on hypotheses drawn from the nature of the modes, it is possible to sketch a theory of the composition of the novels of *U.S.A.* that has considerable significance for the quality of the completed work. A general belief about an era leads Dos Passos to the choice of narrative and biographical figures who exemplify the belief, with these figures conceived of from the first in juxtapositional relationships (an

Eleanor and a Moorehouse together in Paris, a Hearst implicitly
compared to a Moorehouse). The composition of each of the modes
now commences, with each written independently of the others
and with the Newsreels probably the last undertaken. The composition process as it proceeds has a twofold character. As Dos Passos
wrote a narrative or a Camera Eye, he was composing with confidence and authority within the conventions he had established for
that mode. But as he wrote he was also both consciously and unconsciously exploring the juxtapositional possibilities of each modal segment, for he was of course aware that a final and overt act
of juxtapositional composition would be required when the modal
segments were in fact dispersed throughout the novel. Much of
the strength of *U.S.A.* arises out of this combination of a "purity" of
expression within a particular mode—pure in the sense of the ob-
servance of firm and consistent modal conventions—and the far
more indirect suggestiveness of the modal mix.

   The effort and care that Dos Passos brought to the writing of
each of the modes are revealed by the extant drafts of the narratives of *The Big Money.* For each narrative figure, Dos Passos initially sketched, in broad terms and in only a few pages, the major
events of the character's life, with these divided into narrative segments. His next step was to block out in far greater detail the action of a single segment. The final segment of Dick Savage's
narrative, for example, is outlined in fifteen numbered incidents
(see fig. 13).[11] There would then follow a first holograph draft of
the entire narrative. (Dos Passos' letters reveal that he conceived of
and wrote each narrative as a single "story," and that he gave all his
energy to this narrative until it was completed.[12]) From this holograph a typescript would be prepared, which Dos Passos cut and
revised heavily. A second typescript, itself revised, provided the
text for integration into the full text of the novel. The seemingly
unshaped and artless flow of the narratives, though strikingly different from the mannered symbolism of the Camera Eye, underwent a stone-by-stone preparation similar to that of the prose
poems. And what was true of the narratives was also true of the
biographies and Newsreels.

   Even before he had completed the writing of the individual
modes, Dos Passos was engaged in elaborate planning of the juxtapositional order of the modal segments in the book as a whole. His
early division of each narrative into segments, and his attachment
of specific biographical figures to specific narrative figures (Taylor
to Ike Hall, for example), no doubt supplied him with a rough ar-

rangement for this portion of the novel almost from the beginning of the compositional process.[13] But given the complexity and indeterminancy of the task, he was also led to prepare, at various stages in the composition of the novel, draft tables of contents both to record his ideas and to serve as a basis for revision of these ideas. Between approximately early 1935 and early 1936, he prepared at least seven (that is, seven have survived) draft tables of contents of *The Big Money* (see figs. 6–12). The tables are not numbered or dated, but their sequence can be determined by internal evidence.[14] The tables reveal:

1. Although the narratives supplied the base subject matter and structure for the novel, significant changes in narrative content and order did occur in the course of the novel's preparation. Charley, Margo, and Mary are present in the first table (fig. 6) in the number of segments for each narrative as in the published work, except for the minor change of an increase in Mary's segments from three to four. The major changes that occur as the novel goes forward are: the complete cutting of the narrative of Ike Hall (an automobile worker who had appeared as a minor figure in Mac's narrative in *The 42nd Parallel*); the substitution of a Richard Savage for a J. Ward Moorehouse segment at the close of the novel; and a shift in the order of the narrative segments to achieve an even greater early emphasis on Charley Anderson and a later one on Margo and Mary. The Hall material was no doubt cut at a late stage (see figs. 11–12) to shorten the novel (even without it *The Big Money* is still the longest novel in the trilogy), though Dos Passos had completed most or all of the narrative. (He later published several of its segments separately.[15]) Its loss means that the novel lacks a "pure" working-class figure parallel to Mac in *The 42nd Parallel* and Joe Williams in *Nineteen-Nineteen* and in contrast to the middle-class or upward-striving figures in *The Big Money*. The change from Moorehouse to Savage is not so much a change in subject matter—the stress is still on New York advertising and "artistic" life—as in angle of vision through which to depict this world. And the shift in emphasis in the placing of narrative segments appears to follow from Dos Passos' recognition that Charley's New York and Detroit experiences epitomize the early stages of the 1920s boom, while Margo and Mary's movie and radical activities more fully reflect a later phase.

2. Although the biographies were also a key element in the early planning of the strategy of *The Big Money,* they reveal a greater volatility than the narratives. Six of the nine biographies in

the completed novel were planned from the beginning (Taylor, Duncan, Ford, Veblen, Hearst, and Frank Lloyd Wright), but in attempting to choose the other three Dos Passos eliminated at various stages George W. Norris, John D. Rockefeller, Huey Long, Coolidge, and Vanzetti before finally selecting the Wright brothers, Valentino, and Insull. Dos Passos' "raw" juxtapositional planning was in terms of the relationship of narrative to biographical figures, as is indicated by the first three draft tables of contents. So, even in the first table, Taylor (the inventor of industrial engineering) is juxtaposed against Anderson and Ike Hall (a user and a victim of the assembly line), Margo is juxtaposed against Duncan, Charley against Ford and Coolidge, Mary against Veblen, and so on. The flexible spine of the novel is thus constructed. But the organizational strategy of the novel, which required that fictional and public archetypes be balanced, usually for ironic effect, lent itself to change in the selection of examples as the compositional process went forward and new possibilities for ironic effect came to mind. And since the biographies were far more adaptable to change than the narratives, it was they that underwent the greatest change in the course of preparation of the novel.

3. Although the first table contains the first Camera Eye and the first Newsreel, the splicing in of these two modes did not in fact begin until the fourth table for the Newsreels and the fifth for the Camera Eye (figs. 9–10). Three overlapping internal conventions determined the placing of these modal segments. First, and most mechanically, Dos Passos used them as a form of punctuation in the structure of the novel, in that at least one Camera Eye or Newsreel occurs between narrative segments. When a lengthier "pause" in the narrative movement is desired, at the point of introducing a new narrative figure, for example, a group of Newsreels and Camera Eyes will appear between narrative segments.[16] Second, Dos Passos sought to place Camera Eye segments and Newsreels at points where the external events depicted in them coincided roughly, and sometimes precisely (as in the abortive 1919 May Day Paris uprising), with events present in the narratives. And last (as I shall discuss fully in the next chapter), he sought to place them at points at which an underlying theme of the Newsreel and especially of the Camera Eye segment was relevant to a theme in the juxtaposed narrative segment or biography.

4. Dos Passos undertook a reshaping of the final portion of the novel at a late stage of revision, as is revealed by the major differences between the conclusions of the next-to-last and last

tables (figs. 11–12). In the first of these two, the ending was: Mary French, Camera Eye, Huey Long, and Ike Hall. Dos Passos cut the Ike Hall narrative, shifted Savage's segment to a place just before Mary's, added a Newsreel, substituted Insull for Long, and added the Vag epilogue. The revised conclusion was thus: Savage, Newsreel, Camera Eye, Insull, Mary, and Vag. Aside from the Vag addition, which served primarily as an epilogue to the trilogy as a whole, Dos Passos' purpose in revising the conclusion appears to have been to sharpen its irony. The earlier ending was more emphatically downbeat in that Ike Hall and Mary French—a down-and-out workingman and a worn radical dispirited by ideological disputes—were expressions of the mood of the 1930s. A biography of Huey Long, a potential American dictator of the early 1930s, would have contributed further to this mood. With the omission of Hall and the addition of Savage and Insull, the tone becomes more mixed, since the conclusion now contains figures who have seemingly climbed to success. The more openly depression aura of the first ending now gives way to material and themes more characteristic of the trilogy as a whole, in that the ironic depiction of the American success story dominates many of the narratives and biographies. It was perhaps the reintroduction of this theme in the revised conclusion that led Dos Passos to one of his final revisions (as indicated by the penciled-in addition to the typescript of the final table), the addition of the Vag epilogue. For Vag (as I noted earlier) is in archetypal form a final story of an American who believed in the myth of success.

Dos Passos' use of juxtaposition for thematic effect can be divided into three rough categories: a grouping of a large number of varied modal segments around a major theme or event; a more specific, more closely knit grouping, usually limited to several segments; and a precise thematic link across two segments. The draft tables of contents reveal something about the evolution of each of these effects. The first table (fig. 6), for example, indicates, as is shown by the penciled-in divisions in the left-hand margin, that Dos Passos thought of the material of the novel in relation to large chronological/thematic units, even though these units and their titles do not appear in the finished work. (It will be recalled, however, that *The 42nd Parallel* was divided into five parts in the 1930 edition.) "The bright lights," for example, deals with the apex of the mid- and late-1920s boom. Margo, Charley, and Moorehouse are at the height of their success, a success validated by the biographies of Coolidge, Rockefeller, and Hearst, while Mary, Norris, and Veblen represent the unheeded critical voices of the period. This theme, stated here grossly, will of course resonate far more subtly in the finished work. But this later complexity has its origins in Dos Passos' early grouping of a substantial number of narratives and biographies around a large-scale general idea.

Dos Passos' search for tighter, more specific juxtapositional effects (the second and third kinds noted above) is also evident from the beginning in his juggling of narrative/biography relationships to refine thematic implication. This simultaneous effort both to sharpen and to deepen reached a peak with the blending in of the Newsreels and Camera Eye segments. These modes, as I have already noted, have their own internal coherence—the reflection, in chronological order, of major public and private events—and thus were probably written independently of the planning and composition of the narratives and biographies, as is suggested by their absence from the first three draft tables of contents. But once stated, this notion of "independence" must be qualified by the fact that the same creative mind, compartmentalized only to a degree, wrote all the modes. A good many Newsreel segments were therefore no doubt "composed" because of Dos Passos' realization that their events would also be present in the narratives, as with the Florida land boom. And Dos Passos' choice of specific instances of the Camera Eye persona's experience in New York as a radical writer was also no doubt influenced by his awareness of the relationship of these activities to the lives of Charley, Savage, and Mary in the city and to Margo's career as an artist.

The first draft table of contents reveals an obvious example of a planned and specific juxtapositional effect when Charley's arrival in New York to face an uncertain future after heroic war service is followed by the parallel arrival of the Camera Eye persona (Camera Eye 43) and by a Newsreel (XLIV) that also deals with a number of returns from Europe to an unquiet America. Much more often, however, the Camera Eye and Newsreel segments are truly "spliced in," in the sense that their relationship to their adjacent biography and narrative segments is neither planned in advance nor precise. Rather, as in the creation of certain kinds of surreal and abstract paintings, Dos Passos was hoping for an inner resonance that might or might not follow from the mixing of modal segments only loosely connected in external character. In order to gain this effect, however, he needed to experiment, to try out relationships. Hence the seven tables of contents, as Dos Passos sifted the mix that constituted this potential, both to express more cogently already planned juxtapositional themes and to bring to the surface unforeseen juxtapositional inference.

The general nature of Dos Passos' experiments in the creation of thematic implication between modal segments can usefully be illustrated by a return to the "only words against / POWER SUPERPOWER" passage that I discussed earlier in connection with the theme and form of the trilogy as a whole. The process of juxtapositional experimentation that produced the passage is as follows. First, Dos Passos decided to substitute Insull for Huey Long as a final biography in the trilogy. (He had listed Insull as a possible biographical figure in early notes but had not included him in the first six draft contents.) In making this change, he was perhaps attracted by the link between a reference to "the manipulator of the holding company" at the close of the Harlan County Camera Eye and Insull, an infamous holding-company magnate of the 1920s. A second step was the revision of the characteristically ironic title of the Insull biography, "Immigrant Boy Makes Good," to a title that links the Camera Eye and the biography even more tightly, in that "power" is doubly present in both segments. The coal miners produce the raw material of power, but power in the sense of economic and political strength belongs to the owners. And Insull's career, as a director of electricity and gas companies, also illustrates the double meaning of the term. Hence the new title, POWER SUPERPOWER. The third and final step occurred even later in the writing process and requires an explanation in detail.

The setting-copy typescript of Camera Eye (51) (fig. 14)[17] reveals that in this version Dos Passos was thinking of the "we have only words against" passage entirely in relation to its relevance within the Camera Eye. Even his cutting of the last two lines of the segment still leaves "their guns" as the object of "words against." The setting copy of Camera Eye (51) and the opening of the Insull biography in the setting copy (fig. 15) have two additional important characteristics. First, because Dos Passos' method of composition had been to write in independent modal units, he maintained even in the setting copy, for ease of further rearrangement of these units, their separate physical identities. So Camera Eye (51), though paginated now as part of the setting copy (pp. 616–18), has a body of white space at its conclusion, and the following biography of Insull begins at the top of a fresh page with its title. Thus there is still no immediate visual connection between the concluding line of Camera Eye (51) and the title of the biography.

In addition, the setting copy of Camera Eye (51) and the Insull biography reveal that galley proof would, for the first time, have brought the conclusion of the Camera Eye and the title of the biography into inescapable visual juxtaposition. The presence of galley mark 162 on page 616 and of 163 on page 620 indicates that the segments would have been set in close proximity on galley 162. Not only would Dos Pasos have seen this physical juxtaposition at this stage—we know that he carefully read and revised proof for *The Big Money*[18]—but he would also have realized that the juxtaposition would be maintained in the printed book, since each new segment did not begin on a new printed page, but was run-on from the preceding segment. It was thus while reading galley that Dos Passos must have seen for the first time the possible relationship between the close of Camera Eye (51) and the title of the Insull biography, realized that that relationship would be preserved in the printed book, and took the leap into a precise but immensely suggestive juxtapositional theme by cutting "their guns."

The process by which Dos Passos reached this explicit crossing of modal barriers is characteristic of analogous but less dramatic and less specifically verbal instances throughout the trilogy. Dos Passos' desire to have the conclusion of *The Big Money* express a theme close to a major theme in the trilogy as a whole had led him to recast the ending of the novel, including the introduction of a new biography with a stronger relationship to its immediately preceding Camera Eye. Once present, this relationship was further tightened and sharpened by a revision of the title of the biography and a final strategic cutting. In approximate form, this was Dos Passos' method throughout, though the degree of interpenetration between specific adjoining modal units, even after their mutual reflection had been increased by shifting, revision, and cutting, differs considerably from instance to instance. In some sections, a large idea planned from the beginning controls the broad statement of theme in a large number of modal segments. In others, at the opposite extreme, a precise event, symbol, or verbal motif connects two segments. Or there is some mix of these extremes. In addition, the degree of planning versus serendipity differs greatly. In this instance, both are present. The shift to Insull and the change in title were the result of conscious efforts to

restructure and to sharpen; the discovery of the "words against /
POWER SUPERPOWER" passage was the fortuitious product of
the earlier experimental industry. Dos Passos, in short, had no uniform way of producing juxtapositional theme, and he produced
juxtapositional theme that varied greatly in openness, depth, and
intensity. He had realized that the nature of his enterprise required
a combination of planning and of seizing upon opportunities that
arose when potentially mutually reflective units were already in
place. He took advantage of both methods to produce the immense
variety and density of juxtapositional implication that is *U.S.A.*

Geography of Nineteen Nineteen

Plan for The Big Money

Characters for last volume (no. 1)

Characters for last volume (no. 2)

Paul Johnson

Taylor

Queenie Henderson

The Wright Brothers

I. Ward Moore Louse

Thorstein Veblen

Henry Ford

John D. ?

Morrell   —

The forgotten man

Characters for last volume (no. 3)

prelude

Production

climax

The high lights

Down under the boom

THE BIG MONEY

Lives	Headliners	Camera Eye	Newsreel
CHARLEY ANDERSON 1			
(he docked on a Sunday)	43		
	THE AMERICAN PLAN		
IKE HALL 1	43		
(Ike had been making big money)			LXIV
CHARLEY ANDERSON 2			
(American Beauty)			
	aot — ISADORA		
MARGO DOWLING 1			
(Broad Channel to the isle of romance)			
CHARLEY ANDERSON 3		*The Campus at*	
(Home to the Ford Agency)		*Kitty Hawk*	
MARGO DOWLING 2	TIN LIZZIE		
(Siboney)			
CHARLEY ANDERSON 4			
(Want Ads)			
	NORMALCY		
IKE HALL 2			
(A man and his kids — easy monthly payments)			
MARGO DOWLING 3			
(the road to success)			
CHARLEY ANDERSON 5			
(business opportunities)			
MARY FRENCH 1	THE BITTER DRINK		
(sympathizer)			
CHARLEY ANDERSON 6	NURSIS OF IMPERIA		
(Big time stuff)			
	OIL KING		
MARGO DOWLING 4			
(Coming attraction)			
CHARLEY ANDERSON 7			
(Florida boom)			
MARGO DOWLING 5			
(Hollywood opening)			
J. WARD MOOREHOUSE	(apotheosis)	↑ *Peddler of ideas*	
	POOR LITTLE RICH BOY		
MARY FRENCH 2	(red rercolution?)		
IKE HALL 3	(the boys the jazzage and the crime wave)		
	ARCHITECT OF THE WORLD		
MARY FRENCH 3	(after radicalism what)		
IKE HALL 4	KINGFISH THE FIRST		
(The forgotten hours)			

The Hall 4

Keas and Jim
Savage

Vag, as he goes it
As nobody will
him a job.

THE BIG MONEY

MARGO
DOWLING 3

Table of Contents for The Big Money (no. 2)

Table of Contents for The Big Money *(no. 3)*

Table of Contents for The Big Money (no. 4)

THE BIG MONEY

Table of Contents for The Big Money (no. 5)

Table of Contents for The Big Money (no. 6)

Table of Contents for The Big Money (no. 7)

Table of Contents for The Big Money (no. 7)

P1. (Everything except J.W.) Talk about Bingham account

Office Dick & J.W.

Miss Williams secretary

P2. Situation with Ed Goiscom
old time copy writer

P3 Cables of Eleanor   from F_

P4 Dick meets J.W. at the Princess Romanshivili.
She still uses the name of Eleanor Stoddard
— but everybody knows she's the

Princess Romanschili —

P4 Leaves them with J.W. talks to him
about Gertrude doing up
good feeling of understanding comes up
between them

P5. Dick works all night on his copy

P6. Is at the office next morning bright

an early —

P7 Eveline Hutchins calls — Tell her I'm
out says Dick — She's right there —

Plan for Dick Savage Narrative

marching behind the flag up the switchback road to the
mine ~~they shoot down our brave men~~ those that the
guns spare they jail)

    ⊏⊐   the law stares across the desk out of angry
eyes his face reddens in splotches like a gobbler's
neck with the strut of the power ~~that~~ submachineguns
sawedoff shotguns teargas and vomitinggas the power that
can feed you or leave you to starve

    ~~the sheriff~~ sits easy at his desk his back is
covered he feels strong behind him he feels the prosecuting
attorney the judge an owner himself the political boss
the mine superintendent the board of directors the
president of the utility the ~~owner~~ manipulator of the holding company

      he lifts his hand towards the telephone

      the deputies crowd in the door

      we have only words against their guns

      ~~before he lifts the receiver~~

      ~~we must talk to the sheriff~~

Setting Copy Typescript of Camera Eye (51)

In eighteen eighty when Thomas Edison's agent
was hooking up the first telephone in London, he put an
an ad in the paper for a secretary and stenographer. The
eager young cockney with sprouting muttonchop whiskers
who answered it

had recently lost his job as office boy. In his
spare time he had been learning shorthand and bookkeeping
and taking dictation from the editor of the English
<u>Vanity</u> <u>Fair</u> at night and jotting down the speeches in Par-
liament for the papers. He came of temperance smallshopkeeper
stock; ~~He was eager to make money, ambitious for power;~~
already he was butting his bullethead against the harsh
structure of cast that doomed boys of his class to a life
alpaca jackets, penmanship, subordination. To get a job
with an American firm was to put a foot on the rung of a
ladder that led up into the blue.

He did his best to make himself indispensable;
they let him operate the switchboard for the first half
hour when the telephone service was opened. Edison noticed
his weekly reports on the electrical situation in England
and sent for him to be his personal secretary.

Samuel Insull landed in America on a raw March
day in eightyone. Immediately he was taken out to Menlo Park,
shown about the little group of laboratories, saw the

Setting Copy Typescript of POWER SUPERPOWER

5

U.S.A.

The Trilogy

Several of Dos Passos' most perceptive critics have commented on the mix of concrete immediacy and conscious obliqueness in *U.S.A.* Sartre, for example, noted that despite the great air that Dos Passos' fictional world has of being grounded in fact, that world is "not real; it is a created object. I know of none—not even Faulkner's or Kafka's—in which the art is greater or better hidden." Edmund Wilson, after reading *The Big Money,* made essentially the same point when he praised Dos Passos' fiction for being "transparent"—that is, "experience . . . shows through and conveys its significance to the reader without any apparent effort on [Dos Passos'] part to underline it."[1] Both Sartre and Wilson were, in different ways, responding to one of the major characteristics of *U.S.A.*—that it appears to be an almost direct transcription of American life (especially in the Newsreels and narratives) but that it nevertheless communicates the author's full interpretive reading of American life. We are not merely being immersed in experience (though the work wishes to create the illusion that we are), but are rather being led, through the author's "hidden" art, to an understanding of the "significance" of what we are encountering.

Dos Passos' "art" in *U.S.A.* consists of a stylization of experience that is expressed in three overlapping—indeed, often indistinguishable—formal characteristics of the trilogy: the four internally consistent but sharply differentiated modes; the relationships between segments of the same or different modes; and the pervasive irony, present both as a formal characteristic of each mode and as a product of juxtapositional theme, that arises out of the distinction between what Americans have believed or hoped about their country (as depicted in the "direct" transcription of their beliefs) and what is in truth the material and spiritual condition of American society.

Although Dos Passos always conceived of this effort to portray twentieth-century American life in fiction as a single literary work, and was eventually to publish its three novels as one volume under a single title, the effect of writing three separate novels over almost a decade inevitably resulted in a somewhat varying shape and cast to each of the novels. As I have already noted, Dos Passos' suspicions of the far left hardened during the course of writing the trilogy and climaxed with a sharp critique of the movement in *The Big Money*. In addition, the changing historical focus of each novel caused some variation in fictional form among the three works. Thus, *Nineteen-Nineteen,* with its emphasis on the portrayal of Americans abroad during the war and with much of its action occurring in and around Paris, has a greater unity of event and a tighter interrelationship among narrative figures than either of the other novels in the trilogy. And, finally, Dos Passos' developing certainty of method and depth of theme result in *The Big Money* being, by general consent, the best novel in the trilogy.[2] But despite these and other differences among the three works—most of which I will comment on more fully later—each novel is part of a single bold and unified conception. The reader of the trilogy is thus required to perform two simultaneous interpretive acts at any one moment in the trilogy. He must be aware of the implication of the fictional event he is experiencing in its immediate context, a context that will include adjacent segments of other modes. And he must be aware of an ever-increasing ripple of implication of the event within the trilogy as a whole. Of course, this combined interpretive act occurs in the reading of any extended fictional work. What is different about the task in the reading of *U.S.A.* is both the extreme length of the work (and thus the amount of awareness that must be "held in suspension") and the expression of theme in widely different modal forms (and thus the degree of awareness required).

An obvious example occurs in the opening of *The 42nd Parallel*. Mac is an itinerant printer, and as we read his narrative we are immersed in his life both intrinsically, as a "story," and as an archetype of the pre–World War I radical experience. We are also aware, though on a less fully conscious level, of the relationship of Mac's story to some of the accompanying biographies (especially that of Big Bill Hayward), and we are even less consciously aware of the connection between his narrative and the events depicted in the early Newsreel and Camera Eye segments. As the trilogy moves forward, however, the implications of Mac's narrative deepen in response to a variety of emerging complex threads in the work as a whole. Mac's rootless working-class life, for example, is comparable in several significant ways to the experience of the characters who are also the initial narrative figures in the other two volumes of the trilogy, Joe Williams in *Nineteen-Nineteen* and Charley Anderson in *The Big Money;* and Mac's radical ideas and activities differ meaningfully from those of Ben Compton in *Nineteen-Nineteen* and *The Big Money.* So too, Mac's sexual and marital experiences are echoed by those of Joe, Charley, and Ben; and Mac's inability to break through to a full radical commitment in the face of middle-class temptation is in sharp contrast not only to Big Bill Hayward but to the later portrayed IWW radical martyrs Joe Hill and Wesley Everest and to the emerging successful resolution of this conflict in the Camera Eye persona. In these and in additional ways, Mac's narrative contains a potential resonance that is gradually fulfilled as the trilogy proceeds, just as other events and characters in *The Big Money* echo themes introduced and pursued at earlier points in the trilogy. The "hidden art" of *U.S.A.* thus lies not only in Dos Passos' ability to craft theme out of immediate juxtapositions but in his comparable ability to extend and deepen these themes in the course of a work that appears to be merely rendering the flux and diversity of American life.

The 42nd Parallel has a loose but nevertheless readily discernible overall structure. It begins with an extended account of Mac, a figure characteristic of prewar working-class radicalism, and it closes, a generation later, with the initial narrative segment of Charley Anderson, a figure of working-class origins who will push into the entrepreneurial-capitalist class during the postwar boom. Between the appearance of these two characters, the novel is dominated by the linked narrative figures of Janey, Moorehouse, and Eleanor. Although of diverse origins and backgrounds, these three characters come together in New York during the last portion of the novel at the point of America's entry into the war. Their shared enthusiasm for the war signifies the failure of American ideals to prevail over the hysteria engendered by the war spirit. The biographies have a similar basic movement. They begin with the "heroic" figures of Eugene Debs, Luther Burbank, and Big Bill Haywood, each of whom fought for freedom of belief and action. They continue with public figures who either manipulated or betrayed this ideal (William Jennings Bryan, Minor Keith, and Andrew Carnegie) or who unconsciously collaborated with its perversion (Thomas Edison and Charles Proteus Steinmetz). The biographies end with La Follette, who is similar to Debs (the initial biographical figure) in that both are prewar liberal idealists who have been hounded and beaten down because of their opposition to the war. The Camera Eye in *The 42nd Parallel* contains segments that reflect both the miscellaneous nature of memories of childhood and the movement of the persona toward an initial recognition of and early resistance to the conditions of American life that have enclosed or persecuted the narrative and biographical figures. And the Newsreels, in their documentation of the public images of American life from 1900 to 1917, render the sound and fury and essential emptiness of the kind of American public discourse that is more subtly dramatized in the free indirect discourse of the narratives and the ironic method of the biographies.

   The 42nd Parallel opens with seven narrative segments devoted to Mac. Since Dos Passos' usual practice in the trilogy, with the exception of the four initial Charley Anderson segments in *The Big Money,* was not to have more than two consecutive narrative segments concerning the same figure, his heavy concentration on Mac at the opening of *The 42nd Parallel* raises questions both about this specific instance and about his organization of the narrative segments in general. In this instance, it could possibly be held that the device of devoting seven consecutive segments to a single figure results from Dos Passos' uncertainty about his juxtapositional form at the onset of the project—that he was not to realize the advantages of alternating segments of different narratives until well into the first novel of the trilogy. In fact, as we know from the evidence of the manuscripts, although Dos Passos' method was to write a narrative as a single sequence, he also—at a later stage in the preparation of each novel—juggled the segments of the sequence for juxtapositional relevance and emphasis. Since this was his practice for the other narratives of *The 42nd Parallel,* he was of course also free at this later stage to break up the "block" effect of the seven Mac segments by interspersing other narrative segments. The explanation for the seemingly anomalous concentration on Mac at the opening of *The 42nd Parallel* lies rather in his role in the novel. Mac is a largely isolated figure. Aside from a somewhat forced moment of interlacing, when Janey and Moorehouse (as well as George H. Barrow) encounter Mac in Mexico

City during the early days of the revolution, Mac's lack of contact with the other narrative figures represents the vestigial and almost anachronistic role of the American radical in the emerging push toward a capitalist hegemony during the first two decades of the new century. Mac is characteristic of a phase of prewar American life—a phase that reached its peak when Debs gathered almost a million votes in the 1912 presidential election—but this radical tendency in turn-of-the-century American life was always under intense pressure, and it came to an abrupt halt with the war, as is symbolized by the imprisonment of Debs himself.[3] It is thus both historically and thematically appropriate that we are initially immersed in Mac's narrative (over 100 pages of it in the seven segments) and that, except for a final glimpse of him in a last brief segment toward the end of the novel, we move on to other figures who represent the emerging new ethos of American life.

Dos Passos' ordering and siting of narrative segments in *U.S.A.* thus has a kind of common-sense inevitability. Figures whose lives characterize a specific moment of American life have their segments clustered at that moment. Mac is an extreme example of the practice, while Margo and Mary are more characteristic, in that their predominance in the second half of *The Big Money* (an era in which films and far-left radicalism are important new cultural phenomena) is achieved without a long sequence of narrative segments devoted to a single figure. Not that we lose sight of narrative figures once their own narratives cease. With the exception of Mac and of the two figures who die in *Nineteen-Nineteen* (Daughter and Joe), all of the remaining nine narrative figures of *U.S.A.* are present in *The Big Money.* Those who do not have their own narrative segments (Janey, Moorehouse, Eleanor, Eveline, and Ben) appear in varying degrees of prominence in the narratives of other figures. Dos Passos' method was to devote narrative segments to a character until he or she was fixed as a type and was also no longer central to the historical moment. Then the character was not dropped, but was rather absorbed into the narratives of other figures. This technique permitted Dos Passos to draw upon our awareness of the character for thematic purposes without committing himself to redundant additional narrative segments devoted to the figure. The technique works particularly well with Moorehouse. He lacks a narrative segment after *The 42nd Parallel,* but his continuing presence in the trilogy, as he frequently reappears in the narrative segments of other figures, serves a major thematic role in the work as a whole.

The Mac portion of *The 42nd Parallel* also reveals Dos Passos' characteristic creation of narrative figures out of a mix of sources. While in Mexico in early 1927, Dos Passos met Gladwin Bland, a former IWW member who had settled in Mexico before the revolution and was now comfortably well off.[4] Bland told Dos Passos the story of his life, and from this account Dos Passos drew much of the Mac narrative. But whatever Bland told Dos Passos about the specifics of his life, Dos Passos wished to shape this detail into a pattern expressive of the rise and fall of the IWW as a revolutionary force in America in the decade or so before our entrance into the war. Thus, Mac's involvement in the radical movement stems, not from intellectual conviction, as is true of Ben's commitment to the Communist party during the 1920s, but from Mac's absorption of radical ideals from friends and family and from his firsthand experience of the injustices of the American system. Once recruited, Mac participates in the most violent and successful IWW-led campaign, the western miners' strikes of 1906 and 1907, which saw the rise of Big Bill Hayward. Bland had led a wandering life before settling in Mexico, and so does Mac, but in incorporating this aspect of Bland's experience into Mac's narrative, Dos Passos was also influenced by the picaresque tradition. He had been deeply and permanently affected by the picaresque narratives of Pío Baroja, in which the adventures of a youth who becomes a socialist printer serve as the basis for a satiric portrait of the underside of Spanish life.[5] Dos Passos' depiction of Mac within the conventions of the picaresque contributes to the commingled sexual farce and satiric bite of the Bingham portion of Mac's narrative. For such a dominant aspect of Mac's narrative as his rootlessness, Dos Passos was thus drawing, not upon a single source, but upon the impulses stressing mobility in Bland's account of his life, in the typical experience of the IWW radical, and in the conventions of picaresque narrative.

Both Mac's role as an archetypal prewar radical and the nature of the interaction of his narrative with other modal segments in *The 42nd Parallel* are suggested early in the novel when Mac and the Camera Eye persona, in adjoining segments, are taken on train journeys. The novel had opened with "beginnings"—the new century and the early childhood of Mac and the Camera Eye persona. It now proceeds to a more significant beginning for Mac and the persona, their immersion in radical ideas endorsed by parental figures as they undertake journeys into new worlds. On the train to a new life in Chicago, Mac's weak father begins to be replaced by the radical printer Tim O'Hara as Mac's mentor. And the Camera Eye persona, previously under protection of the mother, is beginning to experience the radical independence of mind of the father. "Why Lucy," his father says as the family is on its way by train from Washington to New York, "if it were necessary for the cause of humanity I would walk out to be shot any day." He then inquires of his son, "you would Jack wouldn't you?" (FP, 13). This interplay contains on the surface only parallel train rides by young boys beginning to come under the influence of strong masculine guides. But there is also set in motion a far deeper interplay that will have significance not only for the relationship between Mac and the Camera Eye persona but for that between the persona and the many other radical narrative figures. For unlike Mac, who quickly adopts Tim O'Hara's beliefs, the Camera Eye persona will evolve slowly, with many false starts, in the direction of his father's strength and independence. He will indeed not be able to answer his father's question for a quarter of a century. The readily gained or halfhearted or excessively doctrinaire beliefs of Mac and Ben, or of Savage and Charley Anderson early in their lives, are, in one sense, foils to the Camera Eye persona's slow and difficult journey toward a fully committed humanistic radicalism. In addition, the mobility of Mac and the Camera Eye persona, symbolized by their early train journeys, reveals the poles of implication for mobility in the trilogy as a whole. For Mac, mobility will mean rootlessness and the capacity to be victimized by others; for the Camera Eye persona, it will mean the potential for keeping options open, for the preservation of freedom of choice.

Trains continue to dominate the early lives of Mac and the Camera Eye persona and also serve as a link to the initial biography of the trilogy, that of Debs, most of whose career was spent as a leader of the railroad workers. Deb's career as a radical is the opposite of Mac's. For Dos Passos stresses in the biography, not Debs' early ascendancy, but rather his later imprisonment for opposing the war and his betrayal by the working class. "But where were Gene Debs' brothers in nineteen eighteen when Woodrow Wilson had him locked up in Atlanta for speaking against war" (FP, 27). They had deserted Debs for the good wages and full employment of a war economy. They "wanted a house with a porch to putter around and a fat wife to cook for them." This desertion encapsulates Mac's life story. At first he had resisted petit-bourgeois comforts—wife, family, home—because they represented a betrayal of radical ideals, but he had finally succumbed fully. He too,

along with the entire American radical movement, had in effect betrayed Debs. There runs through the early portion of *The 42nd
Parallel*—until the introduction of the Janey, Eleanor, Moorehouse
center of the novel—the theme of a native American radical tradition of truth-saying and of the use of truth for human betterment.
This is the tradition behind the independence of mind of the Camera Eye persona's father, behind the IWW with its western roots,
and behind the courage and radical beliefs of the first three biographical figures, Debs, Hayward, and Burbank. But in each instance there is present as well in American society a powerful
confining or restricting force that leads to the suppression of this
radical truthfulness, a suppression that is symbolized most of all by
Debs' imprisonment. The Camera Eye persona finds himself
bound—as a "Rover Boy"—by class values and behavior; Mac
finds himself unable to resist the blandishments of the "good life";
and Debs, Hayward, and Burbank are harried and in part or wholly
overcome by narrow political or religious beliefs. In structuralist
terms, the polarities of American life in the early portion of *The
42nd Parallel* are either a dangerous commitment to independent
thought or a safe acceptance of the status quo, with both possibilities paradoxically leading to decline or defeat. Dos Passos has thus
portrayed the beginning of the new century as in truth an ending.
A native tradition of open and courageous struggle for freedom of
belief and action is under attack, usually successful attack, by
middle-class American society.

I have already discussed the conflict in the early life of the
Camera Eye persona between an independence of mind associated
with a lower-class masculinity and a conforming, restrictive code
of belief and behavior associated with a feminine allegiance to
class roles. This theme in the Camera Eye is powerfully juxtaposed to an analogous struggle in Mac. In Camera Eye (11), the
youthful Camera Eye persona is attending a church service in
Pennsylvania. It is a well-to-do church, filled with girls who sing
"chilly shrill soprano." But "who were the Molly Maguires?" the
Camera Eye persona asks repeatedly (*FP*, 108), and of course receives no reply, in this setting, to a question about violent radicalism in the Pennsylvania mining areas of the 1860s and 70s. And
so, though not baptized, he takes communion. In the preceding
narrative segment, Mac faces a parallel situation. He is helping to
fight an important IWW-organized miner's strike in Nevada, led by
the charismatic Big Bill Hayward, when he receives a letter from
his girl, Maisie, in San Francisco saying that she is pregant. This is

the major crisis in Mac's life. On the one side are his class ideals
and commitments, including the IWW doctrine that "a wobbly
oughtn't to have any wife or children, not till after the revolution"
(*FP*, 104). On the other is Maisie, a girl who is depicted as a caricature of the feminine aspiration to middle-class status through the
acquisition of a husband, home, and family. Mac's narrative now
becomes a version of a medieval morality play. Hayward and Maisie
are the good and evil angels who seek to persuade Mac as Every-
man to adopt a course of action that will determine the fate of his
soul. "Big Bill talked about solidarity and sticking together in the
face of the masterclass and Mac kept wondering what Big Bill
would do if he'd got a girl in trouble like that" (*FP*, 102).

The Camera Eye persona, though still conforming at this
point, will continue to seek answers to his questions; but Mac's decision to return to San Francisco to marry Maisie is decisive. Although he will later desert Maisie when her demands become
excessive, he has determined the shape of his life. He will eventually descend far enough into a middle-class frame of mind to set up
shop in Mexico City as a businessman with Concha—who "made
him very comfortable" (*FP*, 309)—in the midst of the Mexican revolution. As he will do many times in the course of the trilogy, Dos
Passos symbolizes the death of the self that is the self-betrayal of
the best part of one's nature by an accompanying physical death.
On a freight car taking him to San Francisco and Maisie, Mac
meets an old hobo—the Mac of the future if he had kept to his
ideals—who dies during the trip (*FP*, 110–12).

Dos Passos introduces in his account of Mac and Maisie the
major theme of the relationship between sex and belief. This
theme will take on greater weight and complexity as the trilogy
proceeds—especially in the Moorehouse and Savage narratives
and in the narratives of almost all the women figures—but it appears in the Mac narrative in its most obvious form. For the working-class radical, sex is a trap, since it can lead to the confinement
of belief and action within the prison of middle-class marriage, as it
does for Mac—first reluctantly with Maisie and then willingly with
Concha. Maisie, who thinks only of money and belongings, epitomizes this threat. After their marriage, she is angry whenever Mac
attempts to renew his radical interests, "as if she thought he was
going out with some other woman" (*FP*, 114). These rival claims of
sex and belief in Mac's life also constitute an unresolved conflict in
Dos Passos himself that appears throughout the trilogy. On the one
hand, Dos Passos depicted many figures for whom sex is a great

danger, whether because it entails marriage and the assumption of middle-class roles (as with Mac, Joe, and Charley) or because it detracts from the pursuit of one's ideals even outside marriage (as with Ben and the Camera Eye persona). In these accounts, Dos Passos seems to be endorsing a Marxist/Veblenesque notion that seduction by the middle class indeed often takes the form of a sexual seduction. On the other hand, Dos Passos almost uniformly symbolizes an inner emptiness and lack of value by a sexual coldness or perversion, as he does in depicting the lives of Janey, Eleanor, Moorehouse, and the later stages of Savage's career. There is also a group of feminine figures—Daughter, Eveline, and Mary French—who wish to love but who discover that the sexual or emotional vulnerability accompanying this desire is a major handicap. In short, *U.S.A.* is permeated with a powerful distrust of human sexuality, a distrust that ranges in origin from a clearly identifiable and in part satirized political belief (as with Ben) to a far deeper source in Dos Passos' own psyche. In that recess, sex seems to be a kind of demon that damns one if it is permitted to hold sway and damns one if it is exorcised. Dos Passos' failure to portray a positive role for man's sexual nature perhaps has its source in his attitude toward his parents. For his recognition of the unreconcilable conflict between his mother's conservative nature and his father's overt and active sexuality, and his realization that he was the illegitimate product of their union, could only have resulted in a powerful ambivalence about the role of sex in human affairs. Whatever the success of Dos Passos' own marriage to Katy Smith in 1929, this view of sex was so fully engrained in his deepest nature that it pervades the portrayal of every narrative figure in *U.S.A.* It is even present, in a negative way, in the triumphant "masculinity" of the Camera Eye persona at the conclusion of the trilogy, for that triumph is of a masculinity of political and artistic commitment and not of explicit sexuality. *U.S.A.* thus reveals Dos Passos' continuing reflection of those aspects of Eliot's themes that were in accord with his own beliefs and temperament. For like *The Waste Land, U.S.A.* is a work about the decline in values and belief in modern society that communicates much of the intensity and depth of the theme through sexual metaphors of fear, inadequacy, and entrapment.

There is no known source for either Janey or Joe Williams, though Dos Passos' placing of their childhood in Washington suggests that he may have encountered government white-collar families like the Williamses during his boyhood periods in that city. But

since one of the principal characteristics of both Janey and Joe is
their softness, their lack of impact on others and on the world, Dos
Passos in this instance—as well as with several other narrative figures in the trilogy—probably relied, not on a single prototype, but
on a gathering of impressions and a general conception. The conception he wished above all to dramatize in the depiction of Janey
was that the conventions of lower-middle-class life can transform a
feeling creature into a seeming automaton. Although always intel-
lectually shallow and uninformed, Janey does have a full emotional
nature that early in her life seeks expression and fulfillment. She
wants to be friends with the little black girl in her neighborhood;
she wants to comfort her brother, Joe, in his difficult relations with
their father; and most of all she wants to love Alex, Joe's dynamic
and good-looking friend. But at every turn she is driven back from
the expression of her feelings by conventions of what is proper for
a white southern girl of the period. Her life, in a sense, peaks and
collapses during the day she, Joe, and Alex go on a country outing.
She is as one with the boys on the trip out, sharing and enjoying
with them, but on the return she gets premenstrual cramps and is
embarrassed and drained. "After that Janey never cried much;
things upset her but she got a cold hard feeling all over instead"
(*FP*, 144). Her sexuality—the force that is at the root of her emotional nature but that is something to be ashamed of and disguised—has been successfully repressed. Soon, indeed, Alex—in
another of the symbolic deaths of the self that occur throughout
the trilogy—is killed in an accident. In response, Janey adopts the
role of an iron virgin; men, she believes, are only interested in one
thing. She soon finds her niche as a factotum for Moorehouse,
whom she can worship without danger. His open assertion of the
need for conventional ideas and feelings in all ranges of human
affairs is the articulated counterpart of the role she has cast herself
in. Dos Passos' final major comment on Janey occurs obliquely in
the juxtaposition of her last narrative segment and the biography
of Steinmetz, a man whose own inner life—his socialist beliefs—
was totally negated by his role as an inventor for General Electric.
Like Janey in her usefulness to Moorehouse, Steinmetz became
"the most valuable piece of apparatus" the firm ever had (*FP*, 328).

The shift in narrative focus from the largely isolated figure of
Mac to Janey, who through her relationship to Moorehouse and Joe
will reappear frequently elsewhere in *U.S.A.*, introduces several
narrative devices and conventions that have major roles in the entire narrative portion of the trilogy. One such device is that of inter-

lacing (as I have called it), in which characters who have their
own narratives also appear in the narratives of other figures. In
part, as I have already noted, this device resembles the conventional modern fictional technique of multiple perspective, in which
the depiction of a Joe or a Moorehouse or an Eleanor through
Janey's point of view deepens our understanding both of these figures (whom we encounter elsewhere principally through their
own point of view) and of Janey. But given the striking narrative
strategy in *U.S.A.* of twelve separate narratives of figures drawn
from widely different backgrounds, Dos Passos' interlacing technique assumes a greater thematic significance than is usual.
Something must be meant, in other words, by the coming together
of these characters out of the vastness of the American scene.
Each novel in the trilogy has a core of such interlaced groupings, a
core that constitutes what can be called a thematic cluster in
which the effect of like finding like emphasizes and confirms a basic characteristic of American life of the period. In *The 42nd Parallel* the cluster consists of the gathering of Janey, Moorehouse, and
Eleanor in New York; in *Nineteen-Nineteen* it is the constant interaction of Eleanor, Daughter, Savage, Eveline, and Moorehouse in
and around Paris during the war and the peace conference; and in
The Big Money it is above all Margo and Charley in Florida and
New York. Of course, to stress at this point the device of interlacing is not to limit the interpretation of large-scale themes emerging
from the narratives to those figures who form associations within
the narratives. So, for example, it is impossible not to compare the
careers of the two radicals Mac and Ben, even though the two
never meet. Nevertheless, the interlacing device—because it cap-
tures our attention by the reintroduction of previously known figures in new contexts—is Dos Passos' most immediate and
dramatic means of establishing connections.

   Another device that occurs for the first time in Janey's narrative is the appearance of a minor figure of some importance—here
Jerry Burnham—who will turn up again and again in the narratives of various other figures. Besides Burnham, there are perhaps
three other such figures in the trilogy—George H. Barrow, Judge
Planet, and Don Stevens. These characters have a double function.
Each is a basic type in American public life—the cynical reporter,
the duplicitous labor leader, the corrupt politician, and the hot-
headed radical. The appearance of the figure in a narrative therefore suggests the entrance of themes associated with his character.

In addition the changes that occur in the course of the trilogy in the status or attitude of the figure constitute a barometer of change in that aspect of American life. So Burnham grows even more deeply embittered; Barrow and Planet are increasingly prominent in national affairs; and Stevens moves through various radical enthusiasms until he finds a resting place in the Communist party hierarchy. Occasionally, the reappearance yet again of one of these figures—Barrow especially seems to be omnipresent—seems excessive, as though Dos Passos was thumbing his nose at the limits of fictional probability. But this response misses the point that *U.S.A.* is not conventional realistic fiction. Barrow reappears, not because he is likely to appear again at that juncture, but because the author has use for his kind of falseness at that moment.

Janey's initial two narrative segments herald the arrival of Moorehouse. Moorehouse, in fact, has only three narrative segments in *The 42nd Parallel* and none in the other two novels. (Only Ben and Daughter have fewer.) In addition, he is a remarkably static character, even in a work in which the narrative figures undergo little change in their basic values and attitudes in the course of the trilogy. He wishes from the first to succeed within the conventions of the American success myth and by means of the platitudes of American popular belief (born on July 4, he reads *Success* magazine as a youth), and these desires and means guide him through the remainder of his life. Yet for many readers Moorehouse is the major narrative figure in the trilogy. His centrality stems, on a superficial level, from his role as patron or mentor in the lives of Eveline, Eleanor, Janey, and Savage, and from the public prominence that makes him a presence (though often only a fleeting one) in the lives and thoughts of almost all the narrative figures in the trilogy. But more significantly for the thematic center of *U.S.A.*, and as Dos Passos stresses time and time again, Moorehouse's career as a public-relations counselor epitomizes the manipulation and corruption of language and therefore of belief in American life. Thus, through Dos Passos' portrayal of the destructive importance of Moorehouse in the lives of many of the narrative figures, through the ironic relationship of Moorehouse and the Camera Eye persona as "creative" users of language, and through the equally ironic relationship of Moorehouse's self-serving exploitation of the language of America's civil religion to those biographical figures who are crushed because of their truthful use of this language, Dos Passos establishes Moorehouse as the fullest representation of the betrayal of American values, of the "old words," by those seemingly committed to the support and strengthening of these values.

As Dos Passos acknowledged on several occasions, he based the figure of Moorehouse loosely on the career and beliefs of Ivy Lee, one of the founders (along with Edward L. Bernays) of the public-relations industry in America.[6] He met Lee in Moscow in August 1928 and acquired from him an outline of his life and opinions. Lee, like Moorehouse, got his start by convincing large American corporations guilty of suspect business and labor practices that they would benefit from having their views presented "correctly" to the public. Lee's career was further enhanced by the major role he (like Moorehouse) played in the American Red Cross during the war. By 1919 he was sufficiently identified with corporate management of public opinion to be attacked by Upton Sinclair in *The Brass Check*. It was no doubt Lee's open acceptance of the premise that language was a device for the manipulation of public belief that especially attracted Dos Passos to his possible use as a prototype.[7] Lee wrote in his book *Human Nature and Railroads* (1915):

> We can never be too careful in the terms we use. Sometime ago, a certain public service corporation was in great financial difficulties; it could not pay its bond interest. Its skillful president induced its bondholders to agree to a reduction of the rate of interest on the bonds. The president then announced to the public that there was to be "a readjustment" of the finances of the company. Now "readjustment of finances" is so much better than saying, "Your company is bankrupt," and no one ever suggested that his company was bankrupt. It was a matter of terms, and we must be careful of the terms we allow to be lodged in the public mind.

"What we say to the public," Lee concluded, "must be with reference to its effect, and not primarily with reference to its logical sequence."[8]

Moorehouse, of course, is also a careful user of terms that are chosen principally for effect rather than "logical sequence" (that is, truth). In particular, the terms *cooperation, understanding,* and *education* are Moorehouse's means of disguising the victimization of labor and the public by his corporate client. These terms derive loosely from that portion of America's civil religion that stresses the advantages of the union of individual freedom and shared respon-

sibility in a democratic society. It is appropriate, therefore, that Dos
Passos "introduces" each of Moorehouse's narrative segments with
a biography of a figure who reveals the full consequences for
American life of a misappropriation of a popular faith and its language. The biography just prior to the initial Moorehouse segment
is of William Jennings Bryan. (Indeed, there is a density of Bryan
references leading up to Moorehouse's narrative, as he is also men-
tioned twice in Newsreels and once in Janey's narrative.) For
Bryan, the "silver tongue of the plain people" (*FP*, 171), the traditional rhetoric of Christian belief is a means of leading the
people—at first against the bankers and the gold standard, but
then for prohibition and religious fundamentalism, and finally to
buy Florida real estate. In a similar manner, the career of Minor
Keith, the "Emperor of the Caribbean," rests upon Keith's exploitation of Central America for his own advantage while ostensibly fulfilling a classic American success myth. And Carnegie's life, in
which his later philanthrophy disguises an earlier ruthless acquisitiveness, provides another example of the successful masking of
truth by honorific public images and language.

One of Dos Passos' more obvious themes in these three biographies, a theme reflected in their ironic titles ("Boy Orator of the
Platte," for example), is that of the element of hypocrisy in these
figures' adoption of public roles and language to advance or disguise the true nature of their careers. In one of his most effective
strokes, however, Dos Passos has Moorehouse so fully committed
to the clichés of American belief that no discrepancy between experience and belief can lead him to doubt their truth. This failure
in perception—or conversely this strength of conviction—is paral-
leled in Moorehouse's personal life by his initial sexual experience.
He is at the outset of his career and is already beginning to live a
version of the American success myth in that he is about to marry
the boss's daughter, Annabelle, when he discovers that she is pregnant by another man. He is at first dismayed, but after reminding
himself that "opportunity knocks but once" (*FP*, 193), he goes
ahead with the marriage and the subsequent use of his wife's
wealth to advance his career without any evident difficulty or pain.
Dos Passos was in this instance revealing Moorehouse's ability to
apply Ivy Lee's premises to every level of his life. Moorehouse's recognition of a hard truth is only momentary once the language of
belief—here of the myth of success—takes over and creates its
own kind of truth. For the rest of his life Moorehouse never sees
what is before his eyes—that he is using others to his own advan-

tage, for example, and calling it loyalty, or that corporations are using their employees to their own advantages and calling it cooperation. He fails to understand, not because he is lying to himself, but because his belief is so full and strong that he cannot see the truth. He becomes, in short, a living paragon of the American myth of success, in that he embodies not only its essential beliefs but also its power to control and to blind.

In his depiction of the intimate connection between a character's sex life, his career, and his use of language, Dos Passos was drawing—perhaps inevitably given the origin of *U.S.A.* in the 1920s—on Freudian ideas about the impact of early childhood on the shaping of the unconscious. Daughter (as the title of her narrative implies and as I will discuss more fully later) is the clearest example of Dos Passos' effort to read character and fate along Freudian lines. Her Electra complex is an extreme example of an emotional state that stems from a family configuration found in the lives of a large number of the narrative figures. In this typical family pattern, one parent is either weak or absent (often dying when the child is very young) and the remaining parent or guardian is a dominant but largely harmful factor in the child's development. Some striking examples of narrative figures whose lives are adversely affected by a remaining defective parent are Janey, Eveline, Savage, and Mary (the mother's gentility); Eleanor (the father's crudity); Margo (the stepfather's sexual aggressiveness); and Charley (the mother's religiosity). There are other narrative figures, of course—Ben, for example—for whom family background plays little role except for the conventional desire of the youth to escape parental control. But the trilogy nevertheless contains an extraordinarily large number of instances in which a potentially beneficial parent (a sympathetic mother, a strong father) fails to function in that role, leaving control of the child to a parent whose beliefs and attitudes are harmful to the child.

The Camera Eye persona is of course also burdened with parents of this kind in the strong but largely absent father and the conventional and sickly mother.[9] And as is true of many of the narrative figures, the peripatetic existence of the Camera Eye persona can be interpreted at least in part as a search for a father—for a source of strength and wisdom because of the absence of the father figure in childhood. The narrative figures do not succeed in fulfilling this need. Either they have been too deeply scarred (like Margo), or they find false authority figures (as do Eleanor, Janey,

and Mary), or they are too weak to pursue the search fully (like
Savage). The Camera Eye persona demonstrates, however, that it
is possible to resolve or mitigate the handicap of a dominant
"weak" parent and to push through to a discovery of the strength of
self that is a rediscovery of the strength of the absent parent. From
the earliest portion of *U.S.A.*, therefore, when Mac's sickly mother
dies and Mac is hustled off to a new life in Chicago, Dos Passos
was writing not only sociologically apt accounts of the instability of
the American family and the rootlessness of American life but
also—in a deeper vein—oblique dramatizations of the origin of his
own uncertain and hesitant quest. Or, to put the matter more in
Dos Passos' own terms, he was not writing "objectively" in the narratives and "subjectively" in the Camera Eye, as he claimed to be
doing. Rather, in the depiction of his characters' family backgrounds as well as in several other narrative themes and strategies,
he was creating obverse counterparts to the Camera Eye persona.

Eleanor, who is introduced after the initial Moorehouse segment as the second of the narrative figures who will cluster around
Moorehouse, is a clear example of a character who is a negative
counterpart to the Camera Eye persona. Like her friend Eveline,
Eleanor derives less from a specific source than from Dos Passos'
encounters in uptown New York during the early 1920s with a
number of well-bred Chicago girls who celebrated a fin-de-siècle
style of life and decoration.[10] Eleanor is not, in fact, well-bred but
has rather posited her entire life on the drive to appear so and thus
to escape the memory of the rawness and crudity she associates
with her father and his job in the Chicago stockyards. She seeks
above all to make herself and her life into an interior decorator's
idea of an objet d'art—refined, pure, and "white." She is eventually
to close herself off from all feelings except those related to her
needs to preserve the sanctity of her taste and to solidify her position on the edge of the upper class. Eleanor's antithetical role in
relation to the Camera Eye persona during her early career is
stressed by the two Camera Eye segments that enclose her second
narrative segment. In the first, the adolescent Camera Eye persona
visits "a very fashionable" English lady—"and there were white lilies in the hall" (*FP*, 223)—whom he dislikes intensely. In the second, he meets on his family's Virginia estate the "methodist
minister's wife . . . a tall thin woman who . . . loved beautiful
things . . . and talked in a bell-like voice about how things were
lovely as a lily" (*FP*, 238). "Oh God not lilies," the Camera Eye per-

sona cries at the end of this segment, rejecting not only this image
of a thin aestheticism as it pertains to him but also as it symbolizes
Eleanor's quest for the pure, white, and refined in life.[11]

Eleanor is in many ways a more intelligent and ambitious
Janey. Both think of life as an escape from the emotional center of
being into a drawing room (or office) where behavior is fully defined and always proper. And both are therefore strongly drawn to
Moorehouse, because his beliefs and his style of life are a full embodiment of the platitudinously acceptable. Perhaps the clearest
fictional expression of the union of the three figures under the arid
but protective umbrella of an upper-class ritual is the constantly
repeated occasion in the trilogy of the serving of tea to Moorehouse
and his entourage by his English butler. This kind of predefined,
protected mode of life, of course, precludes the turbulence of the
sexual; indeed, Moorehouse's attractiveness to Janey and Eleanor
stems in part from their recognition of his essentially asexual nature. ("Oh, you're as cold as a fish," his second wife tells him [*FP*,
340].) Moorehouse will eventually—in France—sleep with
Eleanor, but this occurs principally more because Eleanor demands it as a way of countering the threat of Eveline than because
of any great desire on either of their parts.

Janey has dismissed the sexual in her life because it is not
proper. For Eleanor and Moorehouse, their similar dismissal—
though related to conventional ideas about sex—also has a deeper
implication. Both are forceful, intelligent people who out of a poor
background have struggled up the ladder of success. Both have realized the role of sex in this rise—that it can be a positive factor (as
in Moorehouse's two marriages to wealthy women) or a negative
one (as in the interest of poor young artists in Eleanor). Both realize, in brief, that sex is seldom socially neutral. They are therefore
comfortable with each other because they are paradoxically "honest" with each other about the role each plays in aiding the fulfillment of the other's notion of success. Eleanor uses Moorehouse's
wealth and prominence for her own ends, and Moorehouse uses
Eleanor's social graces for his. In perhaps the deepest vein of irony
in their characterization, there is an underlying truth in Eleanor
and Moorehouse's repeated claim (*FP*, 352, for example) that theirs
is a "spiritual" relationship. It is, though principally in the sense of
two spirits that are similar in their self-serving sterility.

As Moorehouse becomes the dominant figure in the central
portion of *The 42nd Parallel*—both through his own narrative and
through his increasing importance in the narratives of Janey and

Eleanor—the various ironic themes associated with him also grow in prominence. He continues to fulfill the letter of the Alger myth as he works hard in Pittsburgh, acquiring a mastery of the public-relations business while preserving himself sexually as he waits for the right girl. She appears in the form of the daughter of a wealthy family that can help him in his career, and he again—as with Annabelle—permits himself to be seduced by her. As Moorehouse lives out this sullied archetype of success, he is also mastering in both his personal and his professional life a corrupt language of feeling and belief, a language in which platitude and cliché disguise the emptiness or falseness of feeling and belief. Here, for example, is his letter, on the death of her father, to the rich man's daughter whom he believes may be a useful consort:

> Dearest Gertrude,
> In this moment of grief, allow me to remind you that I think of you constantly. Let me know at once if I can be of any use to you in any way. In the valley of the shadow of death we must realize the Great Giver to whom we owe all love and wealth and all affection around the jocund fireside is also the Grim Reaper . . .   (FP, 256)

At this very moment Moorehouse is also beginning to evolve the public-relations formula he will use for the rest of his career, a formula that announces the overt appearance in the trilogy of the theme of the "old words." He tells two of his potential supporters: "The great leaders of American capital . . . are firm believers in fairplay and democracy and are only too anxious to give the worker his share of the proceeds of industry if they can only see their way to do so in fairness to the public and the investor" (FP, 271). Dos Passos' broad caricature of the "art of rhetoric" in Moorehouse should not obscure our understanding of the depth and range of his theme that a frame of mind that can construct a corrupt language of belief can also create a false language of feeling. And Moorehouse, who builds "successful" but essentially harmful personal and business careers out of his unconscious manipulation of the language of belief and feeling, is the principal illustration of this tragic national weakness.

Moorehouse's appeal to Janey and Eleanor thus stems largely from his ability to supply platitudes of language and role to fill the emptiness of their lives. This thematic centrality of Moorehouse in the second half of *The 42nd Parallel* is confirmed by the fictional strategy of this portion of the novel. Eleanor comes to New York and meets Moorehouse, who becomes her protector, while Janey goes to work for Moorehouse and also settles in New York. Meanwhile, in the Newsreels and biographies, as well as through frequent allusions in the narratives, the war in Europe assumes greater and greater prominence. The novel, in other words, begins to push toward a climax in which its major characters are in the nation's major city at a moment of national crisis during which the dominant feature of the principal narrative figure—his ability to obscure truth by a misuse of the "old words"—will also become the national ethos.

Dos Passos depicts in a number of instances the limitations placed on the expression of the ideal of freedom in America even before our entrance into the war. The Camera Eye persona, for example, while visiting Quebec or at Harvard or at a radical meeting (Camera Eye 24–26), discovers that conventional belief and behavior exercise a stranglehold over his desire to break away into an independent life. In the biographies, Edison and Steinmetz are portrayed as imprisoned within the American industrial system. And even Mac, in his last narrative segment, toward the close of the novel, is absorbed in the beliefs of Moorehouse and George H. Barrow during their visit to Mexico City. But it is America's entrance into the war that puts the severest strain on the American belief in freedom and indeed crushes all expression of this belief. The power of war enthusiasm to control and dominate all other sentiments is initially depicted in Eleanor's final narrative segment, which is itself the last narrative segment in *The 42nd Parallel* to be devoted to the Moorehouse cluster of narrative figures. On the eve of our declaration of war the personal and professional lives of these figures are in disarray. Eleanor and Moorehouse are in financial difficulties; Mrs. Moorehouse is threatening to divorce Moorehouse because of Eleanor; and Janey is also deeply resentful of Eleanor. But then America enters the war and all these dilemmas and controversies dissolve in an outpouring of mass patriotic fervor that brooks no individual or divisive expression of belief or feeling. In a series of patriotic tableaus, Eleanor and Moorehouse announce that they will volunteer for war service; a hotel orchestra plays "The Star Spangled Banner" endlessly to a cheering audience; and as Eleanor, Janey, and Moorehouse watch a parade of soldiers, "Miss Williams leaned over and kissed Eleanor on the cheek. J. W. stood looking out over their heads with a proud smile on his face" (*FP*, 358).

The more sinister side of this hegemony of war sentiment is revealed in the closing portion of the novel. The final biography is that of La Follette, a statesman fully committed to the underlying ideals of American life, whose career is destroyed by his opposition to the war. (There are also a number of allusions during these final segments of the novel to the parallel figure of Debs.[12]) The final Camera Eye finds the persona on his way to France to serve in the ambulance corps. In his initial experience in wartime France he wakes up in a Bordeaux hotel room to discover a French secret serviceman going through his luggage. And Charley Anderson, in the final narrative segment of the novel, is in a New York restaurant on the day war is declared and also encounters a band incessantly playing "The Star Spangled Banner." But here the refusal of one couple to stand up each time the anthem is played causes a riot. The emptiness of this mindless war enthusiasm in this instance and several others is nicely suggested by the relationship of the war spirit to a failure in language. On this occasion, the crowd in the restaurant wishes to crush any disrespect to the anthem, even though "nobody knew the words" (FP, 409). And in the final scene of The 42nd Parallel, Charley, also on his way overseas to serve in the ambulance corps, tries to start a conversation with a French lookout. "The lookout put his hand over his mouth. At last he made Charley understand that he wasn't supposed to talk to him" (FP, 415). The novel ends with these sentences. The war has confirmed and intensified the suppression of the free expression of mind, action, and spirit in America as that expression is represented through language. Man can speak only the false and self-serving abstractions (as do Eleanor and Moorehouse and Wilson), or he can attempt to speak out boldly and honestly and be beaten down (as are Debs and La Follette), or he can be silent. The Camera Eye persona, as is suggested by his parallel to Charley at this point, also has seemingly chosen the silence of a noncombatant role in the war. But as will become clear later in the trilogy, he will in fact absorb and learn the lessons of the war and will eventually himself be willing to risk all for freedom.

America's entrance into the world war, as depicted in The 42nd Parallel, is thus both a historical event and a mythic construct. (The Paris peace conference and the Sacco-Vanzetti case will play similar roles at the conclusions of Nineteen-Nineteen and The Big Money.) As a major historical event, it dominates the Newsreels and affects the lives of the narrative and biographical figures and of the Camera Eye persona. As a mythic construct, it symbolizes all those forces in America making for conformity to platitudinous values that in reality disguise personal, class, and national self-interest. *U.S.A.* is a historical novel in which, as in most significant historical fiction, history is a vehicle for symbolic expression rather than principally a source of "actual" event and character.

Dos Passos ends *The 42nd Parallel* with the first segment of Charley Anderson's narrative. At forty-six pages the longest segment in the novel, it appears to be anomalous because it introduces a new narrative figure at the close of the work after the long dominance of the Moorehouse cluster of characters. Yet the segment serves several important thematic and structural functions both in *The 42nd Parallel* and in the trilogy as a whole. For *The 42nd Parallel*, Charley represents a return of focus to a working-class figure, but one who is separated from Mac by a generation and who thus signifies the change in national spirit from the beginning of the century to the immediate prewar period. For the entire trilogy, Charley's workingman status in *The 42nd Parallel* and his reappearance as an entrepreneur in *The Big Money* signifies the full flowering of the American capitalist ethic in the postwar years.

Charley has no specific prototype, but appears rather to have been derived from a composite tinkerer/inventor/entrepreneur American type. Dos Passos' major effort in his depiction of Charley's early life was to establish his credentials within the American myth of success. From the heart of the Midwest, of poor but hardworking and honest parents (his mother's religiosity is central here), he has little interest in formal education but (like Edison or more significantly Ford) proves himself adept at practical mechanics. Like Mac he soon drifts into life as an itinerant workman, but he differs from Mac in that he is less a political than an economic and social being. He easily absorbs political ideas from his immediate surroundings, at one moment echoing IWW sentiments, at the next stoutly supporting the war. What remains constant is his desire to succeed in terms defined by the American success myth— to have money in his pocket (Charley always likes the feel of cash) and to marry a girl whose social status will confirm his success. The vital difference between Charley and Mac is well caught toward the close of Charley's narrative segment in *The 42nd Parallel*, when Charley encounters Ben Compton in New York. Ben, who is the true heir of Mac's early IWW idealism, and who will reappear fully in that role in *Nineteen-Nineteen*, quotes to Charley Debs' famous aphorism that he wished "to rise with the ranks, not from them." Charley's attitude, however, is, "I don't want to spend all my life patchin' up tin lizzies at seventyfive a month" (FP, 411).

In his essential nature, Charley is therefore far more similar to Moorehouse than to Mac. Both he and Moorehouse want to work within the system, to fulfull the myth, rather than to build "a new society in the shell of the old" (FP, 95), as the IWW dream has it. But there is also a vital difference between Moorehouse's and Charley's pursuit of the dream of success, a difference that is the source of the distinction between Moorehouse's "triumph" in this pursuit and Charley's tragic failure. For even in this first narrative segment Charley reveals the human inadequacies that will—in contrast to Moorehouse's almost inhuman coldness—make him in the end a victim of the world he wishes to conquer. In his portrayal of this aspect of Charley's character, Dos Passos was perhaps influenced by Theodore Dreiser's An American Tragedy, which had appeared in 1925. Clyde Griffiths and Charley Anderson share two basic characteristics. Each has a burning desire to escape from a dreary poverty into material success, and each lacks the strength and shrewdness required to avoid the pitfalls present in any attempt to fulfill this desire. In Charley's case, weakness takes two forms, one of which is strikingly similar to Clyde's essential limitation. Charley's early experience at Vogel's garage, where his brother exploits him, reveals that he is not adept at economic infighting. As someone later tells him in The Big Money, his luck—in being a war hero and in his inventive talent—will carry him only so far. After this point he is vulnerable. But even more significantly, to Charley—as to Clyde—sex is both a means toward and a confirmation of success. He thus views socially superior women in semireligious terms, as prizes for which no effort is too great, and this overwhelming desire also makes him vulnerable, as it did Clyde in the pursuit of the Eden-like Sondra. Charley's weakness in this regard is illustrated in his first relationship, with Emiscah in Minneapolis. She is a step above Charley on the social ladder and thoroughly exploits his interest in her. Both of Charley's weaknesses will coalesce and climax in The Big Money, when he is destroyed financially and personally by the combined efforts of his business partners and his upper-class wife. Charley's only refuge from sexual exploitation is, paradoxically, the "honest whore," of whom Margo will be the supreme example. (The prostitute who befriends him in New Orleans in The 42nd Parallel anticipates Margo.) Because they both acknowledge the nature of their transaction, a camaraderie replaces the disguised motives of his pursuit of the girl of his dreams.

Charley's narrative sequence in *The 42nd Parallel,* though not interlaced with other narratives in the novel, is powerfully related to them thematically. Charley has begun to reject the older working-class-radical model provided by Mac, and his is to be a more tragic pursuit of the American success myth that Moorehouse and Eleanor are also seeking to fulfill. In addition, through some maneuvering by Dos Passos, Charley's narrative ties in at its close with the general movement of the novel toward a New York climax at the moment of America's entrance into the war. Charley too has landed in the city, more by drift than purpose, but once there is caught up in the war enthusiasm. The conclusion of his narrative finds him—like Eleanor, Moorehouse, and Janey, like the Camera Eye persona, and like the American public in its heart (as reflected by the song "Over There" in the last Newsreel)—heading for Europe to participate in the war. Each of the novels of the trilogy ends with a major historical event—America's entrance into the war, the Armistice (and peace conference), and the Sacco-Vanzetti case—that is also, thematically, an anticlimax in the light of Dos Passos' ironic undercutting of the conventional public attitude toward the event. For *The 42nd Parallel,* America's joining in the war to protect the ideals of American democracy disguises the self-interest of those enthusiastically supporting the venture and also is a basis for the suppression of the expression of American ideals. The various departures for France are thus not true beginnings but rather confirm the major failings of American life that the novel as a whole has depicted.

Nineteen-Nineteen is a more sharply focused historical novel than either *The 42nd Parallel* or *The Big Money.* Its time span (except for the early lives of some of the narrative and biographical figures) is roughly that of the two years from America's entry into the war to the conclusion of the peace conference in the spring of 1919. The war and its aftermath are thus the principal preoccupations of the historical, fictional, and autobiographical figures depicted in the various modes as well as the major subject of the Newsreels. Dos Passos later recalled that "Paris really was the capital of the world that spring of the Peace Conference."[13] His sketch of the "Geography of *Nineteen Nineteen,*" which places Paris and the characters living or passing through the city at the hub of New

York, Rome, Constantinople, and Alsace, is a graphic illustration of his effort to translate this belief into fictional character and event.[14] Aside from Joe Williams and Ben Compton, all of the narrative figures—usually in interlaced narratives—as well as the Camera Eye persona are present in Paris. The effect of this historical and fictional concentration is not to make *Nineteen-Nineteen* a different kind of work than *The 42nd Parallel* or *The Big Money. Nineteen-Nineteen* is still an integral part of *U.S.A.* in theme and form. Its effect is rather that of a clearer expression of theme—what Dos Passos called "a certain crystalization" of his view of American life[15]—because of the emphasis on a single major event, the war.

Joe Williams, the first narrative figure in *Nineteen-Nineteen*, is Janey's brother and thus shared her youth in white-collar-class Washington. But for Joe's adult life as a merchant seaman, Dos Passos drew primarily, it seems, on the experiences of his friend Tom Cope. Cope, whom he had met while they both served in the ambulance corps in France, spent a year and a half as a seaman in the early 1920s, during which time he and Dos Passos maintained their friendship.[16]

It is difficult to determine whether or not Dos Passos intended from the initial appearance of Joe in Janey's narrative to devote a separate narrative to Joe. Of the twelve narrative figures in *U.S.A.*, three—Joe, Eveline, and Ben—appear in other narratives before they receive separate narrative treatment. (A fourth would have been Ike Hall, who appears in Mac's narrative and whose separate narrative was cut by Dos Passos at a late stage in the preparation of *The Big Money.*) The most likely explanation for the device is that Dos Passos saw its usefulness once he was required to invent "new" narrative figures for *Nineteen-Nineteen* and *The Big Money,* in that he could for these later novels turn to minor figures already introduced in *The 42nd Parallel* for fuller development. So, for working-class figures in *Nineteen-Nineteen* and *The Big Money,* for example, he had available Joe Williams and Ike Hall, who had already appeared in the Janey and Mac narratives of *The 42nd Parallel.* But whatever the origin of the device, it served several useful functions in the fictional strategy of *U.S.A.* The principal one was to contribute to the underlying formal character of the trilogy of distinctive but overlapping perspectives on reality. Thus, a figure initially perceived by us from one angle of vision, that of the major figure in whose narrative he appears, is seen in a strikingly new perspective when his own point of view—through free indirect discourse—becomes the means of understanding. The shift in narra-

tive point of view from Janey to Joe, for example, transforms Joe
during his seaman years from an uncouth roughneck (as rendered
in Janey's narrative in *The 42nd Parallel*) to an inarticulate but pathetic seeker of Janey's unforthcoming love (as rendered in Joe's
narrative in *Nineteen-Nineteen*). In addition, the device afforded a
degree of narrative efficiency, since Dos Passos could compress or
omit portions of a figure's life already accounted for in the narrative
of another character, as he does, for example, in dealing with Joe's
youth or Eveline's Chicago years.

Joe's life as a seaman resembles Mac's as an itinerant printer
in that the "adventures" of both characters have the buoyancy of a
picaresque narrative. Joe gets in and out of scrapes, a good many of
which (such as that in Central America when he is anxiously seeking the latest baseball scores from an American homosexual just as
anxious to get him into bed) are basically tall tales. Once the war
starts, however, these difficulties become more threatening as Joe
undergoes a seemingly unending cycle of illnesses, torpedoings,
and imprisonments. Although even these events have a comic element (Joe getting torpedoed once again becomes a running joke),
their more insidious dimension is borne out by Joe's death in a
drunken brawl in St. Nazaire on the day the war ends. Despite
Joe's apparently free and knockabout existence (represented by his
breezy postcards to Janey from exotic ports), his life—as is empha-
sized by the nature of his death—has been empty and meaningless.

One source of Joe's lack of direction lies in his relationship to
his family, a relationship complementary to that of Janey. For
whereas she had accepted the repression of self demanded by
lower-middle-class proprieties, Joe had rebelled violently to join the
navy. In that act he found only motion, however, not direction. Joe
thus becomes one kind of archetypal American workman—not the
kind typified by Mac or Ben, with their radical beliefs and faith,
nor by Charley, with his eagerness to climb beyond his class, but
rather the kind whose mechanical skill lends the appearance of a
hold on life but who is in fact vulnerable to every preying force in
his world. This aspect of Joe is revealed in the first incident of his
narrative. Having deserted the navy in Buenos Aires and needing
ablebodied-seaman papers to get work on a merchant ship, he is
promptly tricked and cheated by the forger of the papers. Throughout his life, Joe's basic human needs—for work, for love, for freedom, for (in short) a decent life—make him exploitable by those

seemingly supplying these needs. Instead of freedom, he finds confinement—often literally so, as in the long incident when he is falsely imprisoned as a spy by the British. Instead of work and of pay commensurate with his abilities, he is constantly cheated and mistreated by his employers. Instead of love, he finds prostitutes and venereal diseases on the one hand and bourgeois demands for marriage and possessions on the other. If Joe's life were not so inherently pathetic, it would be a parody version of the Marxist notion of the exploitation of the proletariat in a capitalist society. Joe has escaped the bonds of family into "freedom" only to find that life is one long beating down of his spirit. No wonder that the drunken binge becomes his principal means of self-expression.

For a brief period Joe attempts to fulfill the working-class version of the American dream. On the rebound from a series of whores and drinking bouts, he thinks, "God, he wanted money and a good job and a girl of his own" (*NN*, 56). These wishes translate into Della, a figure resembling Mac's Maisie in her ruthless sexual blackmailing of Joe. Herself a working-class girl when Joe meets her at Norfolk, Della and Joe are seemingly powerfully drawn to each other. He tries to make love to her, but she says "not till they were married and he said with his mouth against hers, when would they get married and she said they'd get married as soon as he got his new job" (*NN*, 65). With their marriage, and with the coming of a war prosperity, Della raises the stakes. Joe must give up his prospective career as a ship's officer and get a better-paying job ashore. When Joe resists, Della pushes on to brighter prospects and Joe leaves in disgust. In this and in other efforts by Joe to do more with his life than fulfill the cliché of the whoring, drunken sailor, he is defeated by the ironclad class and economic realities of American life, which make use of his desires to shape and control and eventually crush him.

The common American workman, Dos Passos implies through Joe's narrative, is a marginal and replaceable unit in the industrial system. But his weakness and expendability do not prevent him from sensing what he is, and Joe's increasing bitterness and self-destructive anger as his narrative and life draw to a close dramatize his tragic self-recognition. This self-awareness reaches its climax in a striking symbolic detail connected with Joe's death, when in a flash of vision Joe sees not only this impending event but also the meaningless violence and emptiness of the life that the event signifies. Joe has gotten into a fight over a prostitute in a

St. Nazaire bar. As he is backing out of the barroom, he "saw in the [barroom] mirror that a big guy in a blouse was bringing down a bottle on his head held with both hands. He tried to swing around but he didn't have time. The bottle crashed his skull and he was out" (*NN*, 238).

Like Mac in *The 42nd Parallel,* Joe is largely an isolated figure in *Nineteen-Nineteen.* Except for his association with Janey and his single meeting with Dick Savage in wartime Genoa, he does not interlace with other figures in the novel. Yet Joe's basic character and fate resemble so closely those of two other figures in the novel that the three can usefully be said to constitute another kind of cluster—one in which the characters do not interlace but nevertheless share a major thematic emphasis. Thus—unlike the group of figures revolving around Moorehouse—Joe, Eveline, and Daughter do not appear in each other's narratives in *Nineteen-Nineteen.* They have in common, however, a tragic American innocence. They are "open" characters in the sense that they accept their emotional and sexual natures and seek fulfillment of these as much as circumstances allow. Eveline and Daughter want love above all; Joe, freedom. But they are without strength or shrewdness, and for them something ventured is everything lost. Daughter's love for Dick and his desertion of her despite her pregnancy is the archetype of the victimization of the naive and openhearted by the more ruthless and circumspect. So all three go to bitter deaths (Eveline in *The Big Money*), victims of a failure to realize that to desire is to make oneself vulnerable. None of the major figures in the trilogy is killed in combat, but the deaths, and the nature of the deaths, of these three figures who participated in the war represents the impact of the war on this aspect of the national character. For Joe's death in a brawl, Daughter's in a needless plane accident, and Eveline's by an overdose constitute the effect of the obliquely imposed but nevertheless powerfully destructive moral disaster that was the war on the openness and innocence of the American spirit.

Joe, Daughter, and Eveline are adversely affected not only by their innocence but by more distinctive characteristics of their class and sex—Joe by his working-class origins and Daughter and Eveline by being middle-class women. In contrast to these figures, the Camera Eye persona in *Nineteen-Nineteen*—with the deaths of his parents and with his breaking out of the bellglass of Harvard into wider ranges of experience—is beginning to come to grips with the limitations placed on his insight and understanding by his own background, even though his emergence into maturity will not occur until *The Big Money*. Many of the biographies and narratives of *Nineteen-Nineteen* thus have either an ironic or an exemplary relationship to the dilemma faced by the Camera Eye persona in this novel and in *The Big Money:* Is he to be restricted by his background and hobbled by his personal weaknesses, or is he to fight through to an independent vision and life despite both his background and his weaknesses?

This theme dominates the juxtapositional strategy of the early portion of *Nineteen-Nineteen*. Joe Williams' two initial narrative segments enclose the initial Camera Eye of the novel, in which the death of the persona's parents is announced, and are in close juxtaposition with the first Richard Savage narrative segment and the biographies of Jack Reed and Randolph Bourne. These biographies—as well as that of Paxton Hibben somewhat later—and the Savage narrative as a whole serve as almost precise moral beacons for the Camera Eye persona. The biographies point the way to the potential salvation of self through the pursuit of truth, the narrative to damnation through a soul-destroying moral dishonesty and personal ambition.

That Dos Passos wished us to view the Camera Eye persona, Jack Reed, and Savage comparatively is clear from his emphasis on their common Harvard background. Harvard for each figure is a confirmation of class roles and attitudes. These can be accepted as a self-aggrandizing system of satisfying poses and comfortable values, or they can be rejected as both false and confining. (For Bourne, a Columbia graduate, his physical deformity can perhaps be taken as Dos Passos' tongue-in-cheek depiction of a handicap parallel to that of a Harvard education.) The Reed biography, which occurs immediately after the first Camera Eye concludes with the announcement that "tomorrow I hoped would be the first day of the first month of the first year" (*NN,* 12), plays the role of indicating the direction of "tomorrow" despite the disadvantages of a Harvard background. Reed is the opposite of the "playboy" image that was conventionally attached to the Ivy League graduate of his day and that Dos Passos ironically uses as the title of the Reed biography. He immerses himself in social problems and conflicts in an effort to find solutions outside of conventional class belief. He is therefore clearly distinguished from the seemingly "masculine" Harvard figure of Theodore Roosevelt, whose biography will follow

Bourne's. Reed had vigorously confronted the primary task facing the American writer despite the fact that he too, like the Camera Eye persona and like Savage, had heard Copey recite. He

> kept meeting bums workingmen husky guys he liked out of work. . . .
>   in school hadn't he learned the Declaration of Independence by heart? Reed was a westerner and words meant what they said.   (NN, 14)

Reed's death in Moscow, fighting for the revolution, is thus—unlike the deaths of Joe, Daughter, and Eveline, and the death of the soul that is to be Savage's fate—a true martyrdom.

There is an element of boyish hero-worship in the Reed biography, as if Dos Passos' otherwise not fully acknowledged longing for his father's masculine and aggressive independence of mind and action in defense of the "old words" could here be expressed openly and fervently. Richard Savage's narrative, however, is far more complex and often ambiguous in its emotional tone, since Dos Passos worked into Savage's life and attitudes many of the worst fears he had had about himself, as if to depict them were to finally exorcise them. Indeed, given the close similarity of many of Savage's experiences to those of the Camera Eye persona in *Nineteen-Nineteen,* and given as well Savage's narrative centrality—he also figures prominently in Eveline's and Daughter's narratives—he is no doubt the major narrative figure in the novel.

Dos Passos wished to depict in Savage what he believed to be the worst potential of his own background—that of a youth whose Harvard aestheticism reflected both his superficial rebelliousness and his weak posturing and whose later experiences confirmed the uselessness of rebellion and the advantages of deception and conformity. In a sense, the model for this figure was Dos Passos' entire generation of literary aesthetes at Harvard—the group that had dominated the *Harvard Monthly* and that had collaborated on *Eight Harvard Poets,* a small book of verse that had been published with the aid of Dos Passos' father. This was the group that had combined art interests with antiwar sentiment, had gone overseas in the ambulance corps, and had drifted into various kinds of postwar middle-class roles.[17] It was also a group with a strong homoerotic current, though seldom any overt homosexuality. But Dos Passos also chose a far more specific model in his friend Robert Hillyer. He and Hillyer had been friends at Harvard and had deepened their association when they collaborated on the early portion of "Seven Times Round the Walls of Jericho" while serving in the ambulance corps at Verdun during the summer of 1917. Indeed, Dos Passos worked so much of his awareness of Hillyer's life into the portrait of Savage that Hillyer reacted with shocked indignation when he finally came to read *Nineteen-Nineteen* in 1944. Dos Passos' reply to his old friend—that Savage was principally a "synthetic character" and that he didn't think "there's much Hillyer in Savage"—disguises the extent of Dos Passos' use of Hillyer as a model.[18] Like Hillyer, Savage was born in New Jersey, was an Episcopalian with a family military background, went to Kent School, wrote poetry at Harvard, and served overseas—first in the ambulance corps and later as an officer and army courier during the peace conference.[19] Dos Passos' principal departure from the external events of Hillyer's life in the portrait of Savage to 1919 was in placing Savage on the Italian front as an ambulance driver during the winter and spring of 1917–18. (Here Dos Passos drew upon his own experiences.) And there is no evidence of Hillyer having an affair in Europe resembling that between Savage and Daughter.[20] As far as later careers are concerned, Hillyer was to become a conventional and conservative minor poet and a Harvard instructor, activities that Dos Passos perhaps found roughly equivalent in verbal texture to Savage's career in public relations. But given Dos Passos' portrayal of Savage in *Nineteen-Nineteen* as the deserter of a pregnant sweetheart, as a latent homosexual, and as essentially dishonest and self-serving, Hillyer did not need to reach into Savage's postwar career for material in the characterization to object to.

But Hillyer, in his understandable anger, was missing the point of the Richard Savage narrative. Dos Passos' intent was not to attack Hillyer, whom he continued to regard as a friend, but to use Hillyer's experiences because they at once resembled his own and yet also contained directions that he himself—in the role of the Camera Eye persona—was not to take. This is the reason for the many explicit parallels in *Nineteen-Nineteen* between the Harvard and European experiences of the Camera Eye persona and Savage. For Dos Passos, too, had been raised by a conventional-minded mother, had participated in Harvard aestheticism, and had had early ambitions for himself as a poet. These characteristics shared with Hillyer and Savage comprised a potential for personal

disaster, and the portrait of Savage is a chart of that disaster. This
is the way I have not come, Dos Passos was, in effect, saying,
rather than this is the way Hillyer had come.

Savage's character is revealed in two early incidents. Raised
in genteel poverty by his "refined" mother, Dick is drawn to older
women of artistic sensibility and so has an affair, at sixteen, with a
woman of this kind, a minister's wife. Since Dick is also very religious at this stage of his life, he excuses this "fall" and others by
telling a friend that "physical things didn't matter and that repen-
tance was the key of redemption" (NN, 83). Meanwhile, he continues "sinning [on] Sunday evenings" (NN, 84), when the minister
is conducting services in another town. Dick exhibits here the
quality of mind that will permit him while at Harvard to radically
revise a poem in order to have it conform to popular taste, to serve
as an officer despite his opposition to the war, and to work for
Moorehouse despite his recognition of Moorehouse's vacuousness.
He will always find a means—often, as in this instance, one involving a verbal formula—to validate otherwise contemptible acts.
And though he is perceptive enough to sense what he is doing, he
is not strong enough either to combat or to accept fully this aspect
of his nature.

In a second revealing early incident, Dick is befriended by
Hiram Halsey Cooper, a man of wealth and importance who will
aid him at various points in his career.[21] Cooper is a bachelor, and
his covert homosexual interest in Dick is strongly suggested when
he displays to Dick his first editions of Beardsley and Huysmans.
Throughout Dick's narrative, homosexuals will be attracted to him.
(Dos Passos includes enough of these incidents and allusions to
comprise an explicit theme.)[22] In addition, Dick is sufficiently homosexual in manner to be called a "fairy" by another character
(NN, 466), and he pursues a homosexual encounter at the conclusion of The Big Money. This aspect of Dick's portrait angles in two
directions. No doubt Dos Passos had himself felt the strongly homoerotic character of the Harvard aesthetes and the Monthly group,
though it appears that only one of the Monthly editors during Dos
Passos' time, Stewart Mitchell, was an acknowledged homosexual.[23] And Dos Passos himself had had a late-adolescent infatuation
with Rumsey Marvin, a boy several years younger than he, during
his Harvard years.[24] During the 1920s, and especially before his
marriage in 1929, Dos Passos had actively (though perhaps unconsciously) sought to counter the association of homosexuality with
his shyness concerning women and his nearsighted unathleticism

by adopting some of the mannerisms of Hemingway's aggressive masculinity.[25] His association of homosexuality with Savage may thus have been another example of his use of the figure to dramatize qualities potential in him but firmly rejected.

It was perhaps this anxiety about possible homosexual tendencies within his own temperament that led Dos Passos to use homosexuality as a negative moral symbol in his portrayal of Savage, even though he had elsewhere (especially in *Manhattan Transfer*) depicted sympathetically the dilemma of the sexual deviant. Homosexuality therefore joins abortion and venereal disease in *U.S.A.* as sexual characteristics that are ambivalently portrayed. On the one hand, they are aspects of human sexuality that arise out of uncontrollable personal and social conditions and are thus depicted either neutrally or sympathetically, as with Mac's and Joe's VD and Mary's abortions. On the other, they are also specific instances of the general taint of sexuality and thus constitute evidence—as I suggested earlier in commenting on the relationship of Dos Passos to Eliot's use of sexual symbols—of a flawed moral and spiritual universe. Dick's latent homosexuality has something of this dual character. Given his absent father, genteel and protective mother, and "pretty boy" good looks he cannot be faulted for this aspect of his nature. Nevertheless, Dos Passos links Dick's homosexuality to his basic weakness of character, both in his lack of honesty in failing to acknowledge it to himself (and hence his dishonesty about himself in general) and in the association of homosexuality with the opposite of the masculine moral strength of a Jack Reed or the father of the Camera Eye persona.

With Dick—at the conclusion of his first narrative—going off to serve in the ambulance corps, with the Camera Eye persona (in his second segment) already at the front in France, and with the stress in the Bourne biography on his opposition to Wilson and the war, war material and war themes become dominant early in *Nineteen-Nineteen*. This centrality, and an accompanying greater clarity of theme given Dos Passos' strong opposition to the war, is nowhere more evident than in the biographies of the novel. Although most of the biographical figures had extremely varied and lengthy careers—Theodore Roosevelt and J. P. Morgan, for example—each biography is slanted in contents and emphasis toward the figure's relationship to the war. This lends a black/white character to the biographies here, unlike the other two novels, where figures such as Burbank or the Wright brothers or Isadora Duncan are rendered with a mixture of tones. In *Nineteen-*

Nineteen, the biographies divide sharply into those figures who reject the war (Reed, Bourne, and Hibben) and those who support it (Roosevelt, Wilson, and Morgan), with the stress on the war reaching a final crescendo in the "biography" of the Unknown Soldier, "The Body of an American." Only in the last two biographies of *Nineteen-Nineteen*—those of Joe Hill and Wesley Everest—does this preoccupation slacken in order to introduce the complementary theme of the suppression of radical movements during the war and postwar periods.

We have encountered Eveline Hutchins, who joins *Nineteen-Nineteen* as a narrative figure once the war theme is fully established, as a minor character in Eleanor's narrative in *The 42nd Parallel*. Eveline, both in *The 42nd Parallel* and in the early portion of her narrative in *Nineteen-Nineteen*, appears to be present to complement her "friend" Eleanor. Whereas Eleanor is steely cold and grasping, Eveline is romantic and vulnerable. (In portraying Eveline, Dos Passos may have drawn upon Kate Drain, an attractive woman he admired in Paris during 1918–19, who in 1919 married John Howard Lawson after becoming pregnant by him.)[26] Although Eveline "participates" in the war in the sense that she works in a Red Cross office in Paris, her life in Paris is little different from what it would have been in Chicago or New York, in that her principal preoccupation remains her own love affairs. Her nature and experiences would thus seem to be peripheral to the central theme of *Nineteen-Nineteen*, whatever interest she might have as a feminine type. But in fact Eveline's role as an American feminine type is the very source of her relationship to the "war center" of *Nineteen-Nineteen*.

As a pampered daughter in a prominent Chicago family (her father is a "successful" clergyman), Eveline is bred to fulfillment in life through men. Her early bohemianism and interest in art are principally means for meeting attractive men, as is her later war service. Her life is empty without a passionate affair—"She'd go crazy if something didn't happen to her soon" (*NN*, 124), she exclaims when still a girl—and she thus has affairs with at least eight men in the course of *Nineteen-Nineteen* and *The Big Money*.[27] Dos Passos' irony in his depiction of Eveline's ingenuous romantic nature is largely sympathetic, since she is unconsciously locked into a quest for romantic love through a combination of temperament and class role. She already has the social prominence and security that Eleanor so desperately wants. Only through love can a woman of her background and class achieve the identification of self that she seeks, and in this quest she is constantly exploited by those who recognize that her need is greater than theirs. Her life is like Joe's in that it comprises the cycle of innocence and pain of a child cuddling up for affection and receiving a slap instead. Or, to put it another way, hers is a variation on the fate of Blanche Dubois, in that she is always dependent on the kindness of lovers. One significant relationship of her narrative to the central theme of *Nineteen-Nineteen* thus lies in Dos Passos' similar portrayal of the force of class-determined roles and attitudes in her condition and in that of the "Harvard cluster" of Richard Savage, the Camera Eye persona, and several of the biographical figures. Put oversimply, if the Camera Eye persona recognizes and seeks to resist the bellglass that is his class background, Eveline unconsciously and tragically pursues the fate that is hers as a woman of her class.

There is yet another relationship between Eveline's narrative and the central themes both of *Nineteen-Nineteen* and of *U.S.A.* as a whole. Eveline is apolitical and asocial in her love life. She sleeps with the poor and radical Don Stevens and with Moorehouse. But the men she falls in love with do have one attribute in common— each is an example of a stereotyped role for a lover, from her early affair with an artist to her later ones with a dashing radical and with a soldier. (Moorehouse fulfills a deeper need, that of the caring father.) When she finally marries, at the close of *Nineteen-Nineteen,* it is because she feels that she can no longer attract "romantic" lovers, and she is contemptuous of her husband, Paul, because—despite his love for her—he seems so commonplace. Eveline's life is thus a parable of the dangers of pursuing a false notion of a special category of "old words," those of love. *U.S.A.* is principally about the "old words" of political idealism. But in his major feminine characters, and especially in Eveline, Dos Passos also depicted the corruption of a different but parallel faith in human relations. Eveline's notion of love, in which a form of ecstasy must be achieved with a romantic partner (all other experience to her is "tiresome"), is as much a falsification and corruption of a faith and belief as Moorehouse's idea of industrial cooperation is a falsification of the ideal of democracy. And Eveline in her life is playing out a series of "romances" with conventional figures from conventional love plots as much as Moorehouse is playing out a stereotype of the American dream of success. The difference between the two figures, and thus the source of the difference in Dos Passos' degree of satiric irony in their narratives, is that Moorehouse's essential innocence renders him powerful, Eveline's makes her weak. At the close of *The Big Money,* Moorehouse is a "national institution" (*BM,* 509), while Eveline, empty and depressed, dies of an overdose.

Eveline's arrival in Paris at the close of her second narrative segment reflects the shift to Paris of the geographical focus of *Nineteen-Nineteen.* (The Camera Eye persona, Dick, and Eleanor are already there, and Moorehouse is soon to arrive.) It is now late 1917 in the Newsreel and Camera Eye segments and in the "contemporary" sections of the narratives, and the moral hysteria and blackmail of the war temper are in full control. At its grossest but also most common level, this temper is well displayed by the English magistrate who berates Joe because "this was wartime and they had no right being drunk and disorderly on British soil but had ought to be fighting shoulder to shoulder with their brothers, Englishmen of their own blood and to whom the Americans owed everything, even their existence as a great nation, to defend civilization and free institutions and plucky little Belgium against the invading huns who were raping women and sinking peaceful merchantmen" (*NN,* 45). It is also present in a wonderful scene when Joe, having discovered his wife, Della, in an obvious sexual relationship with an army lieutenant, beats him up, only to be told by Della that "she'd have him arrested for insult to the uniform and assault and battery and that he was nothing but a yellow sniveling slacker and what was he doing hanging around home when all the boys were at the front fighting the huns" (*NN,* 168). But on a more significant level than these satiric accounts of the obviously self-serving use of the propagandistic clichés of the war, Dos Passos also depicts the immense lie that was the war—the discrepancy between the official explanation of the causes, nature, and purpose of the war and the understanding of the war by those experiencing it directly. Those who do know the war at firsthand and who are morally honest denounce, though ineffectually, the war code or convention of the lie. So Joe, after encountering the profiteering and jerry-building of the shipping industry, announces to Dick that the war is "a dirty goldbrick game put over by governments and politicians for their own selfish interests, it's crooked from A to Z" (*NN,* 200), and Jerry Burnham, now a U.P. war correspondent, can bemoan the fact that he is forced "to send out prepared stuff that was all a pack of dirty lies" (*NN,* 218).

These passages display Dos Passos at his most declamatory, as though he were still writing (as he had in his journals of 1917–

18) out of the immediate deep anger of his discovery of the falseness of war rhetoric. For the most part, the theme is rendered far
more obliquely in *Nineteen-Nineteen* by a number of dramatized
contrasts between the official language and the reality of war. One
such contrast lies in the distinction between the physical fact of
death in the trenches, as depicted graphically in several Camera
Eye segments and in a portion of Dick's narrative, and the heroic
and idealistic rhetoric imposed on the war by those safely distant
from the reality. (This of course had been a device and a theme of
an entire generation of American novelists of World War I, including Dos Passos in *Three Soldiers*.) Moorehouse and his Paris group,
in their stylish Red Cross uniforms and with their patriotic rhetoric
at a succession of dinner parties, teas, and flirtations, epitomize
this distinction. But it is also present in the ironic self-recognition
by the Camera Eye persona that his own role as a "gentleman volunteer" (*NN*, 141) ambulance driver in the midst of the carnage
helps maintain the distance between polite conventions involving
warfare and its true nature. And in a further representation of the
difference between the language of war and its actuality, Dos Passos again dramatizes the theme initially rendered in *The 42nd Parallel* of the suppression of liberty in the name of liberty. So Joe
meets a bum in Union Square who has been recruited by the secret service to spy on "reds, slackers, German spies, guys who can't
keep their traps shut" (*NN*, 174), and Dick is thrown out of the
ambulance corps for expressing doubts about the war.

Dos Passos' most effective device for portraying the distinction between belief and reality during the war is his attachment of
a jaundiced sexuality to war motives and activity. This was no
novel technique, of course. Thersites at the close of *Troilus and
Cressida* dourfully announces Shakespeare's joining of the moral
corruption of "war and lechery" throughout the play. And Dos Passos' own generation of world war writers, Cummings especially,
had often ironically depicted the distance between the high moral
fervor and rhetoric of a crusade to save democracy and the actuality of sexual conduct abroad during the war. Dos Passos himself, as
early as his *One Man's Initiation* and *Three Soldiers,* had used this
distance as a vehicle for expressing the falseness of the image of
war as a religious quest. *Nineteen-Nineteen* is thus pervaded with
instances in which the war as bordello is a principal motif. As one
of Dick's ambulance corps comrades says in shocked delight after
their first evening in Paris, "This ain't a war. . . . It's a goddamn
whorehouse" (*NN*, 98). So, too, in a Camera Eye segment immedi-

ately following the biography of Theodore Roosevelt, a biography
that stresses Roosevelt's belief in America's role in a "righteous
war," the journey of the Camera Eye persona to Italy (to herald the
arrival in Italy of America as savior) is prefaced with the announcement that "11,000 registered harlots . . . infest the streets of
Marseilles" (*NN*, 148). And so in Italy Dick experiences a gross
parody of the "rape of Belgian nuns" motif when a group of Italian
officers sexually assaults and persecutes a frightened servant girl.

Dick's experiences on the French and Italian fronts bring out
the best in him. He is appalled by the fighting at Verdun and vows
to return to America to start an underground newspaper that will
"tell the people what the war was really like" (*NN*, 189). On his
way to Italy with his ambulance unit, he gets drunk with Joe Williams in Genoa and shares Joe's distrust and contempt for the
"crookedness" (*NN*, 198) of the war. (Dick's experiences, once Hillyer returned to America in mid-1917, closely track Dos Passos' own
until early 1919, when Hillyer returned as an army officer, after
which they again resemble Hillyer's until Dick's return to America.) In Italy, Dick gets into a scrape—as did Dos Passos—that
epitomizes the false and destructive in the war temper. In a letter
home he had quoted with approval Joe's distrust of the war; he is
therefore to be dismissed from the Red Cross for his seditious opinions. As a Red Cross official tells him, "anybody who gets in the
way of the great machine the energy and devotion a hundred million patriots is building toward the stainless purpose of saving civilization from the Huns will be smashed like a fly" (*NN*, 209). In his
anger at this perversion of the ideal of freedom, Dick constructs "a
daydream of himself living in a sunscorched Spanish town, sending out flaming poems and manifestoes, calling young men to revolt against their butchers" (*NN*, 211). He even buys a compass to
help him cross the Pyrenees into freedom and open revolt. But in
fact he meets an old college friend, gets drunk with him, and finds
himself returning to America in order to join the army as an officer,
as prearranged by his mentor, Hiram Cooper. During the voyage
home he accidentally discovers the compass in his pocket. "Guiltily, he fished it out and dropped it overboard" (*NN*, 213). The opportunity for Dick to plot an independent course, one involving
danger and sacrifice, has been lost. His life now lies clearly
charted before him, and a compass is not required. He will always
flow with the tide, but he will do so with a tortured conscience,
guiltily.

Since both the Camera Eye persona and Dick are no longer

in combat areas, the Parisian salon world of Eveline, Eleanor, and Moorehouse—and later of the returned Dick—becomes the center of action of *Nineteen-Nineteen* through the remainder of the war and until the end of the peace conference in the spring of 1919. Dos Passos' strategy of reporting the war and the peace conference through the flow of lives across Eveline's and Eleanor's apartments results in the ironic trivialization of the momentous, in that the concerns of this world are narrowly personal. Whatever the whispered conversations in corners about the fate of nations, Eveline is preoccupied with her current affairs and Dick and Eleanor with their own well-being.

The war phase of *Nineteen-Nineteen* comes to an ironic climax with the Armistice, an event that occurs in a number of segments from its announcement at the close of Newsreel XXVIII (*NN*, 230) to the early portion of Eveline's last narrative segment (*NN*, 291–95). These juxtaposed repetitions of the end of the war distinguish between the superficial celebrations of the event (in the Newsreels and among Eveline's Paris crowd) and the profound emptiness that is its essential meaning. So for Joe Williams, in an obvious ironic play on the notion of a glorious and triumphant conclusion to the war, the Armistice celebration at St. Nazaire results in his death. And for the Camera Eye persona the Armistice finds him emptying slop cans on board a troopship bound for France. The theme that the war has served primarily to advance such qualities as those rendered metaphorically by Joe's violent and meaningless death and the persona's subjection to despotic control is reinforced by one of the major biographies of *Nineteen-Nineteen*, that of Wilson, which occurs immediately after Joe's death and the return overseas of the Camera Eye persona. Dos Passos uses the Wilson biography for two important purposes—to establish a link between the falseness of the war and the falseness of the peace conference, and to suggest the similarity between the corruption of language of Moorehouse, which dominated *The 42nd Parallel*, and that of Wilson, which is central to *Nineteen-Nineteen*.

Some of Dos Passos' vehemence toward Wilson is explained by Dos Passos' sharing in the common need to use historical figures to symbolize powerful national emotions, as in the focusing of one's hatred for the enemy on its leader during a war. Wilson, whatever the complexity of the man and his policies, thus becomes for Dos Passos a single-faceted embodiment of the evil of America's participation in the war. But Dos Passos also used the biography to express his own personal sense of betrayal by Wilson. As he noted elsewhere, he, like many of his generation, was "violently" for Wilson in the 1916 election because he kept us out of the European war.[28] Dos Passos never forgave Wilson for his swift change of policy after his 1917 inauguration.

Wilson, as portrayed by Dos Passos, is above all a man of words. His father was "a teacher of rhetoric in theological seminaries; the Wilsons lived in a universe of words linked into an incontrovertible firmament by two centuries of Calvinist divines" (*NN*, 241), and Wilson was brought up "between the bible and the dictionary" (*NN*, 241). He thus enters political life with a powerful self-righteousness. His political actions and beliefs—culminating in his leading the nation into a righteous war—are God's work. They were also Wilson's means of climbing the ladder of success. Wilson is therefore a more public equivalent of Moorehouse in his largely unconscious use of cant to advance his own interests. He is naively blind (like Roosevelt) to the possible source of his self-righteousness in his class assumptions and prejudices, and he is vulnerable—as he will be during the peace conference—to those who can manipulate this ingenuous self-righteousness for their own purposes. He thus sums up, in one satanic iconographical figure, the complementary themes of the American suppression of freedom in the name of freedom ("If you objected to making the world safe for cost plus democracy you went to jail with Debs"— *NN*, 246) and the American faith that to mouth a belief in "justice . . . and . . . liberty and . . . peace" (*NN*, 250) is to support the operative truth of these terms in American life. He is self-deceived, as is the American nation at large.

Daughter, whose initial segment appears after the Wilson biography, derives in part from Dos Passos' relationship to Crystal Ross, a young American graduate student he met in 1922. Of Texas background, Ross had had an especially close family life. Dos Passos courted her sporadically in Europe and America, including a visit to her family in Texas, until he was finally turned down in 1925.[29] (There is perhaps an echo of this refusal in Daughter's refusal of the radical journalist Webb Caruthers.) Dos Passos' personal relationship to Ross may account for Daughter being more a psychological than a sociological type. As the title of her narrative implies (and she is the only narrative figure whose narrative is not titled with a proper name), Dos Passos stresses, even more than he had done with other figures, the importance of Daughter's family in the determination of her nature. Raised as "Dad's onlyest sweetest little girl" (*NN*, 256) in a family of vigorous and protective Texas males (her mother is dead), she early develops a deep attachment to her father. The potential harmfulness of this attachment is revealed in her late adolescence by her chaotic unwillingness to acknowledge her love of Joe Whalen, an older man whose mature strength makes him a father figure. Dos Passos also draws upon Daughter's Texas origins to cast her as a special kind of American innocent. A headstrong young woman, she is almost entirely a creature of feeling rather than of thought. Thus, though she shares the usual provincial American's prejudices about foreigners and the urban working class, she responds openly and honestly to injustice when she encounters it at firsthand in a New Jersey textile strike. It is clear from her several brushes with death even before her arrival in Europe that her personal characteristics of suppressed guilt and impulsive honesty make her a candidate for disaster. The fulfillment of this potential, through her relationship with Dick, is the link between her narrative and the remainder of the novel.

Dick's return to Europe and Daughter's arrival signal the shift of *Nineteen-Nineteen* to the seemingly disparate but in fact closely intertwined subject matters of the peace conference and the various love affairs of the principal narrative figures. Present or passing through Paris at this point are not only Eveline, Eleanor, Moorehouse, Janey, Savage, and Daughter but also the minor figures of Jerry Burnham, George H. Barrow, and Don Stevens. While a glow of self-congratulatory righteousness hangs over the political and economic maneuverings of the peace conference (conveyed largely through the Newsreels and Moorehouse), a more convincing dramatization of the ethical character of the moment is communicated by the bitingly ironic biographies of Wilson and J. P. Morgan and by the romantic preoccupations of the major narrative figures.

The love affairs of Eveline and Moorehouse and of Daughter and Dick are initially fulfilling for the woman figures. Eveline finds a refuge in Moorehouse's seeming strength and authority from a series of casual relationships with weak men, and Daughter is drawn by Dick's charm and by his interest in her. In both instances, a woman who is open and unsophisticated in her feelings falls in love with, and is later abandoned by, a man who is empty and false but who also plays successfully for the moment the role of romantic lover. Dos Passos was suggesting by these essentially similar affairs that a basic consequence of our national innocence, of our desire to believe, was that it could be preyed upon (seduced

if you will) by the clever and self-serving. He was in effect retelling
the story of Henry James' Daisy Miller, the impulsive young American girl who is destroyed by her own innocence in a cosmopolitan
European setting. But Dos Passos' Daisies symbolize—given the
context of the peace conference—a political as well as a romantic
innocence. This association is made explicit late in Dick's relationship with Daughter, when his desertion of her, and her subsequent
death, are closely linked to Dick's joining of Moorehouse's entourage.

Dos Passos' use of love themes in *Nineteen-Nineteen* to symbolize large-scale limitations in the American psyche is characteristic of his technique in the trilogy as a whole. Dos Passos has been
criticized for failing to portray love convincingly, and especially, as
in his depiction of Daughter, for lacking "the gift of evincing the
intense energy of sexual passion."[30] But this criticism fails to acknowledge his ironic stylization of sexual experience. For Dos Passos in *U.S.A.*, a man and a woman falling in love and sleeping with
each other is not only a personal event but also part of a larger
pattern of events in the social and moral fabric of the nation as a
whole. This epic cast of mind will occasionally result in excessive
caricature or in a symbolic clarity verging on moral allegory, as in
the portrayal of Maisie and Della or in the implication of Eleanor's
frigidity. At their best, however, as in the Dick-Daughter relationship, Dos Passos' love stories in *U.S.A.* illumine the tragic dimensions both of distinctive individuals and of the national experience
as a whole.

Indeed, it was probably to enhance the inherent narrative
power of the love affair between Dick and Daughter that Dos Passos pushed on quickly to its climax in two consecutive narrative
segments. In Dick's narrative we learn of his return to Europe and
his involvement in the Moorehouse group, his courtship and winning of Daughter during a brief few days in Rome, and his refusal
to come to her aid in her pregnancy despite her complete dependence on him. Daughter's narrative swiftly reprises some of the
same material involving her relationship to Dick in Rome and Paris
(where she has come to plead with him) and then goes on to her
desperate seeking of a means of self-destruction. The two segments in conjunction comprise the full moral collapse of Dick. He
is now, as an officer in Rome and Paris, distant from the actuality of
war, and he adopts increasingly the poses and attitudes of his
class.[31] More significantly, Dick is quickly drawn into Moorehouse's orbit. In particular, he forms an unspoken alliance with

Eleanor, as both sense their complementary (rather than rival) need of Moorehouse to further their own self-interest. In a momentary flush of sentiment, Dick contemplates marrying Daughter. But Eleanor—sensing this "weakness" in Dick—successfully reminds him that "an unsuitable marriage has been the ruination of many a promising young fellow" (*NN*, 393). In a "denial scene" worthy of a morality play, Dick refuses to acknowledge to Eleanor that he and Daughter are deeply involved (thus denying his own commitment to Daughter), and from this moment his and Daughter's fates are sealed. He has deserted Daughter's "honesty" for the "falsity" of the Moorehouse camp, and will soon be rewarded, with Eleanor's aid, by the promise of a good job with Moorehouse. And Daughter, realizing at last Dick's shallowness and cruelty, will rush to her death. As Dos Passos the moralist assumes full control over Dick's destiny, he also ensures that Dick's betrayal of all that was potentially worthwhile in him for material advantage will be paid for by inner pain. Dick's homosexual tendencies now become more evident, and as he becomes dependent on lies, he increasingly experiences the doppelgänger effect of hearing his own voice "like somebody else's voice in his ears" (*NN*, 389).

Eveline's affair with Moorehouse bears even more directly on the false motives within the peace conference, because of Moorehouse's personal participation in the conference. Moorehouse, while with Eveline on the Riviera, had insisted that "people had misunderstood [the] beautiful friendship [between him and Eleanor] that had always been free from the sensual and the degrading" (*NN*, 310). Back in Paris, however, he is cold and distant, and the distraught Eveline discovers him in bed with Eleanor. But Moorehouse had spoken and acted consistently in the two major areas of his life. His use of the language of a "spiritual" relationship to obscure the truth of his relationship with Eleanor is similar to his dependence on a rhetoric of world cooperation to obscure the selfish national aims of the participants (including himself) in the peace conference.

A final historical event associated with the war, the abortive revolutionary rising of May Day 1919, runs through a number of modal segments toward the conclusion of *Nineteen-Nineteen*. As in his depiction of America's entrance into the war (at the close of *The 42nd Parallel*) and of the Armistice, Dos Passos undercuts a presumably heroic or celebratory moment by a series of events and attitudes that dramatize the essential falseness of the moment. It is spring in Paris, but the note of hope in the season has been destroyed by the realization that the peace conference continues to reflect the deeply divisive national self-interests that were the cause of the war itself. A possible alternative to self-interest—a revolutionary socialist society, as in Russia—is a possibility, with the Newsreels blaring the danger of simultaneous risings throughout Europe on May Day. But the event itself, as depicted at the close of Eveline's last narrative segment and in Camera Eye (40), is a failure. The workers do not rise. Instead, middle-class life—as represented by Eveline beginning the affair with Paul that will end in marriage, and the Camera Eye persona going on (in Camera Eye (41)) to attend an anarchist picnic—is again triumphant.

The conclusion of the "European phase" of early-twentieth-century American history is heralded by Daughter's death in Paris in the spring of 1919. Daughter, after being rejected by Dick, finds a temporary haven in the attentions of George H. Barrow. Barrow's joining of a faith in Wilson and the peace conference and a crude effort to seduce Daughter sums up, in caricatured form, the intertwined motifs of the political and the sexual that have dominated the Paris portion of *Nineteen-Nineteen*. In one of the gathering scenes Dos Passos introduces toward the close of each novel in the trilogy, Barrow and Daughter go to a restaurant to have dinner with Eveline and Jerry Burnham and there encounter a party consisting of Moorehouse, Eleanor, and Savage. As usual in this kind of scene, Dos Passos translates moral and emotional reality into scenic geography. The break between Dick and Daughter is symbolized by his absorption into the Moorehouse group, Eveline's isolation is represented by her replacement as Moorehouse's consort by Eleanor, and Daughter's lack of a resource in her need is dramatized by her having turned to the worthless Barrow. It is at this point that Daughter takes final refuge in a drunken French aviator who transforms her back into her "true" role as his "sistair." At her insistence he takes them both on a dawn joyride over Paris that ends in her death.

Daughter's death at the moment of the collapse of the European revolutionary movement is followed by a brief but significant body of material dealing with the analogous failure of the radical left in America during and shortly after America's participation in the war. This portion of the novel contains the narrative of Ben Compton and the biographies of Joe Hill and Wesley Everest. Ben's narrative is unusual in that he is the only figure in the trilogy who receives but a single narrative segment. But since we have already met Ben briefly in the narratives of Janey, Charley, and Daughter, since he will later play a major role in Mary's narrative in *The Big Money*, and since the IWW movement in the West and textile strikes in the East (two of his principal areas of experience) are also present in Mac's and Mary's narratives, Dos Passos apparently felt that he could foreshorten Ben's narrative to one segment without adversely affecting either his impact as a character or the formal balance of the trilogy. Dos Passos encountered the model of Ben, a young Marxist lawyer named Albert Weisbord, during the Passaic textile strike of 1926[32]—the same strike about which he had written his "300 N.Y. Agitators Reach Passaic." He had been sufficiently interested in the type of the first-generation Jewish radical—an important figure in left-wing movements of the 1920s and 1930s—to portray him in Walter Greenberg, a major character in *Airways, Inc.*, the play he had completed in 1928. By 1929, when Dos Passos was at work on *The 42nd Parallel*, Weisbord's career became of even greater interest when he was expelled from the Communist party for failure to follow the party line. By the mid-1930s, Dos Passos had come to believe that a dismissal of this kind was the inevitable fate of the ideological purist when he came into conflict with an inflexible party discipline.

Ben, in his youthful revolt against the older and conventional ways of his family and culture, is a familiar figure in American immigrant fiction. But as Dos Passos tries to suggest by his placing of quotes from Marx at strategic places in Ben's narrative, Ben is also a true believer whose life constitutes the history of a pure radical faith in America. Initially this faith is linked to the IWW, as Ben participates in the western free-speech movement during the early phases of the European war. But he is soon drawn to the Communist party as the fullest expression of Marxist belief, particularly after the Russian revolution of early 1917. Dos Passos' most striking dramatization of the archetypal in Ben's life, however, resides less in the origin and form of his belief than in its consequences. For whether Ben is leading strikes, parading for free speech, or making speeches in support of pacifism, his right to act and speak freely is brutally suppressed. His life is thus a series of beatings and jailings, culminating in a twenty-year prison term for attacking America's participation in the war. His link to the lives of Joe Hill and Wesley Everest in the biographies adjoining his narrative is that they are all—like Sacco and Vanzetti to come—martyrs to the right of Americans to freely express their beliefs, with the state and the mob indistinguishable in their direct assault on this freedom.

As is characteristic of Dos Passos' most persuasively depicted narrative figures, Ben's archetypal role also embodies a deeply individual element that lends to his portrayal a tragic dimension. Ben's commitment to ideology in the face of other, equally compelling but suppressed personal needs is a tragic irony in his life comparable to that of the constant denial of his right to speak in a free society. This aspect of Ben's life is to receive full expression in his relationships to Mary and to the Communist party in *The Big Money*, but it is already present in *Nineteen-Nineteen* in his love affair with Helen Mauer, a fellow radical. Although he and Helen fall in love and live together as any young couple might, their relationship is controlled by Marxist belief. This control is in part comically rendered by Dos Passos, as in his free-indirect-discourse parody of radical "romance" language and belief of the 1920s and 1930s. "There were bedbugs in the bed, but they told each other that they were as happy as they could be under the capitalist system, that some day they'd have a free society where workers wouldn't have to huddle in filthy lodginghouses full of bedbugs or row with landladies and lovers could have babies if they wanted to" (*NN*, 433). But when Ben returns from a jail sentence to find Helen living with an English "comrade," he is bitter and angry despite Helen's appeal to the radical belief that "we're all comrades" (*NN*, 434). Despite his Marxist faith, Ben will always have difficulty structuring his emotional life along lines determined by radical ideology, and he will pay a large price—as we will come to understand—for his "successful" suppression of his basic humanity in the name of orthodox belief.

This "interlude" dealing with the fate of the radical left in America during and shortly after the war—a section that looks forward to the full-scale depiction of American radicalism during the 1920s in *The Big Money*—is interwoven with four segments that bring *Nineteen-Nineteen* and the war theme in the trilogy to a close. (Interwoven in the sense that the biography of Wesley Everest, "Paul Bunyan," plays a role in both sections.) In *Nineteen-Nineteen*, as in the other two novels of the trilogy, Dos Passos makes his conclusion a symbolic restatement of the theme of the novel as a whole. In the Camera Eye's last segment, in the biography of Everest, in Savage's last narrative segment, and in "The Body of an American," Americans are preparing to return or have just returned from the war. Dos Passos sums up in these juxtaposed returns the meaning of our national experience abroad as saviors of American values.

Camera Eye (42) finds the persona moving scrap on and off a railroad car while serving in an army casual labor unit. His service record has been lost, and he and the scrap iron are in limbo—"spare parts no outfit wanted to use" (*NN*, 454). Despite the illusion of having been "reborn" into freedom through his months of temporary duty as a student in Paris, the more powerful and permanent meaning of the war for the Camera Eye persona and for all those others who participated in it is rendered by this scene of anonymous men engaged in mechanical and meaningless actions that are gilded over by a mindless empty sloganizing. ("KEEP THE BOYS FIT TO GO HOME" is the YMCA slogan that runs as a refrain through the segment.) Wesley Everest, on the other hand, has already returned to America after serving in the army, where he won a medal as a sharpshooter, and he has again become a logger on the West Coast. On Armistice Day 1919, Everest and his fellow IWW members are attacked by a mob from the American Legion, and Everest is lynched. So much for Paul Bunyan, whether former fighter for American democracy or not, if he happens to be an IWW man. Savage's very brief narrative segment—only six pages—is devoted primarily to a party given by Eleanor to celebrate the forthcoming marriage of Eveline and Paul Johnson just prior to the return of the Moorehouse group to America. But first we discover Moorehouse at a final press conference announcing "a new era of international cooperation that was dawning in which great aggregates of capital would work together for peace and democracy" (*NN*, 464). At the party, Dick, in his new role, defends Moorehouse against Don Stevens's attack, everyone gets drunk in a sad, empty way at the prospect of Eveline's marriage, and a parakeet, which Eleanor had purchased as a present, dies. The death of the parakeet is a conscious trivialization by Dos Passos of a major meaning of the war. Its demise during this seemingly celebratory moment symbolizes, not those who died in the war, but the failure of moral courage of those who have betrayed themselves (such as Dick and Eveline) within the larger national self-betrayal that has been the war. Only the half-derisive, half-sardonic death of the parakeet, Dos Passos seems to be saying, could adequately render this less apparent but equally significant consequence of the war.

Eleanor's farewell party for Eveline is followed almost immediately (a final Newsreel intervenes) by a far more profound and angry account of a return from the war in "The Body of an American." The form of the segment echoes that of the biographies in general and more specifically of the "U.S.A." prologue and the "Vag" epilogue. The body is that of John Doe, an average American with typical experiences and attitudes. We learn of these in a Whitmanesque catalog of origins and occupations that is notable for the absence of any beliefs by Doe except for the clichés of American culture. The underlying truth of his life in the army—as communicated by the repeated motif of *"Say buddy cant you tell me how I can get back to my outfit?"* (*NN*, 471)—is that he is lost. And out of the lack of value and directionless motion that are the essential truths of the American nation at war comes death in the form of a shell that renders him an anonymous corpse. Woven into this account of the life and death of John Doe, in one of Dos Passos' most bitter uses of the documentary for ironic purposes, are congressional resolutions, newspaper reports, and proclamations that deal with the selection of the Unknown Soldier who will lie at Arlington to symbolize the official high values that brought us into the war. The "biography" ends, "Woodrow Wilson brought a bouquet of poppies" (*NN*, 473). The dead parakeet, Dos Passos seems to be saying, may be the artist's consciously absurdist symbol of the effect of the war experience on specific individuals. But the death of John Doe, and the sanctification of his death by the nation at large, is an unconscious and far more profoundly absurd image of the tragic impact of the war on our national ideals.

The Big Money is more of an independent novel than either of the first two novels of the trilogy. There is a tighter linking of narrative figures between the initial two novels—Moorehouse and his group quickly make the transition from New York to Paris—and the war ethic that dominated the close of *The 42nd Parallel* permeates *Nineteen-Nineteen*. In *The Big Money*, on the other hand, a largely new cast of narrative figures is engaged in acquiring wealth in such new areas of American life as the aircraft and film industries. In addition, Dos Passos' treatment of the American left—a subject common to all three novels—differs in *The Big Money*. His sympathetic and at worst bemused depiction of American radicalism in the narratives of Mac and Ben now becomes far more critical in Mary French's narrative, as his long-brewing disillusionment with the Communist party reached a climax during the mid-1930s, in the midst of writing *The Big Money*.[33] And, finally, Dos Passos achieved in *The Big Money* his most sharply focused expression of the relationship of a national ethos of freedom to the potential death or rebirth of the individual spirit. *The Big Money* can thus be read not only as a powerful climax to the trilogy but, more so than the other two novels, as a work of independent force and integrity.

"COLONEL HOUSE ARRIVES FROM EUROPE," a headline announces in the first Newsreel of *The Big Money*. It is 1919, the war and the peace conference are over, and Americans who served or worked overseas are coming home. Theirs should be a triumphant return—they are victors both in arms and in peace— but the imagery of the arrival in New York of Charley Anderson and the Camera Eye persona conveys a very different mood. Charley is hung over and fogbound in New York harbor, while the Camera Eye persona is confronted by a "crookedfaced customs inspector" who is suspicious of the "French books" he has brought home with him (*BM*, 28). American postwar life, it is clear, cannot be adequately defined by a conventional rhetoric of noble tasks heroically performed.

The theme of discovery—what is the nature of American life of the 1920s, and how can one best accommodate to that life?— dominates the long opening portion of *The Big Money*, a section devoted to the first four segments of Charley Anderson's narrative, the biographies of Taylor, Ford, and Veblen, and the two initial Camera Eye segments. Anderson is an appropriate narrative figure to engage in this effort in definition. When we last encountered him, at the close of *The 42nd Parallel*, he was bound for France to serve in the ambulance corps. He has now returned an aviator, an officer, and a war hero. He has been transformed from an itinerant mechanic on the order of Mac to an identity from which he can advance in ways denied by his earlier class roles. (Dos Passos probably omits a depiction of Anderson's war experiences in *Nineteen-Nineteen* because it is not what Anderson has done in the war that is significant but rather what effect his new identity will have on him after the war.) Charley is thus almost a blank page at the opening of *The Big Money*. His largely apolitical character, in which only the wish to get ahead is apparent, is an empty space on which the 1920s as an era of American life can imprint itself boldly and clearly.

Charley's responsiveness to his times begins almost immediately on his arrival in New York, when he meets Doris, the daughter of wealthy, upper-class New Yorkers. Doris is one of F. Scott Fitzgerald's "golden girls" in her absolute self-absorption and brittle sophistication. She will play the same role in Charley's life as Daisy does in *The Great Gatsby* and as Sondra does in Dreiser's

An American Tragedy. That is, Charley responds to her as a secular icon—as a figure whose wealth and class promise an earthly paradise. Charley, however, despite being a war hero, is broke, and thus has little chance to attract and win a Doris. His return to Minneapolis and a mean job with his brother confirms his distaste for his old status and his determination to live in New York, to be successful, and to win Doris. He will attempt to translate into the actualities of his life Eveline's response to America on her own return from the war. "New York's the capital now," she says, but to live in a capital it is necessary to "make a lot of money right away quick" (*BM,* 65).

The ways in which money can be made in New York are laid before Charley when he becomes a member of the Askew-Merritt airplane motor company on his return to New York from the Midwest. One model is provided by his old war comrade, Joe Askew, a hardworking family man who is committed to the slow proving of their product. Another is provided by Nat Benton, a Wall Street broker and advisor to the firm, from whom he learns that "a lot of money right away quick" can best be made, not by producing things, but by manipulating the companies producing things. And that to make money in this way, secrecy and duplicity are required. And since Doris—or rather what Doris represents—is the prize, Charley soon succumbs to the temptation to take the easy way. He will begin to secretly buy company stock, and he will eventually betray both Askew and the company.

In a further example of one of Dos Passos' basic fictional devices, Charley also begins to take the easy way in his sexual life. He had met Paul and Eveline on the boat returning them all to America. With Eveline now a bored and depressed wife and mother, Charley makes an easy sexual conquest of her despite Paul having aided and befriended him during his early, difficult days in New York. In the betrayal of both Askew and Paul, Charley's always present but undeveloped moral sensibility is deeply though unconsciously troubled. He now begins the cycle of business and sexual "triumphs" followed by prolonged, self-destructive binges that in less than a decade will reduce him to a dissolute, self-pitying shell. In Charley's material rise and spiritual decay during the 1920s, Dos Passos sketched an ethical allegory of the decade independent of the apocalypse of the crash and depression.

A social map of the 1920s, one with immediate relevance to Charley's career, is present in the biographies of Taylor, Ford, and Veblen that are interwoven with Charley's four initial narrative segments. Taylor and Ford constitute the union of engineering genius and cutthroat entrepreneurship that is the dominant economic ethic of the 1920s, and Veblen is the principal critic of this ethic and thus also of Anderson himself. It was Taylor who brought into full expression the "American Plan" of timed industrial processes, leading to the inhuman pressures of the assembly line, and it was Ford who realized the potential of Taylor's ideas for mass production. Ford also reveals the full character of modern entrepreneurial capitalism in which mass production is mass control. ("Henry Ford had ideas about other things . . ."—*BM,* 50.) The two biographies are thus immediately pertinent to Anderson's success story in that he too is a tinkerer who will become a manufacturer and capitalist, and that he too—after his move to Detroit—will begin to think of his employees as assembly-line machines.

The Veblen biography is a suitable climax to Anderson's initial four segments as well as an introduction to Mary French's narrative, which follows. Veblen had sketched in his later writing "a new diagram of a society dominated by monopoly capitalism," a society characterized by "the sabotage of production by business" and "the sabotage of life by blind need for money profits" (*BM,* 101). Like Mary French, Dos Passos had read Veblen while in college,[34] but it was not until the early 1930s that he reread him and discovered in Veblen's interpretation of American capitalism a confirmation of his own beliefs.[35] For Veblen's quarrel was not with the machine or with industrial enterprise but with the trusting of the economic and political consequences of the engineering capacity of America to a business civilization and the profit motive. Veblen's beliefs helped inspire the Technocracy movement, which in the early 1930s—in response to the onset of the depression—had considerable appeal because of its advocacy of a society led by engineers rather than by politicians or businessmen.[36] Dos Passos in Anderson's narrative was dramatizing a rough version of a Technocracy fable, in which Charley Anderson, the American as engineer, is controlled by a business rather than a production ethic, with deleterious consequences both for himself and his society.

Veblen also plays another role in this portion of the novel. Like Frank Lloyd Wright later in *The Big Money,* he stands as a beacon of intellectual and artistic integrity in a largely false age. His method, like Baroja's, is to dissect "the century with a scalpel so keen, so comical, so exact"; thus his career suffers—in the principal motif of the biography—"from [his] constitutional inability to say yes" (*BM,* 93). As a naysayer to the American dream of success in its archetypal twentieth-century form, he tasted throughout his life "the bitter drink" of personal failure, and is therefore another in Dos Passos' gallery of martyred radicals. But the "memorial" of the"sharp clear prism of his mind" (*BM*, 105) remains as an inspiration for a Camera Eye persona or a Mary French, both of whom wish to see themselves and American life clearly rather than through the blurred glass of its false myths.

The theme of self-discovery, of trying out new roles (and thus new costumes) in the "new" world of postwar America, closely links the early segments of Charley Anderson's narrative and those of the Camera Eye persona. Anderson had returned from the war in the uniform of an officer and had immediately realized the usefulness of this costume and identity in providing entry into areas of life previously closed to him. And in a comic confirmation of the advantages of assumed identities, Charley is mistaken by a girl for the famous columnist Charles Edward Holden and thereby gains an easy conquest. The advantages of assumed roles have thus been amply demonstrated to Charley, and his transformation from what he truly is—"only a mechanic"—to capitalist entrepreneur has begun. The Camera Eye persona also experiences the possibility of adopting various advantageous roles after his adventures in Arabia and after the success of *Three Soldiers*. These roles require new costuming—a "tailcoat too small a pair of dresstrousers too large" to attend a party in Damascus, and a "forsomebodyelsetailored dress suit" for a lecture in New York. Rejecting these ill-fitting identities and costumes, he "make[s] himself scarce down a manhole." These are not the positions, he sums up, "for which he made application at the employmentagency" (*BM*, 30–31).

The centrality in the opening portion of *The Big Money* of the related motifs of identity and role is made explicit by Dos Passos' devotion of an entire early Newsreel to Positions-Open advertisements (*BM*, 28–29). The motifs continue to be prominent in the several Camera Eye segments that deal with the persona's wanderings in New York in search of an identity ("has he any?   face"—*BM*, 197) and in Mary French's narrative. For Mary, we quickly realize, is also seeking a more independent and fulfilling role in life than the one imposed on her by her class identity.

There is no known source for the portrait of Mary French, though no doubt Dos Passos met many Mary Frenches—girls of good family attempting to aid the cause of social justice by typing stencils—during the period of his most active participation in radical causes in the late 1920s and early 1930s. Perhaps his placing of Mary as a worker for the Sacco-Vanzetti Defense Committee, a group he also aided, indicates where he encountered either the specific source for Mary or her general prototype. Most probably Mary lacked a specific model, however, given Dos Passos' notion of her as an almost anonymous figure. "Deskworker—one of the little women who run desks," he reminded himself in a note.[37]

Mary's early life is closely related to that of several other figures in *U.S.A.* Like the Camera Eye persona, her family configuration of a father with an active social conscience and a mother whose life is controlled by upper-class values impells her toward a fulfillment of her father's beliefs within her own range of experience. And because her overworked father—a doctor who devoted his life to treating the poor—stirred her sympathy and love, she will—like Daughter—find her personal life conditioned by this relationship and will fall in love with men whom she can mother.

Mary's largely emotional commitment to left-wing causes permitted Dos Passos to express his doubts both about the personal consequences of a faith of this kind and about the direction of the American left in general. As a young woman, Mary, in a reaction typical of her response to human misery throughout her life, views the poverty of south Chicago in human rather than ideological terms. "It was so awful the way the poor people lived and the cracked red knuckles of the women who took in washing and the scabby heads of the little children and the clatter and the gritty wind on South Halstead Street and the stench of the stockyards" (*BM*, 114). Although Mary has attended college, has read Veblen, and will eventually acquire the rhetoric of the left, her career as an activist—from the Pittsburgh steel strike of 1919 to the New Jersey textile strikes to the Sacco-Vanzetti case to the coal strikes of the early 1930s—rests primarily on her instinctive desire to protect and nurture the hungry, to act as a mother, in short, for those requiring aid and comfort. And in each major instance of playing this role in a social cause, Mary also has an affair with a left-winger who himself demands or requires a similar kind of nurturing or comforting. So, for example, she is converted fully to radical union work in Pittsburgh when, sent out by a newspaper editor to confirm a Moorehouse set of clichés about the striking steelworkers (how well off they are and how they are being misled by the Reds), she discovers simultaneously their desperate poverty and a cubbish young striker, Gus, who engages her deeply. Throughout her life Mary will seek to fulfill her mothering need in these interwoven ways. And because she responds to life almost entirely from the heart, with an unqualified openness and fullness, she is to be exploited, betrayed, and defeated both by her lovers and by her causes. Indeed, in the principal pathetic irony of her life, she is forced—by the weakness or blindness of her radical lovers—to abort the children who would have provided the fullest outlet for her essential nature.

An important distinction thus exists between Mary and the Camera Eye persona as figures who escape their origins into a radical activism. Mary's very strength—her feeling nature—is also her weakness, as is illustrated by her affairs with George H. Barrow and Don Stevens. She lives with Barrow and Stevens because each for a time combines a need for her with a radical position. The Camera Eye persona, however, in a segment that immediately follows Mary's Pittsburgh experiences, and in which he himself has experimented in radical activism, quickly comes to distrust the rhetoric and certainties of Barrow or Stevens—"the snatch for a slogan . . . and then the easy climb slogan by slogan to applause" (*BM*, 149). For him, unlike Mary, who is drawn to belief by her need to feel, "doubt is the whetstone of understanding" (*BM*, 150).

The New York experiences of Charley Anderson and the Camera Eye persona—the one searching for the big money, the other seeking an answer to his doubts—and Mary's arrival in New York after the collapse of her affair with Barrow are followed by the early life of the New York born and raised Margo Dowling. Margo will rise to become a Hollywood star, and for that portion of her career, as well as for his general conception of her life, Dos Passos drew upon both his own personal experience of Hollywood and the myth of Hollywood already in place in the early 1930s. Desperate, after a severe illness, for enough money to continue working on *The Big Money*, and also in need of background material for Margo's later career, Dos Passos agreed in the summer of 1934 to go to Hollywood to work on the script of *The Devil Is a Woman*, a film that Josef von Sternberg was preparing for Marlene Dietrich. From this brief exposure (he became ill again and spent most of his time in Hollywood in bed), Dos Passos concocted a vision of Hollywood as a surreal epitome of American desires and fantasies. Dos Passos' Hollywood, like the movies it produced, is a world of the phonily glamorous and exotic in which the sex siren and her artistic director ruled supreme. In Dietrich (with a touch of Jean Harlow) and von Sternberg Dos Passos found apt models for these types.

With the possible exception of Daughter, Margo's basic nature is more powerfully shaped by her early life than any other figure in *U.S.A.* She loves her father, a good-natured Irish drunkard, but feels betrayed when he deserts her and her stepmother, Agnes. Hard times follow until Agnes begins living with the actor Frank Mandeville. Margo turns out to be a pretty, clever girl, and Frank both introduces her to theatrical life and rapes her. These two early experiences with men key Margo's responses to life despite her essentially warm and generous nature. Men are to be distrusted, and since their principal interest in her is sexual, their need and her distrust can be turned into a source of power. Margo's capacity for love has been anesthetized by these early betrayals, but her lack of feeling gives her the ability to use feelings of others for her own ends. And given her attractivenss, shrewdness, and need, these ends move her toward the climactic role of movie star, in which the desire of the nation as a whole to possess her provides her with wealth and fame. Her career will become, in its Hollywood phase, the "art" equivalent of Moorehouse's in advertising and public relations. Both are engaged in the merchandising of mythic areas of the American dream—he of freedom and opportunity, she of love. And both Moorehouse's public relation releases and her movies are equally false in their depiction of the possibilities of life in America.

Although Margo's first segment ends with her as a young girl eloping to Cuba with her boyish husband Tony to escape Frank and Agnes, the nature and direction of her entire career are signaled by the biographies of Isadora Duncan and Rudolph Valentino that enclose the segment. "Art and Isadora" is a tongue-in-cheek celebration of Duncan's attempt to live to the full the ideal of the free artist in opposition to the conventions of society. But though Duncan's bohemian poses are rendered with more than a touch of irony, Dos Passos for the most part applauds her courageous and ultimately tragic independence of spirit and life. She is, in a sense, the artist "old style"—the artistic sensibility struggling in a still largely repressive Victorian world. Valentino, on the other hand, is very much the artist "new style." He is almost entirely a Hollywood-made product. Whatever his own modest talents and distinctive nature, he is recreated into a masculine sex symbol and marketed as such. Dos Passos' devotion of much of Valentino's biography to the frenzy and morbidity surrounding his illness, death, and funeral shapes these events into the symbolic equivalent of his role in the national psyche.

Much of the strength of *The Big Money* lies in the fullness and vitality of Dos Passos' characterization of the three principal narrative figures in the novel—Charley, Mary, and Margo. Although still fulfilling various archetypal roles in the overall design of *U.S.A.*, they differ from many of the other figures in the trilogy in their greater complexity and depth—in their greater humanity, in short. Aside from being less programmatic, each also has a major sympathetically portrayed characteristic—Charley's love of a well-operating machine, Mary's generosity and perseverance of spirit, and Margo's gamine toughness and strength. Thus the defeat of each figure has a greater poignancy than the decline, for example, of Mac or Eleanor. Dos Passos' art in *The Big Money* has therefore reached the full extent of its dual sources of strength. Committed to an experimental method in which a conventional reliance on character and event was to be subordinated to a juxtapositional cubism, he nevertheless found in *The Big Money* a means of combining the strengths of both traditional and modernistic forms of fictional expression.

Having introduced the three major narrative figures and their general spheres of activity, Dos Passos shifts *The Big Money* into a long series of alternating narrative segments devoted to Margo and Charley. We initially follow their separate experiences, until they meet in Jacksonville. Then, after several closely interlaced segments, in which each appears in the other's narrative, Charley dies, and attention is focused fully—in Margo's last segment—on her success in Hollywood. Dos Passos clearly wished by this narrative structure to suggest the underlying similarity of Charley and Margo and of their fates despite the appearances of major differences between the airplane manufacturer who dies following an automobile accident and the successful Hollywood actress.

Charley's life in New York has assumed its definitive pattern. Anxious to push ahead quickly, he begins to speculate in the market, an activity that requires a betrayal of his friend and benefactor Joe Askew. But despite his success, Doris has found a more attractive suitor in a wealthy Englishman from an old family. Charley's response—to get drunk and to push on to Detroit—is characteristic. He has begun the cycle of material advance and destructive self-hate that will culminate in his fatal accident. In Detroit, Charley discovers a surrogate Doris in Gladys, a banker's daughter. She, too, is wealth and class and is a bitch, and Charley, after their marriage, finds himself in an upper-middle-class version of the condition of Joe and Mac—married to a woman who always asks for more. He begins to take refuge in a sentimental self-image. He is only a "dumb mechanic," he often tells himself or his head mechanic, Bill Cermak, who has accompanied him from New York to Detroit. He is not an exploitative manufacturer, a stock market speculator, and a womanizer, but, like the Wright brothers, whose biography immediately precedes the account of Charley's Detroit years, he is only a mechanic. He is washed clean of his sins by his "pure" mechanic's heart.

The key symbolic event in Charley's life occurs at the height of his success in Detroit. For the moment Charley feels on top of the world. He has just made an unrepulsed initial pass at his pretty secretary, he has earned $13,000 in one day on the market, and he is about to fly to New York in a new plane with Cermak. But when Bill speaks to him, as one old mechanic to another, about working conditions at the plant, Charley replies in management formulas that echo Moorehouse's platitudes. "We've got a responsibility toward our investors," he tells Bill. "If every department don't click like a machine we're rooked. . . . we've got to have some patriotism. . . . the industry's the first line of national defense" (BM, 313–14). With this full endorsement of a Moorehouse rhetoric that disguises the ruthless exploitation of the work force by appeals to the rights of investors and the needs of the nation, Charley bids farewell to that part of his nature that had earlier declared to Cermak, "You and me, Bill, the mechanics against the world" (BM, 229). Bill's death, in an accident as they take off for New York, is thus one of the clearest examples of Dos Passos' recurrent use of the device of a symbolic death of the self through the death of another who exemplifies the best part of one's self.

Charley's marriage to Gladys brings into sharp focus two issues related to the frequent description of Dos Passos as a naturalistic novelist. By this designation is frequently meant a novelist's use of "sordid" or sensationalistic subject matter to document in detail a deterministic view of experience, in which man's fate is shaped by social forces beyond his control. These aspects of naturalistic fiction do indeed appear in U.S.A., but the specific nature of their presence in Dos Passos' depiction of Charley's marriage to Gladys suggests that they are, in their concrete fictional rendering, themes and subject matter of considerable complexity and sophistication rather than of a crude simplicity, as is often held. So, for example, Charley becomes involved in a love triangle not long after his arrival in Detroit. He is attracted to Ann Bledsoe, a girl of solid common sense who would obviously be good for him. But when Gladys comes on the scene, with her powerful echo of Doris' sexuality of wealth, and sets out to win Charley away from Ann, he is easy prey and quickly succumbs. Is Charley's "fall," in his marriage to Gladys, his own responsibility or he is a victim of Society? The answer is that it is impossible in this instance, and in many like it in the trilogy, to dissect and categorize precise degrees of responsibility. Society, in the form of Gladys as a social goal that Charley has already been conditioned to desire, no doubt plays a part in his actions. But Charley himself, since he realizes Ann's positive qualities and senses the danger represented by Gladys, should be wary. Is Charley too weak and Society too strong, or is Charley not strong enough in resisting what he knows he should resist? There are no answers to these questions because they are not questions that Dos Passos is seeking to answer. He is rather engaged in dramatizing the ineffable union of human weakness and conditioning force present in most instances of choice. And though one might with some justice claim that the narrative figures in *U.S.A.* appear to be more victims than choosers, Dos Passos' indictment of personal weakness and his celebration of moral courage in the biographies of the trilogy are a clear indication that he held no general belief in the notion of a fully conditioned universe.

Gladys and Charley spend their honeymoon night in a train compartment. Gladys is nervous and apprehensive and asks Charley to postpone making love. But Charley is angrily demanding, and "Afterwards . . . she bled a great deal" (*BM*, 306). This is no doubt a Zolaesque detail, and *U.S.A.* contains a good deal of similar material bearing directly on the physical in experience. But this material, as in the instance of Gladys' bleeding, is far from being principally a sensationalistic documentation of the centrality of the animal in man's nature and existence. Rather, it usually plays a symbolic role in a complex moral theme. Charley, in his own unconscious belief, has bought and paid for Gladys—has paid both in coin and spirit. His brutal taking of her, and her bleeding, are the symbols of his and her degradation in this transaction. And Gladys herself will later make Charley pay dearly for the blood she has shed.

While recovering in Florida from his airplane accident, Charley meets Margo. Her escape to Cuba with Tony had imprisoned her within the narrow life of a married woman in a Latin American country, and she had sought to flee this world as well. The means she had adopted are to serve her self-advancement throughout her career. She tells the young American consul a cock-and-bull story and also allows him to sleep with her, whereupon he helps her to leave Tony and Cuba. Margo has now assumed her full picaro role. She will always invent stories about herself (usually ones in which she is an innocent victim) in order to deceive, and these combined with her only concrete asset—her sexual attractiveness—will give her the advantage over those otherwise stronger than she. Both acts—her lies and her casual sex—are amoral or perhaps even moral, since they are her only means of survival in a hazardous world. They thus resemble Huck Finn's lies and thefts under similar circumstances. In addition, they constitute Margo's "training" for her climactic joining of deceptive innocence and implied sexuality in the romantic parts she will play in Hollywood movies.

On returning from Cuba to New York, Margo soon has the chance to continue perfecting her role when she meets Tad, a Yale halfback from a wealthy family. Although now in a Broadway chorus, she adopts the pose of a pure young girl, knowing that this is the only way to win and hold the conventional and simpleminded Tad. ("I don't need to remind you what type of animal is born every minute" (*BM*, 385), a Florida real estate operator will later tell her.) But at this point another major characteristic of Margo's nature appears. Finding Tad likeable, she permits him to sleep with her on a trip to Florida. And when a down-and-out Tony (now also clearly a homosexual) unexpectedly appears during this trip, she takes him in out of pity. Both acts cause her to lose the golden opportunity represented by Tad. Margo (again like Huck) is often "weakened" by a good heart, a weakness best defined in the course of her narrative by her constant aid of the ungrateful but always needful Tony.

It is at this moment, with Charley openly bitter over the failure of his marriage to Gladys and unconsciously consumed by self-hate because of his betrayal of the "mechanic" in him, and with Margo alone and broke after her misadventure with Tad, that the two meet in Jacksonville. Their union is swift, total, and in a major ironic turn, one of the few happy relationships in the entire trilogy. Both are worldly, wisecracking, and out for a good time, and they are well matched in these ways. But on a deeper level of attraction, each senses a streak of human sensibility in the other, and their relationship thus has a depth transcending their ostensible roles of sugar daddy and kept woman. This deeper level of communion has few outer signs. Each will deceive the other about money and other affairs as the relationship continues in New York and again

in Florida, and there are no moments of open revelation of self between them. Rather, the genuine liking of each for the other is an
unacknowledged refuge before each pushes on to a final destiny.

For Charley, this comes soon in the form of a fatal automobile
accident. It is the height of the Florida land boom of the late 1920s,
and Charley has joined in its speculative wheeling and dealing.
But the bouyant Charley of his early Detroit years, while still out-
wardly evident in much flashing of cash, has in truth given way to
a man flabby in body and mind who drinks too much and who has
recently been outwitted by Gladys, by his former Detroit partners,
and by Margo herself (in her affair with Charley's aide Cliff). It is
this Charley who gets drunk, smashes up his car, and lies dying of
peritonitis in a hospital. Suspecting that Charley's holdings are
mainly on paper, relatives, friends (including Margo), and hospital
officials crowd around him, trying to milk him for cash before he
dies. "It's like a run on a bank . . . ," Charley says in a last wise-
crack, "I guess they think the old institution's not so sound as it
might be" (*BM*, 375). And indeed the "institution" in the senses of
Charley, of the Florida land boom, and of the nation at large is not
"sound." All will soon go under, with Charley's peritonitis (like Valentino's) a symbol of the inner corruption of the organism. A final
symbolic touch at Charley's death is his loquaciousness in the hospital. "He couldn't stop talking" (*BM*, 370), and he dies still attempting to talk. But his talk, like that of Moorehouse, Savage, and
the decade itself (including the "silver tongue" of William Jennings
Bryan, who is selling real estate nearby), is empty cliché. It is only
talk.

The Florida land boom, in which swampy lots (some completely under water) are sold by means of a hard-sell rhetoric, is an
apt launching pad for Margo's assault on Hollywood. She now
knows fully the advantages of disguise, and she, Tony, and Agnes,
though almost broke, adopt the roles of a European-born heiress
and her chauffeur and companion as they seek their fortunes in
the West. The Hollywood portion of *The Big Money* thus depicts
the adventures of fakers in fakerland, in which a comic motif is
that the more outrageous or false a disguise the better its chance of
success. (Margo's final breakthrough in her role as heiress is
achieved by the purchase, on time, of a used Rolls Royce.) Here
the element of caricature present in all of Dos Passos' fiction becomes broad indeed. Dos Passos' Hollywood consists of megalo-
maniacal directors with phony foreign backgrounds, reluctant
upper-class stars, and dumb studlike leading men, all of whom are

committed to kinky sex and studio double-dealing politics while purveying on screen a world of never-never romance. After a slow start, Margo and her entourage reach the required level of phoniness, and she is adopted as a prospective star by Margolies, a director of monumental self-assurance.

Despite recognizing Margolies' fraudulence, Margo allows herself to be drawn into his Svengali-like plans to make her a star, to mate her to his male star Cathcart (Margolies' impotence is strongly hinted), and to marry her as a guarantee that she will remain his property. Tony, who has slipped into his usual dissolute ways, is a threat to these plans, and in a moment of crisis Margo throws him out. In another of Dos Passos' carefully orchestrated symbolic endings to a narrative, Tony is killed in a brawl on the night that Margo sleeps with Cathcart for the first time. The compassionate identification of the picaro with the downtrodden and failures of the world that had marked Margo throughout her narrative is replaced by the cold artificiality of the made object she has become, the Hollywood star. Margo at the close of her narrative is a woman consumed by her new identity. She marries Margolies in a staged Hollywood "elopement," and then—under Margolies' direction—plays a torrid love scene with Cathcart in a meretricious romance. As Margolies assures her, she is "the most beautiful girl in the world, the nation's newest sweetheart" (*BM*, 436). Our sense that Margo has been reduced to an empty mechanism is confirmed in a final glimpse we have of her at Eveline's party in the last segment of Mary French's narrative. Accompanied by Margolies and Cathcart and seen from across a room, she is "a small woman with blue eyelids and features regular as those of a porcelain doll" (*BM*, 553).[38]

Charley's and Margo's narratives thus have analogous shapes. Just as Bill Cermak represents the best in Charley, so Tony brings out the best in Margo. And both Bill and Tony, at crucial moments in Charley's and Margo's lives, are sacrificed to the bitch goddess success. This loss of the best part of self in the pursuit of success constitutes Dos Passos' most severe attack on the myth of success in America. Margo and Charley have achieved their ambitions. But they have done so at the cost of what can be regarded—given the clarity and repetition of Dos Passos' theme—as their souls. The pursuit of success in America is thus a pact with the devil, in which the devil both collects his due and deceives his victim. For Charley in the end, after the long decline following the high point of his early years in Detroit, has little money remaining, and Margo's career—it is strongly suggested—will be ruined by the advent of the talkies.

Dos Passos' return to an emphasis on the myth of success in *The Big Money,* after its centrality in *The 42nd Parallel* and its relative neglect in *Nineteen-Nineteen* because of the prominence of the war theme in that novel, reflects its importance in the trilogy as a whole as well as in the expansive 1920s. His expression of the theme through the parallel and closely interlaced careers of Charley and Margo results in this portion of *The Big Money* taking on some of the shape of a conventional novel. For over 250 pages, the narrative focus moves back and forth between Charley and Margo, and for 150 pages of this material the two figures are interlaced. As though to signal that theme is to be expressed largely through narrative at this point, there is a sharp decline in the number of biographies and Camera Eye segments during this phase of the novel. Once the pattern of alternating narrative segments is established (with Charley's fifth narrative segment—*BM,* 197), there occurs only one Camera Eye (a return from Europe to Havana that is a comic analogue to Margo's sojourn in Cuba with Tony) and the biography of the Wright brothers. Indeed, the last four narrative segments in the Margo-Charley sequence are separated only by single Newsreels. With the completion of Margo's last segment, however, there follows—in one sequence between that narrative and the next one of Mary French—a unit of three Newsreels, a biography, and a Camera Eye, as though to indicate both a shift to a new body of material and a return to a more fully juxtapositional form of expression.

The dominance of narrative in the middle portion of *The Big Money* is not a weakness but rather a sign of Dos Passos' continuing flexibility in the overall juxtapositional form of the trilogy. At this moment, narrative intensity, with a finely tuned interaction between two narratives, was the most useful means of expression, just as at other points an interaction between Camera Eye and biography or between narrative and biography was the most functional. To put the idea somewhat differently, Dos Passos, in his stress on narrative in the central section of *The Big Money,* was not engaging in a belated recognition of the inadequacies of cubistic form. Instead, he was again reflecting the almost infinite adaptability of that form for the expression of a unity of vision beneath the multiplicity of experience.

While the Richard Savage narrative segment in the final portion of *The Big Money* is still devoted to the baleful consequences

of the pursuit of the dream of success in America, Dos Passos is
more occupied in this final section with depicting the mixed character and fates of the various radical alternatives to the pursuit.
This shift in emphasis is announced, immediately following Margo's last narrative segment, by the biography of Frank Lloyd
Wright and by the first of the Camera Eye segments dealing with
the persona's involvement in the Sacco-Vanzetti case. Although
two biographies are still to come—those of Hearst and Insull—Dos
Passos' study of Wright as radical architect is the climactic biography of the trilogy because of its significant relationship both to the
success narratives of Charley and Margo and to the final acceptance by the Camera Eye persona of his own radical role. Wright,
despite personal qualities that would have made success easy, had
kept his talent pure to the detriment of wealth and fame. He is like
Charley in his native American inventive genius. As a youth,

> He walked with long eager steps
>   toward the untrammeled future opening in every di-
> rection for a young man who'd keep his hands to his work
> and his wits sharp to invent.   (*BM*, 429)

But instead of taking this open road, Wright chose to create an independent American architecture out of America's "uses and
needs" (*BM*, 431)—that is, the aesthetics of functionalism—rather
than to emulate traditional styles. He thus becomes an architect of
the "old words." His demand for an American idiom that rejects the
clichés and platitudes of architecture in order to fulfill the basic
needs and aspirations of Americans anticipates the recognition by
the Camera Eye of his own commitment to a similar kind of radical
art: "(Tell us, doctors of philosophy, what are the needs of a man.
At least a man needs to be notjailed notafraid nothungry notcold
not without love, not a worker for a power he has never seen)"
(*BM*, 432). Wright's blueprints, Dos Passos concludes, "as once
Walt Whitman's words, stir the young men" (*BM*, 433). Dos Passos'
invoking of Whitman at this point is a powerful link between the
Camera Eye persona's frustration during an earlier stage of his political and artistic awakening when he sought to play a role in the
achievement of Whitman's "storybook democracy" (*BM*, 150) and
his present response to the lesson offered by Wright. For Wright
had succeeded in establishing in his own art the connection between a radical commitment to American ideals and an art that is

radical in form. The Camera Eye almost immediately confirms in
his own life the role of Wright as "preache[r] to the young men
coming of age in the time of oppression" (BM, 430) when his participation in the Sacco-Vanzetti case leads him to an understanding of his own task in helping to "rebuild the ruined words" (BM,
437) of American democratic idealism.

But this moment of recognition of the task facing the radical
artist—a moment in which the career of Wright and the maturation of the Camera Eye persona affirm the possibility of undertaking the task—is followed immediately by a body of material that
qualifies the note of hope present in the moment. Dos Passos appears to be saying that the acceptance of a radical role by the artist
should not obscure the difficulty of the task facing him, given both
the strength of the forces in opposition and the weaknesses present in the left itself.

The participation of the Camera Eye persona in the efforts to
save Sacco and Vanzetti introduces this major event in the history
of the radical left in America. The case also plays an important role
in Mary French's narrative when we pick up her story—in the first
narrative segment following the completion of the Charley and
Margo narratives—in the mid-1920s in New York, where she is
working for various left-wing groups. At a Madison Square Garden
rally "to welcome the classwar prisoners released from Atlanta"
(BM, 440), she meets Ben Compton, one of those released, and begins a love affair with him. Ben's weakness and need after years in
prison and Mary's mothering instinct result initially in a happy
union. But when Ben regains his strength and again becomes active in radical causes, and when Mary becomes pregnant, the relationship collapses. Ben announces that marriage and a child
"would distract him from his work and . . . there'd be plenty of time
for that sort of thing after the revolution." Although Mary is heart-
broken, Ben is adamant that they must "sacrifice their personal
feelings for the workingclass" (BM, 447). Dos Passos in this incident—as well as in the soon-to-follow response of Don Stevens to
the plight of Sacco and Vanzetti—was dramatizing one of his major objections to the emerging centrality of the Communist party
in the American left-wing movement of the late 1920s and early
1930s. The weakness of the IWW, as illustrated by Mac, had been
an inability to discipline human needs in order to resist the blandishments of bourgeois society. The contrary but even more destructive weakness of the party was its demand that basic human
needs be suppressed in the name of party discipline. To Dos Pas-

sos, Mac slipping into middle-class lethargy was far less harmful to himself and to others than the impact upon both Ben and Mary of Ben's freezing up of his capacity for love and sympathy in response to an ideological correctness and self-righteousness.

After breaking up with Ben, Mary goes to Boston to throw herself into the defense of Sacco and Vanzetti. As is her nature, she responds to the two Italian-American anarchists, not as proponents of a specific cause, but as human beings of an intrinsic courage and dignity—as good men. "There's something so peaceful, so honest about them," she tells Jerry Burnham, who (along with George Barrow and Don Stevens) has been drawn to Boston by the case; "You get such a feeling of greatness out of them" (*BM*, 451). Mary is attracted to Stevens, who reappears as a party functionary. (He has throughout the trilogy played the role of a figure on the extreme left—first as an IWW reporter and then as an outspoken antiwar writer.) Mary has been depressed by the end of her relationship with Ben and by her growing realization that Sacco and Vanzetti would not be saved, but in Stevens's bold activism she takes new hope and strength. Mary's faith in Stevens, however, and in the values he represents, is the basis for the final betrayal of her by the left. Stevens, a cold and ruthless party man, views Sacco and Vanzetti in party terms. He tells Mary, "It doesn't matter whether they are saved or not any more, it's the power of the workingclass that's got to be saved" (*BM*, 458). Mary's acceptance of the principle underlying this statement—that individuals do not count within goals defined by the class struggle—marks the nadir of her participation in the far left. She has now endorsed the same notion that had caused her so much pain when Ben had expressed it in words and action. (It is significant that Ben is a Trotskyite and Don a Stalinist. Despite the enmity between the two camps in the left-wing political wars of the 1930s, Dos Passos was dramatizing a belief that there was little essential difference between them except perhaps for an even greater ruthlessness among the Stalinists.) And in a final ironic turning of the screw, Dos Passos soon causes Mary to discover that she herself—and not just Sacco and Vanzetti—can be discarded by Don in the name of the class struggle. After she and Don have lived for a time in New York, Don leaves for a trip to Moscow and returns married to an English party member—a marriage arranged by the party for party purposes.

Mary's abortion of Ben's child and her acceptance of Don's view of the deaths of Sacco and Vanzetti constitute a "death of the self" in her life comparable to the deaths of Bill Cermak and Tony in the lives of Charley and Margo. The best that is in Mary—her compassionate warmth, as expressed in her desire for a child by the man she loves and in her responsiveness to the human element in the fate of Sacco and Vanzetti—is crushed. As with Charley's and Margo's suppression of the best in their natures, this death of the self can be accommodated within the human will to survive. Mary continues to live afterwards, as did Charley and Margo. But Mary will also pay a heavy price for this loss of self, as she seeks to turn herself into an emotionless drudge. Of course, Dos Passos' depiction of Mary's "fall" is not as caustic as his account of the last phases of Charley's and Margo's lives. Her acceptance of Ben's and Don's beliefs stems from her love for them rather than from personal ambition. And she remains a woman with strong mothering instincts, as is clear from her response to the news of miners' starving children in her final narrative segment. She will continue to "do good" in her various minor roles within radical causes. But the best in her—her ability to love fully and openly—has been deeply scarred. Dos Passos' tone in her final segments is thus the mixed one of sympathy for Mary and contempt for that aspect of the radical left that misuses the responsiveness of someone like Mary to the ills of the human condition.

The Camera Eye persona has also, of course, participated in the futile effort to save Sacco and Vanzetti. Three consecutive and tightly linked segments—Mary French's narrative, Newsreel LXVI, and the penultimate Camera Eye—are devoted to the implications of the deaths of Sacco and Vanzetti for America. Mary and Don fervently sing the "International" on the eve of the execution, signifying their allegiance to the political cause that has been attached to the case by the party. In the Newsreel that follows, the presence of the "International" as the "song" in a segment devoted almost entirely to the Sacco-Vanzetti case suggests that the party has been successful in linking itself to the martyrdom of Sacco and Vanzetti. But for the Camera Eye persona, who has at last achieved the direction he has been seeking throughout the trilogy, the deaths of Sacco and Vanzetti are not a means toward gaining the "power of the workingclass." They are rather a possible means of reviving the potency of the "clean words our fathers spoke" (*BM,* 462). The historical point of reference for the persona is not the "new words" of the "International" and a new political ideology but the "old words of the immigrants" that the "blood and agony" of Sacco and Vanzetti were helping to renew (*BM,* 463). Vanzetti himself, as noted by the Camera Eye persona, had endorsed this belief in the humanistic center of their martyrdom when he wrote that he and Sacco were dying "for tolerance, for justice, for man's understanding of man" (*BM*, 463). Thus, although the persona's announcements that "they have clubbed us off the streets" and "we stand defeated America" (*BM*, 461, 464) are a correct summary of what has been dramatized in the Mary French narrative and reported in the Newsreel, the persona responds not with despair to these truths but rather with an anger born of the knowledge that the "old words" are in terrible jeopardy and must be fought for.

The biography of William Randolph Hearst occurs appropriately between the acceptance by the Camera Eye persona of his role as fighter for the "old words" and the only Richard Savage narrative segment in *The Big Money*. Hearst is an ironic counterpart of the Camera Eye persona. Both were sons of self-made men, both went to private schools and Harvard, and both entered occupations in which the use of words is paramount. But in his career as a yellow-journalism press lord, Hearst viewed language as a device for the control of the emotions of the masses for his own economic and political ends. Dos Passos' portrait of Hearst's obviously shoddy life is thus another of his satiric critiques of false wordmongers that range from Moorehouse and Wilson to—on its lowest level—Savage's effort in his final narrative segment to mount a public-relations campaign on behalf of patent medicines. Dos Passos' allusion to Hearst's favorable reaction to Hitler's Germany (*BM*, 477) is particularly cogent, since the prototype of Moorehouse—Ivy Lee—had been employed by the Nazis.[39] Dos Passos was suggesting the now familiar but then novel idea that there was a basic similarity between the aims and methods of totalitarian states and the control of mass belief through advertising, public relations, and the popular press.

The return to the world of Dick, Moorehouse, Eleanor, Eveline, and Janey near the close of *The Big Money* serves a number of purposes. By focusing on Dick, Dos Passos is able to depict directly the death-in-life fate of the most sensitive and, for a time, most appealing member of the group that had accepted the Moorehouse ethos. Also, the activities of the group permit Dos Passos to render satirically a New York "big money" world of smart sophistication. And finally, Dos Passos is able in this segment and in Mary's last narrative segment to perform the conventional role of the panoramic novelist of stating or suggesting the fates of his large cast of of characters. The Camera Eye persona still has his principal task in life before him, but the narrative figures, Dos Passos implies, are now fixed in their natures and roles. The narratives of *U.S.A.* thus comprise a closed rather than an open-ended work of fiction. Each figure by the end of the trilogy is frozen in a self-destructive or an empty life. Dos Passos' attempt in the final two narrative segments, in which only Mac and the three dead narrative figures (Joe, Daughter, and Charley) do not appear, is to confirm this condition.

Dick's state is characteristic of that of the Moorehouse group as a whole. Ostensibly, he is a great success. He is Moorehouse's right-hand man and heir apparent, and he is pursuing the life of an eligible New York bachelor. But the moral symbolism of the discarded compass is now confirmed in Dick's duplicitous relationships with others and in the chaos of his emotional life. As Moorehouse's "son," Dick finds himself Moorehouse's sycophant defender—his own voice sounding "oily" and "phony" in his ears (*BM*, 482, 484)—whatever the justice of the criticsm. Dick's moral collapse is precisely dramatized in his winning of the Bingham account and in his increasingly overt homosexuality. Bingham, now a physical-culture crackpot and the proprietor of a great patent-medicine firm, is so obviously a quack and a fraud that Dick's collusion in Bingham's efforts to deceive the public is a fully self-conscious betrayal of the commitment to public honesty of his ambulance corps days.[40] And Dick's homosexuality (accompanied by much heavy drinking) is now an acute symbol of his moral decay—less in the fact of his homosexuality than in the forms it takes in his sexual jealousy (and betrayal) of his protégé, Reggie, in the gross pass he attracts from a homosexual priest, and in his drunken "affair" with a black transvestite. Dick is now a figure out of Hawthorne in his almost exact externalization of his moral nature. Our final sight of Dick assuming Moorehouse's role in the office on the morning following a drunken and disastrous night with the black male prostitute "Gloria Swanson" closes the door on his life.

A similar effect of characters locked in their private moral and emotional hells, whatever their ostensible success in the world, is present in the fates of the other figures in the Moorehouse group. Moorehouse himself, though still the confident believer in his own form of untruth, is now also paying the price of a life of emotional aridity. His marriage was, of course, a failure; Eleanor has pushed on to even finer prey in the form of an émigré Russian prince; and Moorehouse is left—as he tells Dick—"a lonely man" (*BM*, 491). Of the remainder of the group, Janey has "a sour lined oldmaidish face" (*BM*, 495) and Eleanor is "shrill," "rasping," and "screechy" (*BM*, 487). (Dos Passos continues with the entire Moorehouse entourage the technique introduced with Charley of prematurely aging each character as a sign of hastened moral decline.)

As usual, Dos Passos' most sympathetic account of a figure in the Moorehouse group is reserved for Eveline. We have encountered her several times earlier in *The Big Money* in Charley's narrative, where her unhappiness as a housewife and mother is dramatized through her shallow and almost entirely sexual affair with Charley. Now, at the close of *The Big Money*, after divorcing Paul and—it is suggested—after many other affairs, her current lover has just left her for another woman. At Eveline's party, Mary can see "the harsh desperate lines under the makeup round [her] mouth and the strained tenseness of the cords of her neck" (*BM*, 550). Her death through an overdose of drugs after her party is like the death of Edith Wharton's Lily Bart in *The House of Mirth*. There may be uncertainty as to whether the death is an accident or a suicide, but there is little doubt of its indication of an unwillingness to face what the future holds.

Although Dos Passos does not fully dramatize the Wall Street crash and the arrival of the depression, there is a clear demarcation toward the close of *The Big Money* between the 1920s and the 1930s. Savage's last narrative segment is still set in the 1920s, with business booming and a Jazz Age hecticness to New York life. But the following Newsreel begins "Wall Street Stunned," the Camera Eye that follows is set in the Harlan miners' strike of 1931, Mary French's last narrative segment contains many references to the miners' strikes of the early 1930s, and "Vag," which concludes the trilogy, is a biography of an archetypal depression figure. But despite this obvious transition into the 1930s, no obvious shift in theme occurs in this concluding portion of the trilogy. The Camera Eye persona finds in Harlan principally a confirmation of his earlier won recognition that words are his only weapon against POWER SUPERPOWER, the narrative figures also confirm the earlier depicted direction of their lives, and the Insull biography is another of Dos Passos' ironic American success stories. Writing in the heart of the depression in the mid-1930s, Dos Passos viewed it, not as a phenomenon that had produced major changes in American life (and thus in the lives of the participants in *U.S.A.*), but as a condition that brought into sharper focus characteristics of American life that had been present since the turn of the century.

Dos Passos' decision to end the narrative portion of *U.S.A.*

with the last of Mary French's segments lends itself to a possible reading of Mary's final act of returning to left-wing activism, despite the collapse of her relationship with Don Stevens, as parallel to the Camera Eye persona's decision to adopt a radical stance as a writer.[41] But to view Mary's return to left-wing union work in these positive terms is to miss Dos Passos' portrayal of the pathetic emptiness of her life in the final segment. Mary has been caught up in the left-wing factionalism of the early 1930s. She is in love with Don and therefore accepts his party-line contempt for Trotskyites and other deviants from party discipline as "social fascists," even though her essentially apolitical nature is revealed by her falling asleep whenever the talk is of "centralcommittee, expulsions, oppositionists, splitters" (*BM*, 535). Ben now turns up. Like all the narrative figures who reappear in this final section of *The Big Money*, he too has aged and is worn and tired. He has been expelled from the party as an "oppositionist" and for "exceptionalism" (*BM*, 539). Mary, fully endorsing Don's position, has no sympathy for Ben or for his confession of regret that they had not made a life together when they had a chance. "I ought to have kept you, Mary," he says (*BM*, 540). In Ben's tragic realization of the deadening effect of ideology on his love for Mary, and in Mary's rejection of Ben's need for understanding despite her compassionate nature, Dos Passos dramatized fully the strictures placed on freedom of feeling by the party's demand for uniformity of belief and expression.

Almost immediately Mary is again made a victim when Don returns from Moscow married to a woman for party convenience. During this last segment, Mary is also appealed to by her mother and her old friend Ada to return to her class origins. She contemptuously rejects these appeals, and is thus left, in a sense, emotionally homeless. She cannot accept the trivial and mindless life of her mother, and she has found herself continually victimized by the callous disregard for the individual that characterizes the far left. No wonder, then, that she tells George Barrow, whom she meets at Eveline's party, that "I haven't any feelings at all any more. I've seen how it works in the field . . ." (*BM*, 553). Each time she has loved in the context of the radical movement—whether Barrow, Ben, or Stevens—she has suffered deeply in ways that symbolize, not her weaknesses, but those of the left itself, from the shallow falseness of Barrow to the party-line hardness of Stevens. Mary herself is stronger than Eveline, and she rejects the triviality both of Eveline's life and of her death. But though she will continue to work for the betterment of the working class, her death-in-life suppression of her capacity to feel—whether for Ben or "in the field"—signifies Dos Passos' own rejection of the party as a means toward greater freedom and social justice in America. For Dos Passos and for the Camera Eye persona the far left is not the answer; "only words" remain.

The "Vag" epilogue confirms the nature and extent of the task facing those who would work for greater freedom and justice in America. The vagrant hitching rides, poor and hungry while the rich ride an airplane overhead, symbolizes not only—as the Camera Eye persona had proclaimed earlier—that we are "two nations" but that the "bottomdog" has been brutally deceived by the rhetoric of the American dream ("went to school, books said opportunity")—a deception purveyed both by Margo ("ghosts of platinum girls coaxed from the screen") and by Moorehouse and Dick ("ads promised speed, own your home") (*BM*, 561). But if words are responsible for the despair of Vag, they can also serve as a powerful weapon of the satiric ironist who is armed with a compelling vision of an America in which the "old words" are used truthfully to help create the fulfillment of the American dream of freedom and opportunity for all Americans.

CONCLUSION

Like many twentieth-century fictional masterpieces—*Ulysses*, for example, or Faulkner's Yoknapatawpha saga—*U.S.A.* seeks to portray a culture in both historical depth and social breadth by means of modernistic techniques. There is thus a modern epic convention, to which *U.S.A.* belongs, in which the traditional aim of the epic to make manifest the history and values of a culture is achieved, not by conformity to a prescribed set of epic rules, but by the author's individual adaptation of the complex fictional devices that have arisen in the twentieth century for the depiction of the interaction of self and society. The success of works in this convention derives not only from the depth of the author's insight into his culture but from the appropriateness and effectiveness of the modernistic fictional forms that he has chosen to render his vision.

Which is to say that *U.S.A.* can be discussed meaningfully in a number of ways but that the final test of its value and centrality in twentieth-century art lies in its nature and quality as a modernistic epic American novel. Dos Passos' model for the epic was principally Whitman as *U.S.A.* seeks to depict in full detail the "varied strains" that are the American experience. To Whitman, too, can be attributed Dos Passos' belief in a semimystical oneness in the multiplicity of America, a oneness that to Dos Passos was above all the nation's history of democratic idealism. There is also of course a Whitmanesque element in the deep exploration of self in the Camera Eye, an exploration that, in the end, is an exploration of what America should be and isn't. Thus, one of the most pervasive and central sources of relatedness, of unity, in *U.S.A.* is in its character as a self-reflexive novel in which the Camera Eye persona's search for identity and role results simultaneously in a vision of self and a vision of America that is the remainder of the trilogy.

As an epic novel, *U.S.A.* is also a historical work, with history—like autobiography—simultaneously both a subject matter and a source of experimental form. In the pseudochronicle modes of the Newsreels and biographies Dos Passos consciously shapes a documentary base, through impressionistic selection and surreal juxtaposition, into an indictment of twentieth-century American life. The underlying motive for this distortion of the "factual" lies in Dos Passos' powerful ironic and thus satiric vision of the immense distance between verbal construct and actuality in twentieth-century America. *U.S.A.* is thus throughout, and not merely in the Newsreels and biographies, the work of a satiric moralist. Dos Passos' caricature of American types, beliefs, and language in the narratives through free indirect discourse and his portrayal of journeys of the self toward self-betrayal and self-destruction are above all a reflection of his condemnation of the failure of America to accept the heritage of its "old words."

Each of the four modes of the trilogy is therefore both a modernistic fictional form and a contribution toward an epic rendering of twentieth-century American life. One of Dos Passos' major achievements in the trilogy arises from his recognition that the four modes could be linked not only by their common reference to an overarching epic intent but by constant juxtapositional allusiveness of epic matter, event, theme, and symbol. *U.S.A.* is a kind of cubistic portrait of America—one in which the effect is of a multiplicity of visions rendering a single object, with every angle of vision related both to the object and to every other angle of vision. It is Dos Passos' relentless pursuit of juxtapositional relationships in the seemingly disparate and fractured modal ordering of the trilogy that is largely responsible for the integral vision of American life in *U.S.A.*

The extraordinary holding power of *U.S.A.* for most readers— the ability of the work to compel attention throughout its extreme length and its complex variety of modes—thus has its origin both in the single-minded intensity of Dos Passos' vision of American life as a whole and in his ability to engage us, as in the death-of-the-self motif that runs through the narratives and the counter rebirth theme in the Camera Eye, in the deepest level of meaning of the relationship of self to community. *U.S.A.* is about a nation of individuals, and in that Whitmanesque paradox Dos Passos found his form and his theme.

NOTES

BIBLIOGRAPHY

INDEX

NOTES

All manuscript material cited in the notes is in the John Dos Passos Papers of the University of Virginia Library. Since the Dos Passos' collection in the University of Virginia Library is cataloged and organized by accession number, with each accession having its own distinctive series of box numbers, I have cited material from the collection in this fashion: acc. no. [ ], box [ ].

Citations from Dos Passos' published works that are discussed at length are from the following texts:

Rosinante to the Road Again (New York: Doran, 1922).

Manhattan Transfer (Boston: Houghton Mifflin, 1925).

U.S.A. (New York: Modern Library, 1939).

Because each of the three novels of *U.S.A.* is paginated separately in the Modern Library standard edition, citations from *U.S.A.* in my text are to a specific novel as well as to page number. The titles of the novels are abbreviated as follows: *FP—The 42nd Parallel; NN—Nineteen-Nineteen; BM—The Big Money.*

The following short titles are used throughout the notes:

Best Times—John Dos Passos, *The Best Times: An Informal Memoir* (New York: New American Library, 1966).

Carr—Virginia Spencer Carr, *Dos Passos: A Life* (Garden City, N.Y.: Doubleday, 1984).

Fourteenth Chronicle.—Townsend Ludington, ed., *The Fourteenth Chronicle: Letters and Diaries of John Dos Passos* (Boston: Gambit, 1973).

Odyssey—Townsend Ludington, *John Dos Passos: A Twentieth Century Odyssey* (New York: Dutton, 1980).

PREFACE

1 Sartre, "Dos Passos and '1919,'" *Literary and Philosophical Essays*, trans. Annette Michelson (London: Rider, 1955), p. 96 (the essay appeared originally in August 1938).

2 George Steiner, *Language and Silence* (1966; rpt. ed., New York: Atheneum, 1970), p. 116.

1   DOS PASSOS BEFORE *U.S.A.*

1 Dos Passos, "Literary Diary," Feb. 23, 1915, acc. no. 5950ac, box 3.

2 Dos Passos, "A Humble Protest," *Harvard Monthly* 62 (June 1916): 119, 120.

3 Dos Passos, "Against American Literature," *New Republic* 8 (Oct. 14, 1916): 270, 271.

4   A typescript of the novel is in the Dos Passos Papers. The work is discussed
    (though not reproduced) by Ruth L. Strickland in her "An Edition of John Dos
    Passos's 'Seven Times Round the Walls of Jericho,'" Ph.D. diss., Univ. of South
    Carolina, 1981.
5   *Fourteenth Chronicle,* p. 119.
6   *Odyssey,* p. 131.
7   Dos Passos to Arthur McComb, Oct. 5, 1918, in the library of the American
    Academy and Institute of Arts and Letters, New York.
8   Dos Passos, "Literary Diary," Nov. 17, [1916], acc. no. 5950ac, box 3.
9   The exact order of the composition of the essays in Rosinante will probably
    never be known, though a rough approximation—based principally on order of
    publication—is possible. The book was completed in the late spring of 1921
    (*Fourteenth Chronicle,* p. 310). Of its seventeen chapters, a portion of one
    chapter—"The Baker of Almorox"—appeared (as I have noted) in August 1917.
    The eight additional chapters of literary criticism and personal essay appeared
    from June 1920 to April 1922, with four published in 1920. Of the eight Telem-
    achus chapters, one, the first ("A Gesture and a Quest") appeared in March
    1921, the remainder in December 1921 and January 1922. It seems probable,
    therefore, that with the exceptions of chapter 3, "The Baker of Alamorox," and
    chapter 16, "A Funeral in Madrid" (see Carr, p. 178), the discursive and per-
    sonal essays were written sporadically during 1919–21, before the Tel chapters,
    and that the Tel chapters were written in a body in early 1921, when Dos Pas-
    sos decided to publish a book on comtemporary Spain.
10 The best discussions of the theme of *Rosinante* remain David Sanders, "The
    'Anarchism' of John Dos Passos," *South Atlantic Quarterly* 60 (Winter 1961):
    44–55, and John H. Wrenn, *John Dos Passos* (New York: Twayne, 1961,) pas-
    sim. The form of the work is seldom discussed.
11 The chronology of publication would appear to preclude these influences, since
    Rosinante was written during 1919–21 (see note 9, above) and *The Waste
    Land* and *Ulysses* were published in 1922. But in fact Dos Passos was respond-
    ing to the mythic undercurrent in Eliot's "Prufrock" (which had appeared in
    1915 and which had heavily influenced *Streets of Night* the following year) and
    to the publication of large portions of *Ulysses* (including the "Telemachus"
    chapter) in *The Little Review* during 1918–20. For Dos Passos' initial reading
    of *Ulysses* in this form, see Joe Flaherty, "Portrait of a Man Reading," Washing-
    ton *Post,* July 13, 1969, *Book World* section, p. 2.
12 *Best Times,* pp. 33–34.
13 See, for example, *Rosinante,* pp. 9, 139.
14 Dos Passos' model for this narrative style appears to have been John Reed's
    account in *Insurgent Mexico* of Reed's adventures in revolutionary Mexico. See
    Dos Passos' laudatory review of *Insurgent Mexico* in the *Harvard Monthly* 59
    (Nov. 1914): 67–68.
15 *Rosinante,* pp. 52–53.
16 *Rosinante,* p. 93.
17 See note 9, above.
18 *Odyssey,* pp. 200–201.
19 See Craig Carver, "The Newspaper and Other Sources of *Manhattan Transfer,*"
    Studies in American Fiction 3 (Autumn 1975): 167–79.
20 The play was performed at Harvard (in 1925) and in New York (in 1926) under

the title *The Moon Is a Gong*. It was published by Harper in 1926 under the title *The Garbage Man;* it also appears under this title in Dos Passos' *Three Plays* (1934).

21 Dos Passos, "What Makes a Novelist," *National Review* 20 (Jan. 16, 1968): 31. For similar recollections by Dos Passos, see his "Translator's Foreword" to Blaise Cendrars, *Panama, or, The Adventures of My Seven Uncles* (New York: Harper, 1931), pp. vii–viii, and "Contemporary Chronicles," *Carlton Miscellany* 2 (Spring 1961): 25–29.

22 Dos Passos, "Grosz Comes to America," *Esquire* 6 (Sept. 1936): 105. Dos Passos also notes in this essay that he saw the paintings of Cezanne, Picasso, and Gris in Paris during 1918–19.

23 *Odyssey,* pp. 222–23.

24 Although Dos Passos saw Eisenstein's major silent films before he began *U.S.A.*, there is some question as to whether he saw them before the composition of *Manhattan Transfer,* since Eisenstein's earliest films were not shown in Western Europe or America until 1925. As Dos Passos recalled in a 1961 letter to David Sanders, "I suspect I got interested in Eisenstein's montage while I was working on *Manhattan Transfer,* though I can't remember exactly. Anyway montage was in the air" (quoted in Sanders, "*Manhattan Transfer* and 'The Service of Things,'" in *Themes and Directions in American Literature,* ed. Ray B. Browne and Donald Pizer [Lafayette, Ind.: Purdue University Studies, 1969], p. 180).

25 See Michael Spindler, "John Dos Passos and the Visual Arts," *Journal of American Studies* 15 (Dec. 1981): 397–98. There is, I believe, no major direct influence of the form of *Ulysses* on that of *Manhattan Transfer,* even though Dos Passos read *Ulysses* in complete form in late 1922 (*Best Times,* p. 131) and though *Ulysses* is often viewed as a significant effort to achieve the effect of cubist simultaneity in fiction (see Stephen Kern, *The Culture of Time and Space: 1880–1918* [Cambridge, Mass.: Harvard Univ. Press, 1983], pp. 76–80). Although both works devote much of their fictional energy to the transmission through montage of the image of a city, *Manhattan Transfer* lacks the overwhelming emphasis on mythic parallels and on stream of consciousness that is central to the form of *Ulysses*.

26 I follow Dos Passos' own practice of not distinguishing sharply between the impact of these two contemporaneous movements on his own work. In fact, however, futurism (which was largely of Italian origin) and cubism do differ in the greater emphasis within futurism on rendering the dynamic nature of a modern machine civilization.

27 Georges Lemaitre, *From Cubism to Surrealism in French Literature* (Cambridge, Mass.: Harvard Univ. Press, 1941), p. 80. Major studies of cubism in painting that have contributed to my understanding of the movement are: Christopher Gray, *Cubist Aesthetic Theories* (Baltimore: Johns Hopkins Press, 1953); Guy Habasque, *Cubism* (New York: Skira, 1959); Edward F. Fry, *Cubism* (New York: McGraw-Hill, 1966); and Max Kozloff, *Cubism/Futurism* (New York: Harper & Row, 1973). For the relationship between cubism and the novel, I am also indebted to Wylie Sypher, *Rococo to Cubism in Art and Literature* (New York: Random House, 1960); Roger Shattuck, *The Banquet Years: The Origins of the Avant-Garde in France, 1885 to World War I,* rev. ed. (New York: Random House, 1968); and Kern, *The Culture of Time and Space: 1880–*

1918. George Knox surveys the impact of Dos Passos' interest in art on his writing in "Dos Passos and Painting," *Texas Studies in Literature and Language* 6 (Spring 1964): 22–38.

28 Lemaitre, *From Cubism to Surrealism*, p. 83.

29 A still-useful early study of the relationship of Dos Passos' work to film is Claude-Edmonde Magny, *The Age of the American Novel: The Film Aesthetic of Fiction between the Two Wars* (1948; Amer. ed. trans. Eleanor Hochman, New York: Ungar, 1972). See also E. D. Lowry, "The Lively Art of *Manhattan Transfer*," *PMLA* 84 (Oct. 1969): 1628–38.

30 See Joseph A. Kestner, *The Spatiality of the Novel* (Detroit: Wayne State Univ. Press, 1978), and Jeffrey R. Smitten and Ann Daghistany, eds., *Spatial Form in Narrative* (Ithaca, N.Y.: Cornell Univ. Press, 1981).

31 *Manhattan Transfer*, pp. 162, 164.

32 Linda W. Wagner, *Dos Passos: Artist as American* (Austin: Univ. of Texas Press, 1979), pp. 50–52.

33 In fact, however, the careful reader of *Manhattan Transfer* will note that juxtaposed narratives are occasionally out of chronological tempo. So, for example, in the early chapters of the novel, Bud Korpenning's sequence of segments spans the first few days of his arrival in the city, while Ellen's juxtaposed segments cover several years.

34 Lois Hughson has studied Dos Passos' method of composition for *Manhattan Transfer* in "Narration in the Making of *Manhattan Transfer*," *Studies in the Novel* 8 (Summer 1976): 185–98.

35 In addition—as is clear from interpolations in the first draft—some narratives were added between the initial version of the draft and its later revision.

36 Iain Colley, *Dos Passos and the Fiction of Despair* (Totawa, N.J.: Rowman and Littlefield, 1978), p. 49.

37 Frank Gado, "John Dos Passos," in *First Person: Conversations on Writers and Writing*, ed. Frank Gado (Schenectady, N.Y.: Union College Press, 1973), p. 52. The interview took place in 1968.

38 See David L. Vanderwerken, "*Manhattan Transfer:* Dos Passos' Babel Story," *American Literature* 49 (May 1977): 253–67.

39 *Manhattan Transfer*, p., 95. All ellipses are in the original.

40 *Manhattan Transfer*, p. 366.

41 Dos Passos, "300 N.Y. Agitators Reach Passaic," *New Masses*, 1 (June 1926) 8. (All ellipses are in the original.) When Dos Passos republished this report (with some minor revisions) in *In All Countries* (1934), he changed its title to "300 Red Agitators Invade Passaic"—a change that reveals even more clearly his effort to parody in the title the style of typical newspaper reporting of radical activities.

2   *U.S.A.*: GENESIS AND BASIC CHARACTER

1 Dos Passos: "The Pit and the Pendulum," *New Masses* 1 (Aug. 1926): 1–11, 30; "Two Interviews," *Official Bulletin of the Sacco-Vanzetti Defense Committee* 1 (Dec. 1926): 3–4; *Facing the Chair: Story of the Americanization of Two Foreignborn Workmen* (Boston: Sacco-Vanzetti Defense Committee, 1927). For Dos Passos' later recollections of the impact of the Sacco-Vanzetti case on him, see *The Theme Is Freedom* (New York: Dodd, Mead, 1956), p. 39, and *Best Times*, p. 168.

2   *Best Times,* p. 166.

3   *Facing the Chair,* p. 45.

4   *Facing the Chair,* p. 58. (Ellipses are in the original.)

5   *The Theme Is Freedom,* p. 103.

6   Dos Passos, "Sacco and Vanzetti," *New Masses* 3 (Nov. 1927): 25. Dos Passos' own immediate response to this resolution was his inclusion in the play he was then writing, *Airways, Inc.,* of an incident involving the execution of a radical labor leader on trumped-up charges.

7   A characteristic comment occurs in the *Bookman* (68 [Sept. 1928]: 26), where Dos Passos wrote: "The only excuse for a novelist . . . is as a sort of second-class historian of the age he lives in."

8   Dos Passos, "Did the New Playwrights Theatre Fail?" *New Masses* 5 (Aug. 1929): 13.

9   George A. Knox and Herbert M. Stahl, *Dos Passos and "The Revolting Play-wrights,"* Essays and Studies on American Language and Literature 15 (Upsala, 1964), p. 16. Dos Passos himself later recalled, in "Looking Back on 'U.S.A.'" (New York *Times,* Oct. 25, 1958, sec. 2, p. 5), the significant influence that the "expressionist" theater of the period had on the "style" of *U.S.A.*

10 Dos Passos, "Contemporary Chronicles," *Carleton Miscellany* 2 (Spring 1961): 26–27. See also David Sanders, "John Dos Passos," in *Writers at Work: The "Paris Review" Interviews, Fourth Series,* ed. George Plimpton (New York: Viking, 1976), pp. 79–81.

11 *Odyssey,* pp. 249, 256.

12 Frank Gado, "John Dos Passos," in *First Person: Conversations on Writers and Writing,* ed. Frank Gado (Schenectady, N.Y.: Union College Press, 1973), p. 43. The interview took place in 1968.

13 Edmund Wilson to John Peale Bishop, August 7, 1929, in Wilson, *Letters on Literature and Politics, 1912–1972,* ed. Elena Wilson (New York: Farrar, Straus and Giroux, 1977), p. 167.

14 The inside cover of one of Dos Passos' notebooks for the trilogy (acc. no. 5950, box 4) contains this note:

The first
30 years   ⎰ The 42nd Parallel ⎱
New   ⎨ Nineteen Nineteen ⎬   *New Century*
Era   ⎱ The Big Money   ⎰
Newera
NEWERA

"New Century" is also similar to the titles of Dos Passos' later lengthy "chronicles" of American life, *Midcentury* (1961) and *Century's Ebb* (1975).

15 Dos Passos to Bernice Baumgarten, of Brandt and Brandt, July 3, 1937, acc. no. 5950aq, box 1.

16 The second novel of *U.S.A.* was initially published under the title *1919.* Dos Passos changed the title to *Nineteen-Nineteen* when the work was republished in 1938 as part of the single-volume edition of *U.S.A.* For convenience sake, I have used the title *Nineteen-Nineteen* for all references to this novel.

17 For the Harlan miners' strike, see *The Theme Is Freedom,* pp. 86–87; for the Madison Square Garden incident, see Dos Passos to Edmund Wilson, March 23, 1934 (*Fourteenth Chronicle,* pp. 435–36), and *Odyssey,* pp. 324–25. Dos

Passos' full and open break with the left occurred in 1937, following the death of his friend José Robles during the Spanish Civil War.

18   Dos Passos to Wilson, January 1935, *Fourteenth Chronicle,* pp. 461–62.

19   See Donald G. England, "The Newsreels of John Dos Passos' *The 42nd Parallel:* Sources and Techniques," Ph.D. diss., Univ. of Texas, 1970.

20   Dos Passos to Donald G. England, March 7, 1969, cited in England, "The Newsreels of John Dos Passos' *The 42nd Parallel,*" p. 6.

21   Dos Passos to Brandt and Brandt, July 15, 1937, acc. no. 5950aq, box 1.

22   The decision to divide the 1930s Harper edition into parts was apparently made late in the preparation of the novel for the press. The divisions are not present in any of the surviving manuscripts of the novel, and no divisions are indicated in the copy of unrevised proof of the novel in the Barrett Collection of the University of Virginia Library.

23   In addition to the changes noted above, Dos Passos also made some minor verbal changes and corrections and brought the punctuation of the Camera Eye and the biographies into greater conformity with his practice in *Nineteen-Nineteen* and *The Big Money.*

24   One anomaly in the format of *U.S.A.* that Dos Passos failed to rectify was that of the varying type fonts and indentation conventions of the tables of contents for the three novels. In its first edition, each novel had a different format for its table of contents. For the second edition of *The 42nd Parallel* in 1937, Dos Passos regularized its table of contents to conform to that of *The Big Money.* But he either neglected or was not permitted to regularize the contents pages of *Nineteen-Nineteen* on its second printing as part of the *U.S.A.* trilogy in 1938.

25   See chapter 4.

26   See, for example, Iain Colley, *Dos Passos and the Fiction of Despair* (Totawa, N.J.: Rowman and Littlefield, 1978), p. 116; Barbara Foley, "The Treatment of Time in *The Big Money:* An Examination of Ideology and Literary Form," *Modern Fiction Studies* 26 (Autumn 1980): 466; and Jonathan Morse, "Dos Passos' *U.S.A.* and the Illusions of Memory," *Modern Fiction Studies* 23 (Winter 1977–78): 554.

27   Earlier discussions of the theme occur in John Lydenberg, "Dos Passos's *U.S.A.:* The Words of the Hollow Men," in *Essays on Determinism in American Literature,* ed. Sydney J. Krause (Kent, Ohio: Kent State Univ. Press, 1964), pp. 97–107; and David L. Vanderwerken, "*U.S.A.:* Dos Passos and the 'Old Words,'" *Twentieth Century Literature* 23 (May 1977): 195–228 and "Dos Passos' Civil Religion," *Research Studies* 48 (Dec. 1980): 218–28.

28   Dos Passos, "Introduction," *Three Soldiers* (New York: Modern Library, 1932), pp. vii–viii.

29   Dos Passos, "The Writer as Technician," in *American Writers' Congress,* ed. Henry Hart (New York: International Publishers, 1935), pp. 79–82.

30   See Lois Hughson, "In Search of the True America: Dos Passos' Debt to Whitman in *U.S.A.,*" *Modern Fiction Studies* 19 (Summer 1973): 179–92.

31   Acc. no. 5950, box 5.

32   John H. Wrenn, *John Dos Passos* (New York: Twayne, 1961) discusses this theme in Dos Passos' work from *Rosinante to the Road Again* to *U.S.A.* See also Blanche Gelfant, "The Search for Identity in the Novels of John Dos Passos," *PMLA* 76 (March 1961): 133–49.

33   Since my effort in this section is to discuss Dos Passos' portrayal in the Camera Eye of his conception of his life leading up to the undertaking of *U.S.A.,* I will

designate the autobiographical figure in the Camera Eye as "Dos Passos" rather than—as I do elsewhere—the "Camera Eye persona."

34 *Fourteenth Chronicle*, p. 3.

35 Dos Passos, in *Harlan Miners Speak: Report on Terrorism in the Kentucky Coal Fields* . . . (New York: Harcourt, Brace, 1932), p. 288.

3   *U.S.A.:* THE MODES

1 Frank Gado, "John Dos Passos," in *First Person: Conversations on Writers and Writing*, ed. Frank Gado (Schenectady, N.Y.: Union College Press, 1973), p. 52. See also David Sanders, "John Dos Passos," in *Writers at Work: The "Paris Review" Interviews, Fourth Series*, ed. George Plimpton (New York: Viking, 1976), p. 81.

2 See James N. Westerhoven, "Autobiographical Elements in the Camera Eye," *American Literature* 48 (Nov. 1976): 340–64.

3 Two surviving examples are Dos Passos' careful revision of Camera Eye (25) on his failure to escape the Harvard ethercone (acc. no. 5950, box 14) and his recasting of a single Camera Eye on his life in New York during the early 1920s into the three separate segments of Camera Eye (45) to (47) (Notebook, pp. 59–64, acc. no. 5950, box 4).

4 Linda W. Wagner, "John Dos Passos: Reaching Past Poetry," *Essays in Honor of Russel B. Nye*, ed. Joseph Waldmeir (East Lansing: Michigan State Univ. Press, 1978), p. 240.

5 The continuing influence of Eliot is clearly evident in Dos Passos' poem "Lines to a Lady," in *The American Caravan*, ed. Van Wyck Brooks et al. (New York: Macaulay, 1927), pp. 454–60. For Whitman's influence on the form of the Camera Eye, see Robert P. Weeks, "The Novel as Poem: Whitman's Legacy to Dos Passos," *Modern Fiction Studies* 26 (Autumn 1980): 431–46.

6 See Dos Passos' collection of his early poems, *A Pushcart at the Curb* (New York: Doran, 1922). The Dos Passos Papers also contains many unpublished early poems.

7 Dos Passos included a factory worker, Ike Hall, in early drafts of *The Big Money* but cut his narrative at a late stage in the composition of the novel; see Chapter 4, below.

8 Even before this meeting, Joe Williams had appeared in Janey's narrative and Eveline in Eleanor's. We do not know at those points, however, that Joe and Eveline will eventually have their own narratives.

9 For my understanding of the device I have relied principally on Roy Pascal's *The Dual Voice: Free Indirect Speech and Its Functioning in the Nineteenth-Century European Novel* (Totowa, N.J.: Rowman and Littlefield, 1977) and Brian McHale's "Free Indirect Discourse: A Survey of Recent Accounts," *PTL* 3 (1978): 249–87.

10 The fullest account of free indirect discourse in *U.S.A.* is by Brian McHale: "Talking U.S.A.: Interpreting Free Indirect Discourse in Dos Passos' *U.S.A.* Trilogy, Part One," *Degrés* (Brussels) 16 (1978): c1–7, "Part Two," *Degrés* 17 (1979): d1–20.

11 Edmund Wilson to Dos Passos, July 16, 1939, in Wilson, *Letters on Literature and Politics*, ed. Elena Wilson (New York: Farrar, Straus and Giroux, 1977), p. 319.

12 Jean-Paul Sartre, "Dos Passos and '1919,'" in Sartre, *Literary and Philosophical*

Essays, trans. Annette Michelson (London: Rider, 1955), p. 94, and Claude-Edmonde Magny, *The Age of the American Novel: The Film Aesthetic of Fiction between the Two Wars* (1948; Amer. ed. trans. Eleanor Hochman, New York: Ungar, 1972), p. 61.

13 Dos Passos, "The Writer as Technician," in *American Writers' Congress,* ed. Henry Hart (New York: International Publishers, 1935), p. 79.

14 See *The Big Money,* pp. 233–36, 314–15, 369–77.

15 See Brian McHale, "Speaking as a Child in *U.S.A.*: A Problem in the Mimesis of Speech," *Language and Style* 17 (Fall 1984): 351–70.

16 Dos Passos to Ernest Hemingway, May 1932, in *Fourteenth Chronicle,* p. 408.

17 George Lukács, *Studies in European Realism,* trans. Edith Bone (London: Hillway, 1950), p. 6.

18 See Barbara Foley, "The Treatment of Time in *The Big Money*: An Examination of Ideology and Literary Form," *Modern Fiction Studies* 26 (Autumn 1980): 447–69.

19 Sanders, "John Dos Passos," p. 82.

20 See note 7 to chapter 2, above.

21 Dos Passos, "A Great American," *New Masses* 3 (Dec. 1927): 26.

22 Scholars have located specific sources for several biographies. See, for example, Philip A. Korth, "John Dos Passos, Ralph Chaplin, and *The Centralia Conspiracy,*" *Society for the Study of Midwestern Literature Newsletter* 9 (1979): 12–16 (for Wesley Everest), and Barry Maine, "Representative Men in Dos Passos's *The 42nd Parallel,*" *Clio* 12 (Fall 1982): 31–43 (for Minor Keith and Robert La Follette). See also Dos Passos' review of several recent biographies of Edison and Steinmetz in the *New Republic* 61 (Dec. 18, 1929): 103–5; he derived considerable material from these studies for his biographies of the two figures in *U.S.A.* In all, documentary material appears in eight of the biographies.

23 See, for example, Dos Passos' extensive yet highly selective notes for the Ford biography: acc. no. 5950, box 4.

24 For *Nineteen-Nineteen,* see acc. no. 5950, box 66; for *The Big Money,* see fig. 4.

25 Gamaliel Bradford, *A Naturalist of Souls: Studies in Psychography* (1917; rpt. ed. Boston: Houghton Mifflin, 1926), p. 9.

26 George Knox, in "Voice in the *U.S.A.* Biographies" (*Texas Studies in Literature and Language* 4 [Spring 1962]: 109–16), also sees the influence of E. E. Cummings in the irregular line and punctuation of the biographies.

27 One of Dos Passos' early notebooks for *The 42nd Parallel* supports this supposition; see *Odyssey,* p. 257.

28 See William Stott, *Documentary Expression and Thirties America* (New York: Oxford Univ. Press, 1973), pp. 120–22.

29 Gado, "John Dos Passos," p. 42; Dos Passos, "Introductory Note," *The 42nd Parallel* (New York: Modern Library, 1937), p. vii.

30 The account in this paragraph derives from my examination of the notebooks and drafts in the Dos Passos Papers and from Donald G. England's study, "The Newsreels of John Dos Passos' *The 42nd Parallel*: Sources and Techniques," Ph.D. diss., Univ. of Texas, 1970.

31 See Dos Passos to Dudley Poore, Aug. 26, 1929 (*Fourteenth Chronicle,* p. 394), in which Dos Passos asks Poore's aid in determining the precise lyrics for a number of songs.

32 Dos Passos to Donald G. England, Mar. 7, 1969, cited in England, "The News-reels of John Dos Passos' *The 42nd Parallel*," pp. 36–37.

33 For the relationship of film newsreels to the contents and form of Dos Passos' Newsreels, see David Seed, "Media and Newsreels in Dos Passos' *U.S.A.*," *Journal of Narrative Technique* 14 (Fall 1984): 182–92.

34 The phrase is Charles Marz's in his "Dos Passos's Newsreels: The Noise of History," *Studies in the Novel* 11 (Summer 1979): 198.

35 The items in Newsreel XLVIII are from the New York *World* during the month of September 1920.

4   *U.S.A.*: THE SHAPING OF THE WHOLE

1 *Best Times*, p. 180.

2 David Sanders, "John Dos Passos," in *Writers at Work: The "Paris Review" Interviews, Fourth Series*, ed. George Plimpton (New York: Viking, 1976), pp. 81–82.

3 Frank Gado, "John Dos Passos," in *First Person: Conversations on Writers and Writing*, ed. Frank Gado (Schenectady, N.Y.: Union College Press, 1973), p. 42.

4 Delmore Schwartz, "John Dos Passos and the Whole Truth," *Southern Review* 4 (Oct. 1938): 361.

5 Acc. No. 5950-j, box 66.

6 A similar though less elaborate plan exists for *The Big Money*; see fig. 2.

7 Acc. no. 5950, box 4.

8 Acc. no. 5950, box 5.

9 Probably because of their brevity, neither the Newsreels nor the Camera Eye segments were paginated until their inclusion in the complete typescript of the novel. The narratives of *The Big Money* also have a somewhat more complicated pagination history than the above summary indicates. Since Dos Passos blocked out each narrative in segments before he began writing, the first typescript of the narrative as a whole had separate pagination sequences for each segment. In the preparation of a second typescript of the entire narrative, however, the narrative was paginated in one sequence, and it was this pagination that was then repaginated when the segments of the sequence were placed in the complete typescript of the novel. The large number of crossed-out page numbers on any page of narrative in the final typescript of *The Big Money* (often five or six) thus stems both from the initial single pagination of the narrative as a whole before its inclusion in the final typescript and from changes in the order of material in the final typescript itself. It should also be noted that Dos Passos limited his composition of each narrative figure to the novel he was then writing. That is, though Charley Anderson and Richard Savage appear in earlier novels of the trilogy, their narratives in *The Big Money* were written independently of their narratives in the earlier volumes.

10 Among Dos Passos' notes for Charley Anderson, for example, is the reminder "Dick Savage and Moorehouse come in here somewhere" (acc. no. 5950, box 4). His notes also contain detailed preliminary plans for the interlacing of Anderson and Margo and for Eveline's various appearances in other narratives.

11 Acc. no. 5950, box 4. I reproduce as figure 13 only the first page of the four-and-a-half page sequence. That this was Dos Passos' method from the begin-

ning of the trilogy is confirmed by the survival of full preliminary notes for the entire Mac narrative (acc. no. 5950, box 66).

12 For example, in an undated letter to Brandt and Brandt, which the firm received on March 30, 1935 (acc. no. 5950aq, box 1), Dos Passos noted that he expected to complete the Charley Anderson narrative in a few weeks and that it would be about 150 pages. The final typescript was in fact 187 pages.

13 That Dos Passos' preliminary division of the narratives into segments encouraged juxtapositional planning is suggested by his early note to himself (Notebook, p. 14, acc. no. 5950, box 4) that the first segment of Margo's narrative should come "between Charley Anderson 2 & 3" and the second "between Charley Anderson 4 & 5."

14 Briefly and roughly, the evidence is: the evolution of the initial narrative segments until they reach their final form of four consecutive Charley Anderson segments; the refinement of the subjects, titles, and order of the biographies; and the gradual filling in and ordering of the Newsreel and Camera Eye segments.

15 See "Tin Can Tourist," *Direction* 1 (Dec. 1937): 10–12, and "Migratory Worker," *Partisan Review* 4 (Jan. 1938): 16–20. Dos Passos' general conception of Hall was that he had an "extremely limited life" (acc. no. 5950, box 4).

16 See *The Big Money,* pp. 421–38.

17 The full setting copy of *The Big Money* is in acc. no. 5950, box 5.

18 It is clear from Townsend Ludington's account in *Odyssey,* p. 351, and from Dos Passos' letter to Hemingway of May 31, 1936 (*Fourteenth Chronicle,* p. 484), that Dos Passos read galley proof in Havana and Miami in late April and early May and page proof in Providence in late May and early June. Although I am assuming that "their guns" was cut in galley proof, it would not affect the argument if it were in fact cut in page proof.

5   *U.S.A.*: THE TRILOGY

1 Jean-Paul Sartre, "Dos Passos and '1919'," in Sartre, *Literary and Philosophical Essays,* trans. Annette Michelson (London: Rider, 1955), p. 89; Edmund Wilson to Dos Passos, July 22, 1936, in Wilson, *Letters on Literature and Politics, 1912–1972,* ed. Elena Wilson (New York: Farrar, Straus and Giroux, 1977), p. 279.

2 See Iain Colley, *Dos Passos and the Fiction of Despair* (Totowa, N.J.: Rowman and Littlefield, 1978), p. 110, for a representative judgment.

3 Dos Passos' reliance on the history of the IWW in the Mac narrative is studied by Melvin Landsberg, *Dos Passos' Path to "U.S.A.": A Political Biography, 1912–1936* (Boulder: Colorado Associated Univ. Press, 1972), and Robert C. Rosen, *John Dos Passos: Politics and the Writer* (Lincoln: Univ. of Nebraska Press, 1981).

4 Dos Passos recalls this source in *Best Times,* p. 170. Bland later corresponded with Dos Passos about the use of his life in *The 42nd Parallel.*

5 The work referred to is Baroja's trilogy *Struggle for Life,* which comprises the novels *The Quest, Weeds,* and *Red Dawn.*

6 See *Best Times,* p. 178. For Lee's life, see Ray E. Hiebert, *Courtier to the Crowd: The Story of Ivy Lee and the Development of Public Relations* (Ames: Iowa State Univ. Press, 1966).

7 Dos Passos had, of course, portrayed figures of this kind in his work before

meeting Lee. I have already noted Phineas Blackhead in *Manhattan Transfer* (see chapter 1, above). In addition, the character Jonathan P. Davis in Dos Passos' play *Airways, Inc.*, which he completed in 1928 just before leaving for Russia, is a real estate salesman with some of Moorehouse's characteristics. Davis is chairman of the "Citizen's Fairplay League, which was founded last year to restore mutual confidence between the real estate operator and the public" (*Airways, Inc.* [New York: Macaulay, 1928,] p. 101).

8   Ivy Lee, *Human Nature and Railroads* (Philadelphia: Nash, 1915), pp. 17–18.

9   Dos Passos' inclination to view his childhood in these terms is even more pronounced in his portrayal of the autobiographical character Jimmy Herf in *Manhattan Transfer*. Herf's father is entirely absent, and his mother falls ill and dies during his childhood.

10 See *Best Times,* p. 137.

11 Eleanor herself is later associated with lilies (*FP*, 354). Dos Passos was also undoubtedly aware of the association of Oscar Wilde (and thus an effete aestheticism and homosexuality) with lilies.

12 See *The 42nd Parallel*, pp. 411, 412.

13 *Best Times*, p. 76.

14 See fig. 1, above.

15 Dos Passos to Malcolm Cowley, Feb. 1932, in *Fourteenth Chronicle*, p. 404.

16 See *Fourteenth Chronicle*, pp. 261–62.

17 The most literary of Dos Passos' Harvard friends were Dudley Poore, Stewart Mitchell, E. E. Cummings, and Robert Hillyer, all of whom contributed to *Eight Harvard Poets*, which—after much delay—appeared in 1917. Other Harvard friends included Frederick Van der Arend, Wright McCormick, Arthur McComb, Cuthbert Wright, and Ed Massey. Poore, Cummings, Hillyer, and Van der Arend served in the ambulance corps. For Dos Passos' Harvard, see— besides *Odyssey*, pp. 67–85—Charles W. Bernardin, "John Dos Passos' Harvard Years," *New England Quarterly* 27 (March 1954): 3–26, and Malcolm Cowley, "American College, 1916," in *Exile's Return* (1934; rpt. ed., New York: Viking, 1951), pp. 27–36. Cowley in particular stresses the fin-de-siècle aestheticism of this period at Harvard.

18 Dos Passos to Robert Hillyer (responding to Hillyer's complaints), Oct. 1944 and Nov. 3, 1944, in *Fourteenth Chronicle*, pp. 543–44.

19 There is no biography of Hillyer, but see the entry by David D. Anderson in the *Dictionary of American Biography,* supplement 7 (1981), pp. 346–47.

20 Dos Passos may, however, be covertly alluding to such an incident in his further use of Hillyer for the character Tad Skinner in his autobiographical novel *Chosen Country* (Boston: Houghton Mifflin, 1951). Skinner is portrayed as a womanizer both before and during his service in the ambulance corps in France.

21 The figure of Cooper seems to derive, not from Hillyer's background, but from Dos Passos' family friend and benefactor James Brown Scott who aided Dos Passos several times during the war in ways that resemble Cooper's later aid of Savage.

22 See especially the incident in Paris when Savage is walking home late one night and "a whitefaced young man who was walking the other way looked into his face and stopped" (*NN*, 361).

23 Richard S. Kennedy, *Dreams in the Mirror: A Biography of E. E. Cummings* (New York: Liveright, 1980), p. 193.

24 See *Odyssey*, pp. 67–68 and passim. Ludington (*Odyssey*, p. 68) notes that "One might speculate that there was something of the physical in Dos Passos's attraction for Marvin."

25 See Donald Pizer, "The Hemingway–Dos Passos Relationship," *Journal of Modern Literature* 13 (March 1986): 111–28.

26 See *Odyssey*, pp. 161–62, and Carr, p. 162.

27 These are José O'Riely, Don Stevens, Raoul, Moorehouse, and Paul in *Nineteen-Nineteen* and Charley Anderson, Savage, and Charles Edward Holden in *The Big Money.*

28 *Best Times*, p. 28.

29 See *Odyssey*, pp. 220–49 passim.

30 Colley, *Dos Passos and the Fiction of Despair*, p. 59.

31 In Dick's returning to Europe as an officer, Dos Passos was not only drawing upon the experiences of Hillyer and several other friends who became officers after serving in the ambulance corps but was also distinguishing between them and his own insistence on joining the army as an enlisted man. This feared and hated immersion in a stifling and mechanical suppression of individual freedom—as he later depicted it in *Three Soldiers*—also ensured that he would not lose touch with the "truth" of the war experience.

32 See Landsberg, *Dos Passos' Path to "U.S.A.,"* pp. 127–31.

33 Dos Passos' growing disillusionment with the Communist party during the early and mid-1930s, culminating in his complete break with the far left during the Spanish Civil War, is one of the most fully studied areas of his career. See Landsberg, *Dos Passos' Path to "U.S.A.,"* pp. 178–83; Rosen, *John Dos Passos: Politics and the Writer*, pp. 74–78; and *Odyssey*, pp. 301–46 passim.

34 Dos Passos to Melvin Landsberg, June 26, 1956, and July 12, 1966, cited in Landsberg, *Dos Passos' Path to "U.S.A.,"* p. 32n.

35 Dos Passos wrote to Edmund Wilson on September 24, 1934, that he had been rereading Veblen. He continued: "I shouldn't wonder if he were the only American economist whose work had any lasting value" (*Fourteenth Chronicle*, p. 443).

36 See William E. Akin, *Technocracy and the American Dream: The Technocrat Movement, 1900–1941* (Berkeley: Univ. of California Press, 1977). Akin notes that public interest in the movement was at its highest during 1932–33. Dos Passos' specific response to Technocracy can be observed in the title and substance of his important 1935 essay "The Writer as Technician," in *American Writers' Congress*, ed. Henry Hart (New York: International Publishers, 1935), pp. 78–82.

37 Acc. no. 5950, box 4.

38 Dos Passos borrowed the porcelain and doll images from his description of Ellen Thatcher in *Manhattan Transfer*, pp. 374, 375, at a parallel moment in Ellen's career as an actress.

39 Hiebert, *Courtier to the Crowd*, pp. 286–88.

40 Dos Passos based his portrayal of the later Bingham on Bernarr Macfadden, a physical culture popularizer of the 1920s. See Landsberg, *Dos Passos' Path to "U.S.A.,"* p. 211.

41 See Robert J. Butler, "The American Quest for Pure Movement in Dos Passos' *U.S.A.,*" *Twentieth-Century Literature* 30 (Spring 1984): 80–99.

BIBLIOGRAPHY

The Bibliography is limited to significant work on *U.S.A.* and to major studies of Dos Passos' career as a whole.

BOOKS

Becker, George J. *John Dos Passos*. New York: Ungar, 1974.

Belkind, Allen, ed. *Dos Passos, the Critics, and the Writer's Intention*. Carbondale: Southern Illinois Univ. Press, 1971.

Carr, Virginia Spencer. *Dos Passos: A Life*. Garden City, N.Y.: Doubleday, 1984.

Colley, Iain. *Dos Passos and the Fiction of Despair*. Totawa, N.J.: Rowman and Littlefield, 1978.

England, Donald G. "The Newsreels of John Dos Passos' *The 42nd Parallel*: Sources and Techniques." Ph.D. diss., University of Texas, 1970.

Hook, Andrew, ed. *Dos Passos: A Collection of Critical Essays*. Englewood Cliffs, N.J.: Prentice-Hall, 1974.

Landsberg, Melvin. *Dos Passos' Path to "U.S.A.": A Political Biography 1912–1936*. Boulder: Colorado Associated Univ. Press, 1972.

Ludington, Townsend, ed. *The Fourteenth Chronicle: Letters and Diaries of John Dos Passos*. Boston: Gambit, 1973.

———. *John Dos Passos: A Twentieth Century Odyssey*. New York: Dutton, 1980.

Potter, Jack. *A Bibliography of John Dos Passos*. Chicago: Normandie House, 1950.

Rohrkemper, John. *John Dos Passos: A Reference Guide*. Boston: G. K. Hall, 1980.

Rosen, Robert C. *John Dos Passos: Politics and the Writer*. Lincoln: University of Nebraska Press, 1981.

Wagner, Linda W. *Dos Passos: Artist as American*. Austin: Univ. of Texas Press, 1979.

Wrenn, John H. *John Dos Passos*. New York: Twayne, 1961.

ARTICLES AND PARTS OF BOOKS

Butler, Robert J. "The American Quest for Pure Movement in Dos Passos' *U.S.A.*" *Twentieth Century Literature* 30 (Spring 1984): 80–99.

Cowley, Malcolm. "The Poet and the World," *New Republic* 70 (Apr. 27, 1932): 303–5, and 88 (Sept. 9, 1936): 134.

Diggins, John P. *Up from Communism: Conservative Odysseys in American Intellectual History*. New York: Harper & Row, 1975, pp. 74–117, 223–68.

Foley, Barbara. "History, Fiction, and Satirical Form: The Example of Dos Passos' *1919*." *Genre* 12 (Fall 1979): 357–78.

——. "The Treatment of Time in *The Big Money:* An Examination of Ideology and Literary Form." *Modern Fiction Studies* 26 (Autumn 1980): 447–69.

Gelfant, Blanche. "The Search for Identity in the Novels of John Dos Passos." *PMLA* 76 (March 1961): 133–49.

Goldman, Arnold. "Dos Passos and His *U.S.A.*" *New Literary History* 1 (Spring 1970): 471–83.

Hughson, Lois. "In Search of the True America: Dos Passos' Debt to Whitman in *U.S.A.*" *Modern Fiction Studies* 19 (Summer 1973): 179–92.

Knox, George. "Dos Passos and Painting." *Texas Studies in Literature and Language* 6 (Spring 1964): 22–38.

——. "Voice in the *U.S.A.* Biographies." *Texas Studies in Literature and Language* 4 (Spring 1962): 109–16.

Lydenberg, John. "Dos Passos's *U.S.A.*: The Words of the Hollow Men." In *Essays on Determinism in American Literature,* ed. Sydney J. Krause. Kent, Ohio: Kent State Univ. Press, 1964, pp. 97–107.

McHale, Brian. "Talking U.S.A.: Interpreting Free Indirect Discourse in Dos Passos' *U.S.A.* Trilogy." *Degrés* (Brussels), 16 (1978), c1–7; 17 (1979), d1–20.

Magny, Claude-Edmonde. *The Age of the American Novel: The Film Aesthetic of Fiction Between the Two Wars.* 1948; Amer. ed. trans. Eleanor Hochman, New York: Ungar, 1972, pp. 105–43.

Maine, Barry. "Representative Men in Dos Passos's *The 42nd Parallel.*" *Clio* 12 (Fall 1982): 31–43.

——. "*U.S.A.*: Dos Passos and the Rhetoric of History." *South Atlantic Review* 50 (Jan. 1985): 75–86.

Marz, Charles. "Dos Passos's Newsreels: The Noise of History." *Studies in the Novel* 11 (Summer 1979): 194–200.

——. "*U.S.A.*: Chronicle and Performance." *Modern Fiction Studies* 26 (Autumn 1980): 398–416.

Morse, Jonathan. "Dos Passos' *U.S.A.* and the Illusions of Memory." *Modern Fiction Studies* 23 (Winter 1977–78): 543–55.

Pizer, Donald. "The Camera Eye in *U.S.A.*: The Sexual Center." *Modern Fiction Studies* 26 (Autumn 1980): 417–30.

Sanders, David. "The 'Anarchism' of John Dos Passos." *South Atlantic Quarterly* 60 (Winter 1961): 44–55.

Sartre, Jean-Paul. "Dos Passos and '1919.'" In Sartre, *Literary and Philosophical Essays,* trans. Annette Michelson. London: Rider, 1955, pp. 88–96.

Seed, David. "Media and Newsreels in Dos Passos' *U.S.A.*" *Journal of Narrative Technique* 14 (Fall 1984): 182–92.

Spindler, Michael. "John Dos Passos and the Visual Arts." *Journal of American Studies* 15 (Dec. 1981): 391–405.

Vanderwerken, David L. "Dos Passos' Civil Religion." *Research Studies* 48 (Dec. 1980): 218–28.

——. "*U.S.A.*: Dos Passos and the 'Old Words.'" *Twentieth Century Literature* 23 (May 1977): 195–228.

Walcutt, Charles C. *American Literary Naturalism, a Divided Stream.* Minneapolis: Univ. of Minnesota Press, 1956, pp. 280–89.

Weeks, Robert P. "The Novel as Poem: Whitman's Legacy to Dos Passos." *Modern Fiction Studies* 26 (Autumn 1980): 431–46.

Westerhoven, James N. "Autobiographical Elements in the Camera Eye." *American Literature* 48 (Nov. 1976): 340–64.

Winner, Anthony. "The Characters of John Dos Passos." *Literatur in Wissenschaft und Unterricht* (Kiel), 2 (1969): 1–19.

Index